THE MANCHESTER JUBILEES

Barely a year old, Newton Heath's No 5698 *Mars* gets a southbound excursion underway from Crewe Station, passing between the carriage shed and Crewe (South) MPD. After a brief sojurn on the Midland Division, *Mars* returned to Newton Heath during wartime and was destined to spend the rest of her days as a Central Division loco, working principally out of Bank Hall MPD. It is perhaps fitting that No 5698 is seen here on the West Coast Main Line, as she is one of the members involved with hauling the last regular passenger workings over Shap as far as Carlisle. **AUGUST 1937 ● E. R. MORTEN**

PAUL SHACKCLOTH

THE MANCHESTER JUBILEES

ISBN 0 9543128 5 5

First published 2012

© Steam Image 2012

Designed and Published by Steam Image, Cheadle Hulme, Cheshire SK8 6NY
Printed by Deanprint Ltd, Stockport, Cheshire SK3 0PR.

FOREWORD

When William A Stanier was appointed Chief Mechanical Engineer of the LMS on 1st January 1932, a priority was to standardise the locomotive classes. One of his first efforts was the 5XP - later known as the Jubilees, or affectionately called the 'red uns' by locomen. This design just pre-dated the more numerous 5MT's - the Black Fives. British Railways changed the Jubilee classification to 6P as of 1st January 1951 and they were further re-classified 6P5F from November 1955.

191 engines appeared between May 1934 and December 1936 as taper boiler versions of the Baby Scot or Patriot locomotives and incorporated a 3 cylinder layout. They were widely dispersed over the LMS with the Manchester Depots receiving 7 members upon entering traffic. Much has been written about the trials and tribulations of the early days, suffice to say that initially they were unsuccessful and beset with steaming difficulties, but the problem was soon resolved by a simple modification to the diameter of the blastpipe orifice.

The original batch (Nos 5552 - 5664) were fitted with small super-heaters and a domeless boiler but the later engines (Nos 5665 - 5742) benefited from having 24 element superheaters, domes and separate top feeds. The result was a locomotive capable of with-standing a hard slogging which many enginemen considered as the best approach to achieve optimum results. They were fast and free running as the surviving performance logs testify - especially over the Midland Lines, and although rumours abounded about them reaching 100mph - they probably did in favourable conditions - it appeared that a Jubilee reached a critical maximum between 95 - 100mph and needed coaxing to reach speeds into the 90's. The highest authenticated speed belonged to No 45579 *Punjab* at 97.5mph on the descent from Luton to Bedford on 29th May 1958.

Aesthetically, they were arguably the most pleasing of all the Stanier products. The rebuilt Patriots and Royal Scots and especially the Duchess Pacifics have their supporters - but the Jubilees held, and still hold, a great affection with so many. The large class had a great many complexities - be it of varying livery or size of numerals, differing tender details or that fascinating array of names which included many heroes of Naval battles along with their ships and countries with Commonwealth connections. They were enigmatic locomotives, perhaps best summed up by an old Newton Heath driver who likened them to the nursery rhyme. 'When they were good, they were very very good, but ...'

Longsight's locomotives nearly always worked out of Manchester London Road on the intensive London and Birmingham services. They also travelled to Shrewsbury and beyond on the West of England trains as well as having regular trips to Leeds, Liverpool, Blackpool and other points north.

The Newton Heath men performed herculean feats on the Manchester to Glasgow service and often subjected their 'Jubs' to merciless hammerings over Shap and Beattock with trains some-times loaded to 15 bogies. It was significant that by 1960 when Class 7 power had become available (Britannias followed by Royal Scots displaced from elsewhere), the former L&Y depot never lost faith with its trusty Jubilees and they enjoyed a final fling before dieselisation. As well as working all over the Central Division, their locos, and the Jubilees in particular, could turn up in the most unex-pected of places. In support of this, it was often said that a Newton Heath man's route knowledge was second to none.

The Trafford Park contingent concentrated their efforts exclusively on express passenger workings between Manchester Central and London St Pancras. As a consequence they rarely strayed off the Midland Main Line and, indeed, it has proved exceedingly difficult to trace a photograph of one off the beaten track, other than at Hope on the Sheffield service or at Crewe Works. All had moved on by March 1960, but the shed was to enjoy something of an 'Indian Summer' when No 45705 *Seahorse* arrived in September 1964 to work the prestigious Buxton Commuter Train.

Patricroft's engines travelled far and wide. Their principal duties were between Liverpool Lime Street and Leeds City with trains destined for Hull and Newcastle. They had regular turns to Chester and Llandudno as well as a daily job as far as Carlisle with the newspaper train to Glasgow St Enoch from Manchester Victoria (11 middle). They also had the habit of appearing at unlikely places, especially after a phase of reorganisation in April 1958 which placed them under Newton Heath's jurisdiction.

Stockport Edgeley and Agecroft MPD's received their members by default late in the day and cannot be seriously compared with the other four depots whose allocations were of long standing. Engines were brought in to eke out their days, often in poor condition and worked almost exclusively on freight and parcels turns. Other unlikely depots also benefited as a result of this cascading, often after short periods of storage. Nevertheless, they had their moments, as several photographs will testify.

Four members survive in preservation. No 5593 *Kolhapur* ran out of Longsight between 1943 and 1951, returning for short spells at Patricroft and Newton Heath during 1964/5. No 5690 *Leander* was never a Manchester engine and although No 5699 *Galatea* went into traffic at Newton Heath, it is No 5596 *Bahamas* and its association with Stockport (Edgeley) for which it is affectionately remembered - and rightly regarded as the 'flagship' engine.

Statistically, 138 of the 191 engines qualified for inclusion and 88 are featured - some more so than others. The criteria was that every candidate photograph had to be allocated at the time. Despite lengthy periods as Manchester engines, some remained remarkably camera shy whilst others were just the opposite. The likelihood of capturing a short term, one-off transfer or loan during war time was nigh on impossible - but there is the odd exception.

Their Majesties King George V and Queen Mary celebrated their *Silver Jubilee* in May 1935. To commemorate the occasion, the LMS, who coincidentally had a nationalistic tendency with regards to naming policy, chose No 5642 to receive the *Silver Jubilee* nameplates. Built in November 1934, this engine was considered to be 'the best of the bunch' and immediately exchanged identities with No 5552, also exchanging tenders with No 5559, thus gaining a Stanier example. In addition, she was adorned with a uniquely distinctive livery of 'glossy' black, offset by a variety of fittings in chromium plate including front numberplate and cab side numerals.

ACKNOWLEDGEMENTS

The publication of this book represents the culmination of many years of research and, fittingly, coincides with the Diamond Jubilee of Her Majesty Queen Elizabeth ll. It was the late Gordon Coltas - enthusiast and nocturnal dark room technician extraordinaire, whose enthusiasm inspired me from the outset. He, like myself and many others, was a lover of Jubilees and was very much involved in the early days of the *Bahamas Locomotive Society* at Dinting.

My intention has been to provide a comprehensive cover of the activities of those Jubilees which qualified for inclusion. To achieve this, I have had to cast my net far and wide, and to all those persons who have responded in various ways, I offer my sincere thanks. They include Brian Arnold, Mike Bentley, Dave Bradbury, Richard Casserley, Howard Chamberlain, Chris Coates, Fred Consterdine, Peter Cross, Eddie Johnson, John King, Steve Leyland, Jim Milner, John Morten, Trevor Moseley, Graham Neve, John Nixon, John Sykes, Chris Tasker, Keith Thompson, Eddie Winfield, Paul Winstanley and members of the Lancashire and Yorkshire Society.

Photographic sources include: F Allcock, J H Aston, Chris Banks, Alan Barnard, Arthur Bendell, Rod Blencowe, Mike Boakes, Harold D Bowtell, B W L Brooksbank, W A Brown, R J Buckley, D Burdon, F M Butterfield, R Butterfield, Roger Carpenter, Don Cash, H C Casserley, John Clarke, Ian Cockcroft, W D Cooper, Richard Cort, Brian Cramer, Bernard Crick, J J Cunningham, Jack Cupit, Jim Davenport, Roy Davenport, J D Darby, Frank Dean, A Devonport, Gerald Drought, J Fairclough, Ray Farrell, Peter Fitton, D. Forsyth, Ronnie Gee, A C Gilbert, B K B Green, R S Greenwood, L Hanson, Dave Hampson, G Harrop, Tom Heavyside, Barry Hoper, R H Hughes, Peter Hutchinson, Paul Jordan, Raymond Keeley, W R M Lees, Brian Magilton, John Marshall, Michael Mensing, Midland Railway Trust, Millbrook House, Brian Morrison, Gavin Morrison, Ray Morten, D Montgomery, J W Neve, Ian Pearsall, Derek Penney, R D Pollard, Bill Potter, Norman Preedy, Tony Oldfield, Real Photos, Peter Reeves, Geoff Sharpe, G M Shoults, Pete Skellon, N Skinner, E E Smith, John Spencer, Tony Steele, John Tarrant, Ken Tyler, Peter Ward, Martin Welch, Graham Whitehead and J Yates.

In addition, once again I have to thank David Postle at the *Kidderminster Railway Museum* for making available images by Ian Cockcroft, Bill Potter and John Marshall. In a similar vein, those by Tony Steele and some of Roy Davenport appear courtesy of *The Gordon Coltas Trust*, others by Geoff Sharpe. Mike Claxton, brother of the late Paul, is another who has gone out of his way to provide a selection of photographs, as have Peter Fitton, Michael Mensing and Gavin Morrison. Assistance is always on hand from Brian Green, who not only provides his own excellent material, but that of the late Jim Davenport. Pictures taken by Harold D Bowtell, J D Darby, R H Hughes, R D Pollard, Peter Reeves and G M Shoults come from within the photographic archive of the Manchester Locomotive Society, to whom I am eternally grateful.

Thanks must be extended to David Young and Arthur Haynes who, as well as making constructive comments, have provided answers to many obscure questions as well as diligently checking over the copy. Finally, to my wife Norma who continues to support and encourage my solitary endeavours.

JULY 2012 ● PAUL SHACKCLOTH

A PERSONAL OVERVIEW

Although they meant little to him at the time, the nameplates of *Mars, Dauntless* and *Glorious* remain fresh in his memory. They flashed by Moston Junction signalbox with great regularity whereas the other engines seemed to plod along and were much dirtier. With no main roads to cross, this was the place where young Paul was allowed to venture to gain his first impressions of steam - but no further. He knew not that they were Bank Hall engines, but next, the equally obscure names of *Tobago, Vernon, Amethyst* and *Boscawen* had been also scrawled on scraps of paper. He was informed by the older lads that these four were from 'just down the road' - but which road?

All would soon be revealed as his horizons were about to broaden. Having gained his mother's confidence, a new, almost desperate plea to venture further afield had been granted, subject to the usual provisos and that his older friend Joe must accompany him. A short cut through Broadhurst Park and Moston Woods, then under the hooped bridge brought them to within spitting distance of Newton Heath MPD. He'd been told there was a wall to sit on - there was - and the rest, as they say, is history.

CONTENTS

THE
LONGSIGHT
LOCOMOTIVES

The peace and tranquility of a summer Sunday in Cheadle Hulme is broken by the passage of No **45633** *Aden* and nine carriages taking the Wilmslow line with the 2.40pm Manchester London Road to Cardiff General. The previous month, *Aden* had been outshopped at Crewe - receiving a Heavy General overhaul and repaint in Brunswick Green livery. On this beautiful summer's day, photographer Tom Lewis could hardly fail to be impressed as the loco fairly glistened in the afternoon sunshine - he probably first observed a red buffer beam in the far distance whilst crossing the 'seven arches' viaduct, straddling the Ladybrook valley. The footbridge at Cheadle Hulme Station, something of a landmark in earlier days, offered covered protection during the LMS period only. Passengers accessing Platforms 1 and 4 were exposed to the elements from the outset and again during the BR period. The booking office was centrally situated at platform level between Nos 2 and 3, the entrance gained by steps and inclined path off Station Road, Cheadle Hulme's main thoroughfare, which passed underneath the station within the limits of the platforms. The Macclesfield line trails in from the right.

15TH JULY 1951 ● TOM LEWIS

9A LONGSIGHT MPD

The 191st and final member of the class, No 5742 *Connaught* was brought into service at Crewe North on the last day of 1936 - the previous sixty having emerged from the nearby Works within the year. It had already enjoyed a spell at Longsight during the war years and beyond, but *Connaught* - now a BR loco - rather surprisingly returned for a nine-month period in October 1950 before once again resuming duties at Bushbury MPD, working as a top link loco on the two-hour Wolverhampton - London Euston expresses. A double chimney had been fitted in 1940 but was removed during a Heavy General overhaul in March 1955. No **45742** drifts through the South Shed yard whilst a visiting Fowler 2-6-4T No **42360** from Macclesfield awaits its next turn of duty. Bound to touch the odd raw nerve of the enthusiast are those steps off the footbridge, just visible on the far right - as is the Foreman's office window! Ejections were commonplace here. Longsight was considered a tough nut to crack. **9TH JUNE 1951 ● TOM LEWIS**

Longsight was Manchester's premier depot for Jubilees with a maximum of 14 on allocation at any one time. Statistically, 71 different engines displayed 9A plates over a 28-year period - meanwhile, others regularly arrived on loan for short periods, usually acting as cover whilst their own were away at Crewe Works. Standing resplendent in the south shed yard is the one that got away to the 'Wessie'. No **45671** ***Prince Rupert***, a one-time Royal Train engine, was Newton Heath's pride and joy prior to transferring across the city during the week ending 19th October 1957. During that year, the South Shed was converted from 8 to 6 roads and used for both steam and diesel repairs, although the yard continued to stable locos in service, as is the case here. **AUGUST 1959 ● AUTHOR'S COLLECTION**

The second loco in the initial batch of five built at Crewe Works was No **5553 Canada,** brought into traffic in May 1934 at a cost of £5,700. Although continually on the move during the LMS period, it managed a five-year stint at 9A during the early 1950's, by now its 14th shedplate change. The loco, basking in the morning sun, stands alongside a Jinty 0-6-0T in the South Shed yard. It would be back off to Crewe North for a fourth spell the following month.

MAY 1956 ● N. R. PREEDY COLLECTION

Loco servicing facilities were concentrated at the Manchester end of the site and the north shed remained the running shed until the end of steam here in February 1965. This dramatic low level view sees No **45595 Southern Rhodesia** coupled to No **46120 Royal Inniskilling Fusilier,** both about to reverse off shed for their next turns of duty. Notice the lamps already affixed in the Class 1 position. Meanwhile, one of the shed's Stanier 2-6-2T's, No **40093** replenishes her tanks after arriving on shed.

1957 ● G. DROUGHT

The shed's first association with the class was the arrival of the new engine, No 5610, brought into traffic on 19th July 1934, which promptly disappeared to Camden the following week! Four months later saw another batch of four arrive, Nos 5626-9, all again moving on after a mere 2 to 3 month period. Resident No **45671 Prince Rupert** rubs shoulders with old Newton Heath stablemate No **45635 Tobago** in the north shed yard, beyond which stands 2P 4-4-0 No **40674**, now withdrawn with chimney sacked over - and which was the one time regular Longsight breakdown train engine.

21ST JUNE 1959 ● R.H. HUGHES

LONGSIGHT CARRIAGE SIDINGS

A familiar feature of operation on summer Saturdays was the continual movement of empty stock between Longsight Carriage Sidings and London Road Station. Coaches that will form a West of England departure are topped and tailed by Jubilees, thus saving a path over this busy section. No **45595 _Southern Rhodesia_** *(left)* will take another train south, possibly a relief to the above whilst No **45644 _Howe_** *(below)* will work at least as far as Shrewsbury.

AUGUST 1957 ● M.S. WELCH

A fine study in locomotive detail is offered with this close-up of No **45631 _Tanganyika._** Records have unfortunately failed to establish whether a speed indicator was carried during the LMS period although a Standard BR Smith example was fitted at Crewe in June 1960 in addition to the Advance Warning System the previous year. The vast majority of the class were similarly modified during this period as they became due for shopping. The significance of Reporting Number W563 is that it was one of a batch which represented a passenger train departure from within the Manchester District of the Western Division. They appeared in the 'Special Traffic Notices' which applied to that day or period as an extension of the working timetable. The boards also offered a visual aid to officials and, dare I say it, keen enthusiasts.

AUGUST 1955 ● AUTHOR'S COLLECTION

A popular vantage point for spotters was the end of Platform 4 which afforded views of the through MSJ&A lines as well as movements within the train shed. The regulars present will not be that impressed with No **45680 *Camperdown*,** a long serving 9A loco and will be hoping that the next arrival is a rarity - preferably a 'namer' on a running-in turn from Crewe Works. Whilst they gaze south, the crew clamber aboard *Camperdown* before her imminent departure.

c1955 ● J. YATES

MANCHESTER LONDON ROAD STATION

This impressive view records another arrival with a stopping passenger train. No **45632 *Tonga*** (fitted with a BR standard chimney) is the motive power. Beyond the signal gantry is Manchester London Road No 1 signal box, one of four within the Station environs which looked after the former LMS section including the ex-MSJ&A lines. A fifth box, built to control the former Great Central lines, features prominently on the front cover photograph.

24TH JUNE 1953 ● B.K.B. GREEN

Returning to the shed tender first is No **45638 *Zanzibar*,** beyond which are the electrified lines of the Woodhead route to Sheffield Victoria.

29TH AUGUST 1957 ● D. FORSYTH

'Each a glimpse and gone forever'. Words that will strike a chord with many enthusiasts and immortalised by author Colin T. Gifford as a book title which became the sequel to his acclaimed work *Decline of Steam*. They are particularly relevant here, looking towards Manchester London Road Station. Glimpsed through an open carriage window of an arrival from Sheffield Victoria is one of the two rebuilt members, No **45736 Phoenix** departing with an unidentified southbound express. After a fleeting three-month visit to Longsight, she was gone forever from the Manchester area but remained on the Western Division until her demise. Prominent in this unusual panoramic view is the protective concrete cover over London Road No 2 signal box - fitted in 1940 as a wartime measure to withstand shrapnel and blast. The smaller No 1 box, which also straddled the running lines nearer the junction with Mayfield Station, was similarly protected.

AUGUST 1960 ● JIM DAVENPORT

The doyen of the class - but not strictly speaking the forerunner. Much has been documented regarding the change of identities with No 5642 and the subsequent special treatment afforded to No **5552**. Suffice to say, the loco was named **Silver Jubilee,** bestowed on 24th April 1935 in commemoration of the 25-year reign of King George V, the first 113 locos having entered service nameless. A little known fact is that she spent more time at Longsight than at any other depot - from the depths of wartime through to the early BR period seven years later. In April 1936 and in all her pomp, No 5552 visited Manchester's Belle Vue Gardens - which were rail connected from the shed yard across Redgate Lane and over a field - in conjunction with an exhibition organised by the LMS, but is seen here at London Road just prior to Nationalisation. **c1947 ● HUGHES JUNCTION**

Again, just prior to Nationalisation, No ▶ 5631 Tanganyika ambles into the station with a stopping train which is perhaps a Manchester portion working forward from Crewe. The cessation of hostilities resulted in a change of emphasis in express motive power at Longsight. From October 1946 the depot took delivery of up to a dozen rebuilt 'Royal Scots' and 'Patriots' which had been recently cleared to work over the Stoke line. During 1947 they lost a similar number of Jubilees but still had eight members to call on, including No 5631. A young girl gazes out of the leading compartment window, oblivious to the camera, but the Permanent Way man is very much aware and gives a surly backward glance.

AUGUST 1947 ● LRGP

ARDWICK JUNCTION

The former Great Central main line curves away to the right towards Ashburys and Gorton, diverging from the former LNWR at Ardwick Junction, one mile south of London Road. No **45631** *Tanganyika* passes the junction signal box on the approaches to Longsight with a Birmingham express. Immediately beyond this point, the railway straddled the premises of the Manchester Corporation Transport Department's Hyde Road Garage and Works. Some vehicles, often ancient and abandoned, stood in the back yard within the vee of the junction and were always of interest to those who appreciated buses - but could only be seen from passing trains. **c.1958 ● AUTHOR'S COLLECTION**

Jubilees in tandem - the pilot is No **45644** *Howe* - the train engine unidentified - have reached Longsight Junction with fourteen bogies in tow. The train may well be the Friday Up *Comet* (5.50pm London Road to Euston via Crewe) which was invariably strengthened and required Class 8 motive power - a Crewe North Duchess Pacific often featured on this turn from the mid 1950's. Locomotives working the diagram returned the following day with the 11.45am London Euston to London Road train, again via Crewe. **c1958 ● M.S. WELCH**

HEATON CHAPEL

The 2.20pm to London Euston makes steady progress through Heaton Chapel Station with No **45617** *Mauritius*. Despite an abundance of Royal Scots and, the later presence of Britannia Pacifics, Longsight continued to find work for their Jubilees on the most exacting of turns. The bi-directional signals controlling Up and Down Fast were operated from a small cabin just out of view, situated between the fast lines.

3RD SEPTEMBER 1952 ● AUTHOR'S COLLECTION

HEATON NORRIS JUNCTION

A favourite photograph and location looking back towards Manchester. Bowerfold Lane bridge offered this commanding view of the railway complex on the approaches to Stockport. The lines curving away to the right offered a multitude of routes from Denton Junction to north Manchester, Guide Bridge and Stalybridge for Yorkshire and beyond. An immaculate No **45578 *United Provinces*** brings its train, once again the 2.20pm Euston express, past the old and new signalboxes. It was unusual to find stabled coaching stock here but this was Easter Monday and the siding acted as an overspill for Longsight whilst the passengers enjoyed the delights of Belle Vue.

19TH APRIL 1954 ● JIM DAVENPORT

The view looking south was equally as impressive. Flanking the former LNWR signals which dominate the scene (other than the Up Fast which is of LMS origin) is the busy Heaton Norris goods warehouse whilst on the right are the premises of the Signal and Telegraph Department. No **45742 *Connaught*** passes through Heaton Norris Station with a train from Birmingham, the exhaust from its double chimney obliterating the station building and No 1 signal box.

14TH MAY 1951 ● TOM LEWIS

STOCKPORT EDGELEY STATION

▲

The crew of No 45680 *Camperdown* observe the 25mph speed restriction and creep off the end of the viaduct into Edgeley Station's No 2 platform with a morning express. Also in view is 'Crab' 2-6-0 No **42789** from Farnley Junction and making for home territory with a mixed freight. Apart from those engines which were regularly observed by local enthusiasts, the gatherings at this point on the station or Bowerfold Lane eagerly anticipated those workings which would often produce a loco fresh off Crewe Works - sometimes a rare Jubilee - occasionally a Princess Royal or Duchess Pacific or the relative anticlimax of a spotless Class Five. Much rarer was the sighting of a Leeds Holbeck or Farnley Junction Jubilee passing through on its way to and from Crewe.

1959 ● AUTHOR'S COLLECTION

▲

Here today - gone tomorrow. Those large St Rollox numbers carried by No **45679** *Armada* were unique for a Longsight engine - but for seven weeks only! Midway through this short period, she awaits departure with a southbound train. Standing in the single bay between Platforms 1 and 2 and on pilot work is Stockport Edgeley MPD's last remaining Jinty, or 'Dobbin' as they were locally referred to, No **47431**.   21ST MAY 1960 ● D. FORSYTH

A pleasing study of No 45578 *United Provinces* on the loop ▶ line on the Down side of the station. Of more than passing interest behind the tender are figures on the boarded crossing leading to the carriage sidings. One carries a flag suggesting signal or points failure. The unmistakeable livery of a Palethorpes van stands along-side, awaiting forward movement to Bradford later in the day.

21ST JUNE 1957 ● B.W.L. BROOKSBANK

Another member which had sporadic periods at 9A was No 45655 *Keith*. This engine is perhaps more often associated with the Midland line and subsequently features later within the Trafford Park chapter. It emerges here from the gloom of Edgeley's short tunnels with W210 - a Swansea to Manchester London Road train. A 'now' and 'then' comparison would still reveal the Armoury drill hall with its distinctive tower looking down over proceedings but little else remains. The tunnels were opened out, not without difficulty, and track realigned with the advent of electrification two years later.   **1ST JUNE 1957 ● TOM LEWIS**

EDGELEY JUNCTION NO 1

The morning 10.37am express to Euston was a favourite for many local photographers. On this occasion Peter Hutchinson trains his camera on No **45556 *Nova Scotia*** at Edgeley Junction whilst his regular companion, Jim Davenport, stood shoulder to shoulder and did the same. Jim's picture appeared in an earlier volume *Stockport in the Days of Steam*, which may account for its familiarity to some. Locomotive exhaust obliterates the rear of the MPD but the capacity of the sidings, in the vee of the main line and the Cheadle branch, appears sorely tested - a fine sight and a reflection of the diversity and volume of freight traffic that passed through the town. Edgeley Junction No 1 signal box is in view whilst the smaller, No 2 box was situated at the throat of the shed yard. The premises and chimney of Thomas Woodrow & Sons, Hat Manufacturers, stand prominent alongside the start of the Buxton branch - a legacy of a once thriving local industry. *Hat Works - the Stockport Museum of Hatting*, is the only one of its kind in the UK dedicated solely to the subject.

19TH APRIL 1954 ● PETER HUTCHINSON

Only four Manchester Jubilees carried domeless boilers during the BR period. Nos 45578 *United Provinces* (December 1952 - August 1957), 45645 *Collingwood* (October 1957 - October 1963), 45600 *Bermuda* (July 1954 - June 1958) and **45555 *Quebec*** (June 1952 - February 1956). The latter approaches Stockport with a stopping train and is passing under the line between Davenport Junction and Cheadle Village Junction, known locally as the 'Khyber'. **19TH APRIL 1954** ● **JIM DAVENPORT**

◀ **This was another rarity.** No 45703 *Thunderer* came on to Longsight's books w/e 30th August 1947 but during its short twenty one month spell managed to appear in three different guises. The earlier Crimson Lake livery gave way to that of LMS 1946 lined black just after Nationalisation on 10th January 1948. On that date, *Thunderer* is believed to be the first Jubilee to re-enter traffic with no legend on the tender - a condition it retains in the photograph. Fifteen months later it received standard BR Gill Sans smokebox and cabside numerals. The southbound express with ex-GWR stock, still in chocolate and cream, is passing under Siddington Avenue Bridge, near the throat of Adswood Sidings.

9TH OCTOBER 1948 ● **TOM LEWIS**

ADSWOOD SIDINGS

No 45587 *Baroda* brings a Birmingham ▶ train past Adswood Sidings and over the former Midland main line which served Manchester's Central Station at a point referred to as 'Cross Bridges'. Siddington Avenue bridge is in the far distance whilst two lines of wagons are all that can be seen within the sprawling Adswood marshalling yard - beyond which stands the Bridge Hall Estate. Loco and scratch set make progress on the Up Fast but the tracks soon converge to Up and Down Main only at Adswood Road Signal box. The line then crosses the Ladybrook valley and on to Cheadle Hulme. *Baroda* spent most of the 1950's at 9A, but had a shedplate attached to the smokebox door on four different occasions.

11TH APRIL 1952 ● **B.K.B. GREEN**

A westerly sun highlighted southbound afternoon trains from the Up side of the same stretch of main line. The contours of No **45603 Solomon Islands,** Fowler tender and a uniform rake of stock make for this most pleasing picture. During April 1950, the loco had been observed at Birmingham New Street, still in LMS Crimson Lake livery with its new BR number but retaining LMS on the tender sides. By October it was in lined black with a large BR emblem on the tender before Brunswick Green was finally applied in April 1952.

8TH SEPTEMBER 1952 ● **B.K.B. GREEN**

CHEADLE HULME

◀ **Approaching the junction at Cheadle Hulme** and easing to take the Macclesfield line are No **45587 Baroda** and an unidentified 'Royal Scot' with a Euston express. Although undated, this was, in all probabilities, a Friday, as it was common practice to send a pilot engine south in order to work a northbound extra from the capital the following day.

1957 ● **M.S. WELCH**

BRAMHALL

The low shadow cast on the fence ▶ protecting Bramhall's Up platform betrays the fact that the train is the 12.05pm Manchester London Road - London Euston express. Yes - the sun shone brightly in the South Manchester suburbs on Christmas Eve in 1949 and rewarded local photographer Roy Davenport with this fine view of No **45740 Munster**, a loco which spent a decade on allocation but remained on the Western Division throughout its lifetime.

24TH DECEMBER 1949 ● **ROY DAVENPORT**

Longsight attracted a number of Jubilees whose stays were brief to say the least. No 45703 *Thunderer* (page 15) was one and **No 45688 *Polyphemus*** was another. Previously a Crewe North engine, it retained the tablet catcher bracket which rather disfigured the cab side number, but had been fitted for that shed's turns over the Stranraer line. The engine retained this plain black livery until June 1952 and had no tender legend for the latter part of its stay, but was to become one of nine subjected to modified draughting in 1957, by which time *Polyphemus* was established as one of the Bushbury elite. The 12.05pm express to Euston is viewed from Woodford Road bridge on the approaches to Poynton Station - a regular Jubilee turn at the time. The fledgling Pownall Green Estate stretches away in the distance beyond Bramhall Golf Course. Note the marker post on the embankment which signifies the northern boundary of the Prestbury Permanent Way gang length.   **AUGUST 1951 ● TOM LEWIS**

PRESTBURY

An impressive view of No 45603 *Solomon Islands* just south of Prestbury Station. This 'Jub' was remembered as a 'good un' by the old hands at 9A and managed to achieve 58,436 miles during 1952 - this despite a five week spell away at Crewe for a Heavy General! Unfortunately, it was away to Camden the following year, just one month after this photograph. The Up Prestbury Starting Signal, which is of early LMS corrugated pattern on a wooden post, is situated on the Down side due to difficulties caused to sighting by the curve.

6TH JUNE 1953 ● AUTHOR'S COLLECTION

Emerging from Hibel Road tunnel and into Macclesfield is No **45587** *Baroda* on a Birmingham train. To the right is the throat of the rather restricted site of Macclesfield MPD, the track leading directly on to a turntable which fed three roads. Hibel Road was the town's principal station until 1960, at which time major changes involved the redevelopment of neighbouring Central at the expense of Hibel Road, which was all but swept away. Of interest are the two water tanks in view. The nearer is of North Staffordshire origin, serving the shed, whilst beyond is a similar structure on land once occupied by the Great Central and North Staffordshire Joint Railway. A sleeper fence divided the properties. The local spotting fraternity still talk of the day in the mid 50's when a Jubilee visited their shed. No 45631 *Tanganyika* limped into Hibel Road Station one morning about 40 minutes late on an Up Euston. She promptly 'sat down' and a pair of Fowler 2-6-4T's were commandeered to take the train forward to Stoke.   1953 ● M.S. WELCH

MACCLESFIELD

A local Permanent Way Patrolman with a keying hammer and walking in the 6ft is seemingly oblivious to the passing of No **45553** *Canada* and a train of at least 12 bogies - the 4.05pm Manchester - London. This view is looking north from the Down platform end of Macclesfield Central Station and towards the junction of the Bollington and Marple line and Macclesfield Hibel Road Station, from where the train had called. Such were the stations' close proximity, the rear carriages are only just clear of Hibel Road's Up platform. No 45553 gets into its stride over Buxton Road bridge on the through road at Central. The large glass frontage of Arighi Bianchi is clearly visible - a building inspired by the Crystal Palace Exhibition of 1851 which, in turn, saw the creation of Joseph Paxton's glasshouse at Chatsworth. It was erected in 1884 by builders George Roylance, who utilised local ironwork cast at Harlow's Foundry. The northern portion just in view (the workshops) were demolished in the 1950's due to the considerable expense necessary for structural repair and the land became a car park. Moves are now afoot to rebuild it once more! When the local Council submitted plans for the new 'Silk Road' bypassing the town centre, they proposed the demolition of Arighi Bianchi's distinctive frontage. Such was the public outcry that common sense eventually prevailed and now road, rail and A.B.'s happily exist side by side.

3RD SEPTEMBER 1955 ● E.R. MORTEN

Schoolboy and infant stand side by side on the flagstones which comprise Macclesfield Central's Up platform. They are admiring a locomotive that was allocated to Longsight during the LMS period only (June 1937 to August 1941) - No **5668 *Madden*** gets away from Hibel Road with a train for the Capital. The coach behind the tender is ex-LNWR 3rd class corridor/compartment stock, ARC roof type and built at Wolverton c1900 to Diagram D268, It comprised seven compartments, six seats in each with lavatory at either end. The prominent building with small centre dome is a typical Victorian silk warehouse, known as the 'Royal Silk Warehouse' and owned by Messrs Brown, Robinson. The building is extant but, alas, no longer for silk.   **1939 ● E.R. MORTEN**

Climbing Moss Bank, two miles south of Central Station is No **45638 *Zanzibar***. Trains of ten carriages and over hauled by Jubilees required assistance up the 1 in 102 gradient here. Macclesfield MPD had a small allocation which consisted almost entirely of Fowler 2-6-4T's and one was always in evidence on these duties as and when required.   **1956 ● M.S. WELCH**

Approaching North Rode Junction, 4 miles south of Macclesfield is No **45644** *Howe* with repeater signals set for the Stoke line. The box here, which unusually faced the vee of the junction, was built by the North Staffordshire Railway in 1849. The picturesque Churnet Valley line branches off to the left, skirting Rudyard Lake before passing through Leek then on to Uttoxeter and thus bypassing the Stoke-on-Trent area. Overnight traffic such as the Huddersfield Hillhouse and Moston to Camden fitted freights used this diversionary route for many years, the latter train sometimes in the hands of a Newton Heath Jubilee.

30TH SEPTEMBER 1959 ● M. MENSING

STOKE-ON-TRENT

Entering Stoke-on-Trent Station with a Manchester to London express is No **5638 Zanzibar.** A feature of the Potteries area were the bottle ovens that dominated the skyline. A number are in view here beneath the bracket signal at the end of the Down main platform. Stoke-on-Trent College is also prominent to the right.   **c.1944 ● KIDDERMINSTER RAILWAY MUSEUM**

A Duchess Pacific from Polmadie, No 6224 Princess Alexandra draws level with No **5740 Munster** at Basford Hall, south of Crewe at 3.55pm on a Saturday afternoon. Both trains have passed through the complex without scheduled stops - the former, on the Up Fast, is working the 10.00am Glasgow Central to London Euston throughout and is running late. Before the outbreak of war, this would have been the prestigious 'Royal Scot' and its spotless locomotive would have appeared suitably adorned with headboard rather than a scruffy Reporting Number - all titled trains had been suspended from September 1939. No 6224 is presentable, however, and is carrying the 1946 lined black livery. The re-timed train was due in the capital at 6.20pm. With safety valves lifting, No 5740, the not so clean Longsight Jubilee, is unusually employed on the 2.15pm *Summer Saturdays Only* Llandudno to Birmingham New Street. Note the vintage ex-LNWR carriage behind the tender.

AUGUST 1947 ● AUTHOR'S COLLECTION

BASFORD HALL

Another unkempt member at the same ▶ location with what was still affectionately referred to by railwaymen as a 'horse and carriage' train - very much a former LNWR parlance. These were lengthy affairs of a great variety of stock and in their heyday worked daily in both directions between Glasgow and London and over other main line routes of the LMR. They were usually remarshalled at Carlisle and Crewe but the traffic was far less regular by BR days. No **45632** *Tonga* is another case of unusual motive power and is probably the third 'horse', having relieved another bringing the entourage south from Carlisle as far as Basford Hall Sidings.

8TH AUGUST 1954 ● B.K.B. GREEN

MADELEY BANK

The Treaty of London between the United Kingdom and Trans-Jordan granting total independence to the latter came into force on 17th June 1946, after which time No **5633**'s *Trans-Jordan* nameplates were removed. It subsequently became the first member to receive the new LMS Block Number 1946 glossy black livery at which time the replacement *Aden* plates were affixed and covered over until the official re-naming ceremony on 4th September 1946 at London Euston. The loco is caught in this condition on Madeley Bank hauling the 2.10pm (Sundays Only) Manchester London Road to London Euston express - a train consisting of 16 bogies. **21ST JULY 1946** ● J. D. DARBY

WHITMORE TROUGHS

◀ **Bowling along in fine style** on the Up Slow line is No **45644** *Howe* working an excursion train. The location is Whitmore troughs, situated 10 miles south of Crewe, and the first of five such sets between here and Euston averaging 35 miles between each. Those serving the fast lines were taken out of use on 14th March 1965 and those serving the slow lines six months later. This would have been one of the loco's last 'crack' turns over the West Coast Main Line as the following year she became surplus to requirements at Longsight. A rather inglorious transfer to Crewe South and into retirement, working almost exclusively on freight duties, was followed by withdrawal three years later. *Howe* then became one of 59 Jubilees to be cut up at Crewe Works.

4TH SEPTEMBER 1959 ● RAY FARRELL

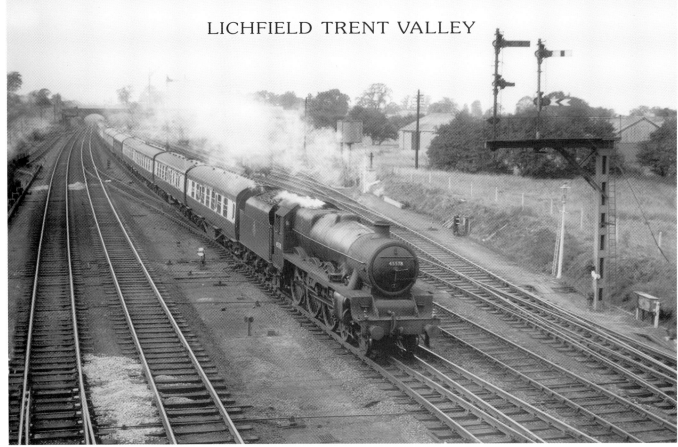

Firmly in control of proceedings is No 45578 *United Provinces,* approaching Lichfield at speed with a Manchester to London express. The capital city always appeared first on the carriage boards, irrespective of direction of travel.   **1ST SEPTEMBER 1956** ● **E.R. MORTEN**

A group of local trainspotters are engaged in conversation with the crew of No **45553** *Canada* at the north end of Lichfield Trent Valley Station. Others merely cast admiring glances before the Jubilee's departure. Whilst the traffic was always heavy here, nearby Tamworth offered even better scope where locos passing overhead on the Midland main line could also be recorded. Large numbers gathered in a convenient field, yet seldom were there problems. On the rare occasion juveniles appeared before a local magistrate accused of railway trespass, their case was dismissed. A Justice Of The Peace ruled as follows. *I consider the collecting of locomotive numbers to be a perfectly legitimate hobby and when pursued intelligently, may serve useful and instructive purposes. It should not be brought into disrepute.* Perhaps he was also a gricer!

c1954 ● **G.W. SHARPE**

The 12.15pm London Road to Euston sweeps through Lichfield Trent Valley Station behind No **45617** *Mauritius.* The leading coach is of interest being of LNWR origin. Hademore water troughs are two miles distant.
17TH JULY 1951 ● **R.J. BUCKLEY**

Heading north out of Rugby on the Trent Valley line with the 3.45pm Euston - London Road is No **45595 Southern Rhodesia.** Although a common feature on Stanier's larger engines, the coats of arms positioned above both nameplates were fitted to two members only - No 45595 and No 45739 *Ulster.* The latter - never a Manchester engine - spent virtually all its BR life on the Midland Division at Leeds Holbeck. Six months previous to this photograph, on November 5th 1957, No 45595 hauled the Up *Lancastrian* (4pm London Road to Euston) and narrowly escaped disaster at Kilsby *(see below)* when a 10 ton articulated lorry plunged 30ft over a bridge and on to the main line. Three minutes later, *Southern Rhodesia* struck the wreckage at high speed and parts of the lorry were carried into Kilsby Tunnel before the train came to a halt. Both lines were subsequently blocked and not re-opened until the following day. The engine was towed to Rugby later in the morning for repairs to bent coupling rods and attention to all cylinders. In the meantime, traffic was conveniently diverted via Northampton. **29TH APRIL 1958 ● M. MENSING**

RUGBY

Weedon Lane bridge, on the southern outskirts of Rugby, offered a fine panoramic view of the main line. No **45644 *Howe*** gets the 12.00 noon London Road to Euston train away past Hillmorton from its penultimate stop. **26TH MAY 1958 ● M. MENSING**

KILSBY TUNNEL

Some two miles further south, London-bound trains encountered the notorious Kilsby Tunnel. During excavation, 26 men lost their lives when unexpected water was struck. 8 months of continuous pumping was necessary and 36 million bricks were eventually used within its 1 mile 660 yard length. Two ventilating shafts of 60 feet diameter - one of which is 120 feet deep - offer flashes of light to alert passengers. An immaculate No **5668 *Madden*** is about to take the plunge with an unidentified train. The loco carries matching 1928 scroll type numerals on both cab side and smokebox door.

1ST JUNE 1938 ● H. GORDON TIDEY

GAYTON LOOPS

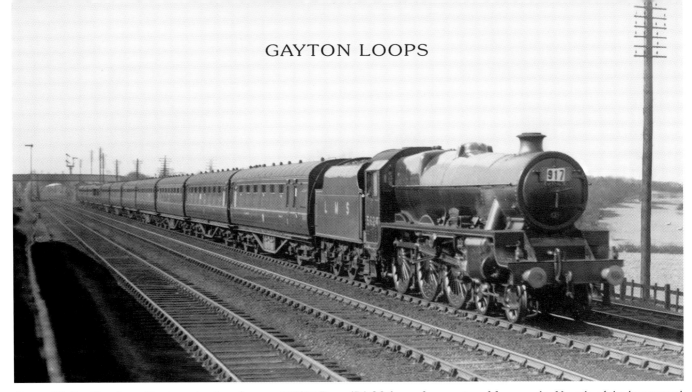

Some 63.5 miles from Euston stands a former LNWR Type 'D' 20 lever frame signal box on the Up side of the line named Gayton Loops. Built during 1876 in conjunction with the 879 yard long loop lines, it is just in view behind the rear coach. The tall signal in front of Bridge No 216 on the Down side was called 'Big Ben'. The box was re-named simply 'Gayton' in 1947. An immaculate No **5624 St. Helena,** with burnished buffers heads south at speed on Easter Saturday, 1937 - a condition suggesting a possible recent Royal Train outing. Although the loco's spell at Longsight in LMS days was officially a loan period, it lasted all of 14 months and received the 1936 sans serif style cabside numerals in the meantime during its first Heavy General overhaul.   **3RD APRIL 1937 ● L. HANSON**

CASTLETHORPE TROUGHS

Another London-bound Jubilee replenishes its tender at Castlethorpe Troughs. Although they are only 6 inches deep, some 2,000 gallons will either be taken aboard or cascaded as overflow as seems the case here, the scoop having been in contact for a mere 20 seconds. With Nos 45556 *Nova Scotia* and 45680 *Camperdown* both indisposed at Crewe Works, No **45578 *United Provinces*** arrived on a short term transfer from the North shed week-ending 26th November 1949 to assist over the Christmas period, but returned for a longer spell three years later. This photograph must be dated shortly after 8th August 1957, as the engine is now fitted with a domed boiler but still carries the first BR crest on the tender, and is in ex-works condition.   **AUGUST 1957 ● H. GORDON TIDEY**

LOUGHTON GOODS SIDING

The longest serving member of all the Jubilees which worked out of Longsight was No **45638 *Zanzibar*.** She arrived from Crewe North Shed during war time but after only four months was loaned to Edge Hill for a similar period. *Zanzibar* then settled down in March 1943 for a seventeen-year unbroken stint, brought to an end only by dieselisation. The author recalls her as always seeming to be on shed whenever he visited and was remembered with a certain amount of disdain. No 45638 treads a familiar road and is passing Loughton Goods Siding, approaching Wolverton with a northbound express. **20TH JUNE 1953 ● AUTHOR'S COLLECTION**

LAMBS SIDING

No **45644 *Howe*** passes Lambs Siding on the approaches to Bletchley with another Down express. Access to this siding, which served the local brickworks, was from the Fast Lines only and under the control of a 20 lever signal box of that name. The Slow Lines were the responsibility of Stoke Hammond and Bletchley No 1 boxes at this point. On the morning of 1st February 1957, *Howe* reached Edinburgh Princes Street and was then serviced at Dalry Road MPD. The occasion was a Scotland v Wales Rugby International, the supporters' train having originated from Neath the previous evening (8.27pm). **6TH MAY 1960 ● AUTHOR'S COLLECTION**

LINSLADE TUNNEL

This overhead view at Linslade, taken in bright sunlight from the castellated tunnel portal, nicely illustrates the contrasts offered by a loco carrying the 1946 black livery in ex-works condition. The LMS lettering, numerals **5556** and nameplate ***Nova Scotia*** positively gleam and are most legible. Loco and first carriage have just passed under the Stoke Road bridge on the Up Fast and are about to plunge into the central twin bore of the 283 yard long tunnel, just north of Bletchley. Passage through the Down Fast, the track to the left of the train, often created problems for enginemen because of the narrow confines of the single track bore. Travelling at speed could potentially cause compression, resulting in the fire blowing back. **2ND OCTOBER 1948 ● B.W.L. BROOKSBANK**

LEIGHTON BUZZARD

◀ **A trio of photographs** epitomising Jubilees hard at work on the West Coast Main Line. No **45723** *Fearless* blasts through Leighton Buzzard Station with a Euston express. A creditable performance log of this long serving engine featured in the April 1956 edition of *Trains Illustrated* working over the arduous North and West route south of Shrewsbury. After brief interludes at Crewe North, interspersed by a longer one at Carlisle Upperby, *Fearless* remained on the West Coast Main Line to the end, eking out her final years at Rugby and Nuneaton MPD's.

1954 ● REAL PHOTOS

Overtaking a southbound local train ▶ near Leighton Buzzard on the Up Fast is No **5741** *Leinster.* The outbreak of hostilities brought about immediate speed restrictions of 45mph which were later relaxed to 60mph on certain lines in October 1939, by which time the railway network had become temporarily Nationalised. This photograph, perhaps taken somewhat surreptitiously, was a most fortunate 'grab shot' as on 21st March 1942, *Leinster* became one of Longsight's wartime Jubilee arrivals. The majority, naturally, eluded the camera at a time of prohibition and shortage of material but records show that Nos 5623 *Palestine,* 5625 *Sarawak,* 5630 *Swaziland,* 5635 *Tobago,* 5653 *Barham,* 5672 *Anson,* 5708 *Resolution,* 5720 *Indomitable* and others graced the allocation list. Whether they all displayed 9A shedplates however remains debatable.

7TH AUGUST 1942 ● H.C. CASSERLEY

CHEDDINGTON

◀ **The 1953 summer timetable** produced an interesting development with the regular rostering of a Longsight engine through to Brighton on the south coast. The duty was the overnight Friday 11.40pm Manchester to Hastings via Brighton and Eastbourne and the 12.30pm return from Hastings the following day. On 1st August 1953 the turn produced Caprotti Class Five No 44686 and the following week, Jubilee No **45595** *Southern Rhodesia.* There was a degree of conjecture about this but her arrival was deemed acceptable by the SR authorities. By 1959, No 45595 was into its ninth and final year at 9A. Shortly before transfer, the immaculate loco is caught tearing upgrade near Cheddington with the 12.05pm London Road - Euston. She returned once more to Crewe North week ending 20th June, this being the seventh time!

JUNE 1959 ● M.S. WELCH

TRING CUTTING

Thundering south through the mile long Tring Cutting with the Up *Mancunian* is No **45553 *Canada*.** The train is nearing the station, after which the final 32 miles to the Capital are virtually all down gradient.
                                                                                     c1951 ● A. BARNARD COLLECTION

No 45592 *Indore* arrived from Crewe in June 1948 after a Light overhaul ▶ still in Crimson Lake livery. She is working a Down express north of Berkhamsted now carrying BR lined black applied ten months later.
                                                                                     JUNE 1949 ● R.K. BLENCOWE

It was surprising to discover that No 45693 *Agamemnon* was officially a Longsight engine - for one week only prior to wartime! Records show that she arrived from Willesden week-ending 29th April 1939 and the following day, a Sunday, prolific photographer H.C. Casserley recorded her working northbound through Berkhamsted on an unidentified train - thus making this photo the most unique in the book. By the following weekend, she was on her travels again - on loan to neighbouring Patricroft for a further week and then to Edge Hill. Two years later she was off to Polmadie, never to return south. Consequently she became one of the few Jubilees to have spent the entire BR period in Scotland (at Corkerhill) and was a much sought after locomotive.   **30TH APRIL 1939 ● H.C. CASSERLEY**
                                                                                     ▼

BERKHAMSTED

The introduction of an emergency timetable after the onset of war led to many weird and wonderful locomotive workings and combinations. Timings were slower and trains often heavier which may account for these two Longsight Jubilees working in tandem. No **5741 _Leinster_** is piloting No **5723 _Fearless_** north of Berkhamsted Station with the 10.15am from Euston to London Road.

15TH MAY 1944 ● H.C. CASSERLEY

Similarly, the Down 'Comet' merely became the 11.50 am to Manchester London Road. No **5625 _Sarawak_** passes by on the working at the same location. This loco spent three periods on the books, once more restricted to LMS days, during which time she suffered minor damage from enemy action at Nuneaton on 17th May 1941.

19TH AUGUST 1939 ● H.C. CASSERLEY

The 5.30pm from Euston to Manchester ceased to be a named train _(The Lancastrian)_ and now stopped at Crewe where a Liverpool portion was detached. A fifteen minute pause was allowed for this before London Road was eventually reached at 10.10pm. No **5666 _Cornwallis_** has singular control of the heavy train, pictured north of Berkhamsted. This loco spent a lifetime on the Western Division but only briefly as a Manchester engine during the LMS period.

14TH JULY 1939 ● H.C. CASSERLEY

◄**A post-war scene showing No 5638 _Zanzibar_** approaching Northchurch tunnel with the 12.15pm Euston to Manchester via Stoke. The engine is working hard on the continuous climb through the Chiltern Hills to the summit at Tring and a fine speed has already been attained. The 347 yard long tunnel situated between Berkhamsted and Tring was widened during the 1870's by two single bores which accommodated the Up and Down slow lines (far left). Brick, rather than stone portals were utilised. Inquisitive passengers are treated to fine views of the Grand Union Canal which runs close to the line for the next sixty miles.

8TH AUGUST 1948 ● H.C. CASSERLEY

Approaching Northchurch Tunnel from the north with the heavy 10.20am ex-Manchester London Road is flagship loco No **5552 Silver Jubilee.** This train ran via Stoke with fifteen bogies, including a combined portion added at Stockport Edgeley from Halifax (depart 9.10am) and Colne (depart 8.10am). The severe weather may well account for the loco's grubby condition as Longsight were instructed to keep her smart. Despite the conditions, the train is running to time with arrival at Euston scheduled for 2.25pm.

7TH MARCH 1947 ● H.C. CASSERLEY

A Longsight Jubilee regularly worked up to London from Crewe with an express fish to Broad Street (7pm ex-Wyre Dock), returning on the 2.40pm ex-Camden Yard express freight as far as Crewe. No **45603 Solomon Islands** makes fine progress north of Berkhamsted with the latter train and appears to be in the BR mixed traffic livery of lined black.

20TH APRIL 1951 ● AUTHOR'S COLLECTION

BOURNE END

Bourne End Signal Box was situated midway between the towns of Hemel Hempstead and Berkhamsted - a distance of 3.5 miles. It contained a 48 lever LNW tappet frame and, whilst having control of all Up and Down movements within its own section, was also able to divert traffic from Up and Down Fast on to the slow lines and vice versa if necessary. A major disaster occurred here on 30th September 1945 when Royal Scot No 6157 *The Royal Artillaryman* came to grief with the 8.20am Perth to London Euston. The train was diverted from Fast to Slow line but the crew ignored the statutory 20mph speed restriction and derailed with the loss of 43 lives. No **45617 Mauritius,** still showing LMS on the tender, thunders by on the Up Fast in this view taken from the box.

JUNE 1949 ● AUTHOR'S COLLECTION

WATFORD TUNNEL

Having arrived with the Up 'Mancunian', No 45587 *Baroda* reverses her stock out of the station from within the shadow of the Euston arrival platforms - despite still showing Class 1 lamps. The fact that *Baroda* is coupled to a Stanier tender dates the photograph as post-March 1959 by which time it was extremely unusual to find a Jubilee on this train. The previous year she had worked the 'Annual Public Excursion' between Euston and Crewe on 6th August 1958, presumably as a way of getting home, as Crewe North Class Five No 44761 returned the train back to the Capital.   **1959** ● **M.S. WELCH**

LONDON EUSTON STATION

Locomotive and crew workings were ▶ quite independent. During 1954, Camden had a single engine working daily to Manchester whilst nine Longsight locos arrived in the Capital on passenger and parcels trains. All were booked for Class 7 power, including their five Britannia Pacifics. Weekend and summer reliefs bought others and accounted for a regular Jubilee presence. Longsight crews covered five daily and one three-days-weekly workings to Euston. Camden supplied men from their 2nd, 3rd or 4th link whilst Willesden crews had three weekend summer jobs to Manchester. No **45578 *United Provinces*** and train occupy Platform 2 shortly after arrival.

1954 ● **N.R. PREEDY**

◀ **In the early BR period, Jubilees were regularly diagrammed for *The Mancunian*** despite Longsight having Class 7 power to call on. The arrival of five BR Britannia Pacifics (Nos 70030-34) by January 1953, however, was significant and the Jubilees' appearance on this service then became more sporadic. *The Mancunian* was inaugurated on 26th July 1927 and withdrawn on 9th September 1939 along with other named trains as a wartime measure. British Railways re-introduced the name, together with *The Comet* on 26th September 1949. No **45718 *Dreadnought*** emerges at speed from the southern portal of Watford tunnel carrying the train nameboard on the smokebox door. This was one of only four expresses entitled to carry the extra Coronation Crown and Cypher headboard but didn't always do so (the others were *The Royal Scot, The Thames-Clyde Express* and *The Ulster Express*). The third titled train operating between London and Manchester over the West Coast main line, *The Lancastrian*, was particularly short lived in the BR period. After its re-introduction on 16th September 1957 (along with the Midland Division's *The Palatine*), it last ran on 8th September 1962. *The Mancunian* survived until 15th April 1966.   **9TH AUGUST 1952** ● **B. MORRISON**

CHEADLE HULME

◄ **The 11.55am Manchester London Road to Plymouth express** takes the Crewe line and rattles through Cheadle Hulme with No **45587 Baroda** in charge. The cattle dock here is a legacy of a once thriving farming community, whilst, also in earlier days, Lord Vernon distributed his coal through Cheadle Hulme from the nearby Poynton Collieries and had a yard opposite the station. Wagons remain in evidence beyond the Macclesfield lines trailing off to the right. *Baroda's* ten year spell at 9A was interspersed by three short periods away at Preston, Crewe North and Bushbury, but she was a regular over the North & West route.

8TH AUGUST 1953 ● B.K.B. GREEN

A member not readily associated with Longsight is the now ▶ preserved No **5593 Kolhapur.** Naturally, this engine's history has been well documented, but an interesting wartime snippet was a special assignment conveying Winston Churchill from Liverpool Lime Street to London Euston on his return from America. Six years later and now sporting black livery, No 5593 ambles through the Cheshire countryside between Handforth and Cheadle Hulme with a Down express.

12TH JUNE 1948 ● TOM LEWIS

The driver of immaculate No 45680 Camperdown finds time to survey the local scenery. Engine and train are passing the independent Cheadle Hulme School and he is perhaps admiring its fine architectural detail. She was one of at least thirteen to reach the BR period still carrying the LMS Crimson Lake livery, arriving at Longsight in October 1947. Although eventually cut up at Crewe in June 1963, a highly detailed miniature 5" gauge locomotive, built by an ex-Longsight fitter, survives in active service and runs on occasional Sunday afternoons at the Stockport Model Engineering Society's headquarters at Grove Park, Cheadle Hulme.

29TH NOVEMBER 1953 ● TOM LEWIS
▼

Cheadle Hulme School features within this elevated picture taken at virtually the same spot, but there the similarity ends as the condition of No **45709** *Implacable* leaves much to be desired. This member, along with No 5662 *Kempenfelt*, suffered wartime damage on 10th October 1940 at Kentish Town MPD.

SEPTEMBER 1951 ● AUTHOR'S COLLECTION

Traces of a sprinkling of snow still remain evident within the vacant MOD Sidings at Handforth, but there are no such signs on the main line over which many trains have already passed in each direction since daybreak. No **45632** *Tonga,* with an uncharacteristically dirty chimney, makes haste with the 10.50am Manchester London Road to Plymouth express. On New Year's Eve 1952, she had appeared at Bradford with the 11.45am from St. Pancras, but arrived too late to return with the 6.05pm Bradford to Derby, so retired to Leeds (Holbeck) MPD light engine.

27TH FEBRUARY 1955 ● B.K.B. GREEN

HANDFORTH

The 6.30pm Manchester (Mayfield) to Crewe local called at all stations except Heaton Norris, arriving at 7.45pm. No **45617** *Mauritius* slowly departs from Handforth with a lightweight train including an assortment of parcels vans bringing up the rear. The balancing Down service, the 3.42pm Crewe to Mayfield, was somewhat quicker, calling at Wilmslow and Stockport only, and an ex-works loco running in from Crewe often featured on both trains.

21ST MAY 1952 ● TOM LEWIS

THE STYAL LOOP

A dramatic lineside view of No 45644 *Howe* making for Wilmslow via the Styal Loop, which offered a convenient path avoiding the busy environs of Stockport. The Up *Mancunian* is about to cross the River Mersey and former CLC line, situated midway between East Didsbury and Gatley Stations. *Howe's* arrival came about as a result of the Anglo - Scottish Jubilee exchanges which involved twelve locos moving in either direction at the end of August 1952. The purpose was to concentrate all the Scottish based engines as having sloping throatplates and larger fireboxes for ease of maintenance at St. Rollox Works - the boilers not being interchangeable. Much to the delight of local gricers, No 45644 arrived from Perth whilst No 45718 *Dreadnought* went in the opposite direction. The other Manchester locos involved were No 45720 *Indomitable* which left Patricroft for Corkerhill in exchange for No 45645 *Collingwood*.

26TH FEBRUARY 1953 ● TOM LEWIS

Approaching the Heald Green Distant Signal is No **5638 *Zanzibar*** with the 9.45am Up London train. Prior to the War, this train was 'The Mancunian' but a further 16 months would elapse before the title was re-introduced.

12TH MAY 1948 ● R. E. GEE

The Up *Mancunian* once again, but now within the Urban District of Wilmslow and approaching the Bollin viaduct serving the Styal route. The train called at Wilmslow Station before joining the Stockport line to proceed non stop to London Euston on a tight schedule. No **45723 *Fearless*** brings her carmine and cream stock appropriately designated, but, for reasons unknown, the locomotive headboard was missing. Unfortunately this was a common occurrence.

21ST APRIL 1951 ● ROY DAVENPORT

This was evidently a favourite location for three cameramen whose quality of work is widely acknowledged. Brian Green and Tom Lewis's views are coupled to this one taken by Jim Davenport of No **45709** *Implacable* with the morning *West of England*. This loco was one of a handful to receive the BR Mixed Traffic livery of black, lined in red, cream and grey, and carried a BR standard chimney (as does No 45632 *Tonga* below).

1953 ● JIM DAVENPORT

WILMSLOW

Crossing the Bollin Valley immediately north of Wilmslow Station is No **45555** *Quebec* with a morning stopping train, possibly the 9.15am Birmingham New Street to Manchester London Road. The Styal line trails in on the right, gaining access to the station by an independent viaduct built sixty years after the one in view. On 28th October 1951, *Quebec* was an unusual occupant of Bristol Barrow Road MPD together with Edge Hill's No 45567 *South Australia,* whilst on 1st April 1953, a derailment caused the diversion of some North to West trains via Wolverhampton, Stourbridge and Worcester - including No 45555 on the 7.26am Manchester - Cardiff.

19TH APRIL 1954 ● ROY DAVENPORT

A familiar viewpoint overlooking the approaches to Wilmslow Station from the south. No **45632** *Tonga* gets smartly away with W212 - the 9.50am Relief Manchester London Road to Paignton. The London Midland engine headcodes were letters and numbers pasted on a board fixed to the upper part of the smokebox door, which often obscured the numberplate. The prefix letter denoted the appropriate Division, in this case Western. Even suffix numbers denoted Up trains, and odd numbers Down trains. These numbers were sub-divided as follows: W1 - 499: Ordinary trains. W500-739: Special trains which passed over other Divisions as well as the Western. W740 - 999: Special trains running over Western Division only.

8TH AUGUST 1953 ● B.K.B. GREEN

A trackside view at the same location from within the goods yard sees No **45624 St Helena** racing south with an unidentified express. Like other large Depots, Longsight wasn't averse to borrowing locos when the situation demanded. Such an occasion occurred on Tuesday, 28th April 1959 when *St Helena*, now of Camden, found herself re-visiting old haunts and was later that day pressed into service working the 5.50pm express commuter train to Buxton, usually a job for a 2-6-4 tank engine.

1952 ● ROY DAVENPORT

ALDERLEY EDGE

Highlighted by a strong morning sun, the Great Western passenger stock betrays the fact that this train is, once more, the Manchester to Plymouth. No **45723 Fearless** has passed through Alderley Edge and makes towards Chelford in the heart of the Cheshire countryside.

26TH MAY 1956 ● TOM LEWIS

A nice panoramic view of Sandbach Station, amidst much interesting infrastructure, looking north - some might say a modellers' delight. With safety valves lifting, No **45680 Camperdown** is impatient to restart the 3.15pm all stations to Crewe from its penultimate stop. This train was another running-in turn and the Longsight Jubilee had recently been through the shops for a Light Intermediate Repair.

14TH JUNE 1957 ● A.C. GILBERT

SANDBACH

CREWE

Threading its way into Crewe Station off the Manchester line is No **45680 *Camperdown.*** This is the familiar pre-electrification scene overlooking the complex of lines at North Junction. There are plumes of steam in the distance, looking in the Chester direction. The tender coupled to an ex-works loco is clearly visible whilst the only other sign of activity appears to be beyond the train on the main line. This is probably a pilot loco and stock awaiting the signal before setting back. On 6th November 1950, *Camperdown* failed here with blower trouble on the 11.55am Manchester - Plymouth and was hastily replaced by Compound 4-4-0 No 1168 (9A) and Class 2P No 40659 (5A).
c1956 ● M.S. WELCH

◄ **Taking the Chester line** and passing between the Works and the throat of Crewe North Shed yard is No **5593 *Kolhapur,*** clearly displaying the 9A shedplate carried from December 1943 to July 1951. **1946 ● REAL PHOTOS**

The wall behind No 45740 *Munster* and leading carriages is unmistakably that at the south end of Crewe Station. It will be recognised not only by those enthusiasts who griced from the platforms, but also many others as it often featured in photographs within their cherished *Ian Allan ABCs.* The train is for the South West but during the evening of 21st June 1952, No 45740 was seen heading a special out of Bristol, probably for Manchester as Longsight's No **45500 *Patriot*** had worked through to Bristol the same afternoon. *Munster* also handled Dynamometer Car tests between Wolverhampton and Euston during March and April 1937. **11TH JUNE 1950 ● B.K.B. GREEN**

▼

A distinctly grubby No 45740 *Munster* passes through the platforms from the North Shed ready to relieve a southbound departure.

20TH JUNE 1951 ● JIM DAVENPORT

In direct contrast, a common occurrence here was that of an ex-works loco running in, passing through the environs of the station with fresh paint glistening - assuming the sun was out. No **45595 *Southern Rhodesia*** presents a glorious sight from the footbridge, skirting around the side of the North shed, having received her last Heavy General overhaul. She remained paired with a Fowler tender (the third) until her next overhaul fifteen months later, a Light Intermediate, at which time a Stanier version, ex-No 48165, became available. Behind the loco and cycle shed are the offices of the District Motive Power Superintendent and stores, between which was the shed entrance. I wonder how many spotters have 'run the gauntlet' here over the years?

20TH JUNE 1957 ● B.W.L. BROOKSBANK

Waiting to relieve a train off the North and West route is No **45644 *Howe*.** The view looking south from almost the same spot as above reveals the impressive screening shielding Platform 1 from the ravages of inclement weather. A multitude of parcels and passengers alike used the facilities here. Bus transport within Crewe was catered for by Crosville Motor Services Ltd and as the railway station was some distance from the town centre, a shuttle service (K20) operated at regular intervals. Other routes passed by or terminated at the station. The Crosville fleet of nearly 1,200 vehicles was composed to a great extent of those of Bristol manufacture, and two examples await departure on Nantwich Road. The station frontage was typically LNWR in design.

AUGUST 1958 ● M.S. WELCH

WHITCHURCH

The Indian sub-continent within the British Empire provided scope to name twenty-one members of the class. The world famous Taj Mahal, situated in the city of Agra, fell within the United Provinces and No 5578 was bestowed with this name on 3rd March 1938. This loco was one of only four Manchester Jubilees to carry domeless boilers during the BR period, these being Nos 45578 *United Provinces* (December 1952 - August 1957), 45555 *Quebec* (June 1952 - February 1956), 45600 *Bermuda* (July 1954 - June 1958) and 45645 *Collingwood* (October 1957 - October 1963). No **45578 *United Provinces*** leaves Whitchurch Station with a local train for Shrewsbury. The line diverging left is the former Cambrian route to Oswestry.　　**6TH AUGUST 1955 ● E.R. MORTEN**

WEM

The Shropshire market town of Wem, situated between Whitchurch and Shrewsbury, is famous for its sweet peas. It was also well known to enthusiasts as a good vantage point to observe ex-works engines 'running-in' from Crewe and one would have thought that the majority of Jubilees might have passed along this way at one time or another. With traces of snow beneath the point rodding, No **45578 *United Provinces*** once more progresses south through Wem Station with a van train. She now has a domed boiler *(compare with above)* and, as the tender carries the second BR totem, the date must be between 22nd October 1958 and her transfer away on 20th June 1959.

JANUARY 1959 ● AUTHOR'S COLLECTION

Rolling off the viaduct and negotiating English Bridge Junction on the southern approaches to the station is No **45632 Tonga** with a Plymouth to Manchester train. Passing by is Britannia Pacific No **70025 Royal Star** which has clear signals for its homeward journey, and standing prominent behind the Cardiff Canton engine is the 14th century Great West tower, part of the Abbey church dating back to 1083.

JUNE 1955 ● G.W. SHARPE

SHREWSBURY

Brewing up in the centre road with parcels vans behind the tender is No **45678 De Robeck.** She is hardly in the best of condition and records show the loco as being on loan from Crewe North for a five month period early in 1951. The 9A shedplate is almost the cleanest item about the engine! Others which enjoyed temporary residence during the BR period were Nos 45613 *Kenya* (Upperby), 45622 *Nyasaland* (Trafford Park), 45643 *Rodney* (Crewe North), 45652 *Hawke* (Trafford Park), 45736 *Phoenix* (Crewe North) and 45737 *Atlas* (Crewe North).

FEBRUARY 1951 ● R.K. BLENCOWE

Standing in Platform 2 is No 45689 *Ajax,* having arrived with a stopping passenger train from Crewe on a filling-in duty.

13TH AUGUST 1955 ● B. MORRISON

One of those classic views showing off the elegant lines of the Jubilee locomotive to best advantage. No **45595 Southern Rhodesia** draws away from the station with a Paignton to Liverpool train. Literally towering over the station and its environs from the west is Shrewsbury Castle, situated on the banks of the River Severn which passes directly beneath the railway, just south of the platforms.

21ST JULY 1954 ● B. MORRISON

The north end of Shrewsbury Station was a popular vantage point and this magnificent gantry carrying an array of ex-GWR lower quadrant signals with distinctive finials has featured in many a photograph over the years. On this occasion, a pair of Longsight locos are framed in perfect light. The points are set and No **45644** *Howe* has the 'right away' from Platform 1 for the Crewe line with a Manchester bound excursion. Meanwhile, unrebuilt Patriot No **45501** *St. Dunstans* stands in the centre road, awaiting the arrival of the next train off the North and West route and is ready to relieve an incoming GWR engine.　　　　**AUGUST 1957 ● AUTHOR'S COLLECTION**

The gantry features yet again in this view looking North East. The signal is off for the Wrexham direction and 'Castle' Class 4-6-0 No **5010** *Restormel Castle* gets slowly away. The train is a Paddington to Birkenhead express and this Stafford Road engine would have relieved a 'King' Class 4-6-0 at Wolverhampton Low Level Station to work on as far as Chester. At the time, Birkenhead MPD had a handful of 'Grange' Class 4-6-0's which were used on the last leg. Occupying the Patriot's position in the previous picture, No **45723** *Fearless* awaits her turn to take a train forward. Strategically, Shrewsbury was an important and busy junction - none more so than on a Summer Saturday when it became a trainspotters' paradise and all manner of ex-GWR, LMS and BR classes could be observed. Prior to 1959, the heavier 'King' Class 4-6-0's had not been permitted north of Wolverhampton but, after trials, the ban was relaxed and they were regularly observed here. Thus, for a short period, it was possible to see a 'King' and a 'Duchess' Pacific working alongside in ordinary service - unique to Shrewsbury!

JUNE 1954 ● M.S. WELCH

41

BAYSTON HILL

From the commencement of the 1949 Summer Timetable, the Longsight engine working the 9.20am Manchester London Road to West of England express continued through to Pontypool Road *(see also page 45)*. No **45638 *Zanzibar*** gets to grips with the gradient and passes the village of Bayston Hill, situated three miles south of Shrewsbury, with the train. Locos were often borrowed by Trafford Park, as was the case on 23rd November 1955 when *Zanzibar* was observed leaving London St Pancras with the 6.40pm Manchester Central train - piloted by a Bournville Compound 4-4-0 No 41194.

13TH APRIL 1950 ● N. PREEDY COLLECTION

CHURCH STRETTON

The North to West cross country route was the principal artery of communication between Lancashire and the western part of the Western Region comprising South Wales, Bristol, Devon and Cornwall. In pre-Nationalisation days it was jointly owned by the LMS and GWR from Shrewsbury as far south as Hereford, and the 51 mile route is, scenically, considered one of the most beautiful stretches of line in the country. In this picture just north of All Stretton Halt near Church Stretton, the Welsh mountains lie to the west, whilst Lawley Hill is prominent. No **45587 *Baroda*** brings the 7.30am Penzance to Manchester (London Road) which includes a catering car sandwiched between two Brake 3rds immediately behind the tender. The first seven carriages are all roofboarded, which display both termini and principal intermediate stations. Note the extra pole situated to alleviate the additional stress of telegraph wires on a curve. **10TH JUNE 1957 ● M. MENSING**

The 3.55pm Shrewsbury to Hereford stopping train consisting of ex-GWR Collett stock in carmine and cream, arrives at All Stretton Halt behind No **45689 Ajax.** The journey involved calling at 16 stations and halts en route and took two hours - hardly ideal work for a Jubilee. Being a Bank Holiday Monday there is every likelihood that the engine was needed later in the day to work north with a returning Whitsuntide extra. Longsight engines of both 6P and 7P classification were daily visitors to the North and West line during the 1950s but on the odd occasion were presented with problems. On 6th September 1956 a collision at Ludlow resulted in the 9.25am Manchester to Swansea running from Shrewsbury via Wellington to Wolverhampton Low Level. No 45680 *Camperdown* was relieved here in favour of a GWR loco for the onward journey via Stourbridge Junction, Worcester Foregate Street and Great Malvern to Hereford. *Camperdown* later returned on the 3.20pm Wolverhampton to Wellington local before proceeding on to Shrewsbury with the empty stock.

10TH JUNE 1957 ● M. MENSING

CRAVEN ARMS
AND STOKESAY

◄ **The gradients on the North and West route are severe.** Southbound trains are immediately faced with a 12 ½ mile climb from Shrewsbury to Church Stretton whilst those in the opposite direction have a slightly longer ascent beginning south of Ludlow. Four miles south of Church Stretton lies the small town of Craven Arms whose station opened in 1853 and was named after the local coaching inn. It was renamed Craven Arms and Stokesay in 1879, reverting to its original name in 1974. Shortly after the war, the elusive No **45741 Leinster** is caught standing at the station with a stopping train. Despite her grubby condition, the loco still retains the original *to traffic* livery of 29th December 1936 complete with sans serif numerals.

10TH APRIL 1946 ● F.M. BUTTERFIELD

The village station at Berrington & Eye was an early casualty on the former Shrewsbury & Hereford Joint Railway, closing in 1958. Fifty years later, the old Station Master's house - a fine example of sandstone - remains extant and in private ownership. No **45587** *Baroda* once again features, easing its way into the platform with the 3.55pm Shrewsbury to Hereford stopping train. **1957** ● **AUTHOR'S COLLECTION** ▶

The Manchester to Cardiff train treads cautiously out of Hereford Station and under the Aylestone Road bridge. With safety valves lifting, No **45578** *United Provinces* was one of the Longsight regulars working through the city throughout the 1950's. Prior to this, there had been a loco change at Shrewsbury on most Up expresses. There is a Great Western presence in the form of a 2251 Class 0-6-0, probably on pilot duty on a centre road within the station vicinity, although a second Stanier tender also manages to creep into view.

5TH JUNE 1958 ● **G.M. SHOULTS**
▼

HEREFORD

The approach to Hereford (Barrs Court) Station from the south was by way of Red Hill and Rotherwas Junctions. No **45631** *Tanganyika* has charge of the 7.30am Penzance to Manchester London Road and is ½ mile distant from Rotherwas Junction where the main line to Newport diverged from the line to Ross-on-Wye. **7TH APRIL 1958** ● **M. MENSING**

LLANVIHANGEL

No 45624 *St.Helena* brings the morning West of England express through the deserted platforms of Llanvihangel Station *(left)*. If on time, the Shrewsbury crew then had a 1 hour 45 minute period at Pontypool Road to rest and prepare their loco for the return working. Photographer Martin Shoults spent part of the afternoon at Llanvihangel recording the traffic. After photographing the southbound train, the following locos passed by in the interim period: GWR 4-6-0's Nos 6908 *Downham Hall,* 6901 *Arley Hall* and 5054 *Earl of Ducie,* ex-LNWR 0-8-0 No 49033 and finally BR Standard 4-6-0 No 75009. *St Helena* then re-appeared in fine style, breasting the summit at the station with the 7.30am Penzance to Manchester *(below).* The seven mile southern approach was much more formidable than that from the north - the climb beginning in earnest from the Usk Bridge at Penpergwm through Abergavenny.

14TH JUNE 1954 ● G.M. SHOULTS

Although relatively camera shy during its five year stay at 9A, No 45624 was a regularly observed loco off the beaten track. On 20th July 1952 she arrived at Aberdeen with the 10.15am from Glasgow and returned on the 5.25pm. On 30th December 1955, *St. Helena* worked the 6.00pm Leeds City to Morecambe and the 8.50 return. On 15th December 1956, she carried Manchester United supporters on a football excursion from Manchester London Road to Bordesley, that being the nearest station to Birmingham City's ground. The route from Crewe was via Market Drayton, Wellington, Wolverhampton (Low Level) and Birmingham (Snow Hill) and the loco went on to Tyseley MPD for servicing. Finally, on 17th March 1957, No 45624 piloted BR Standard Pacific No 71000 *Duke of Gloucester* on the 11.15am London Euston to Carlisle throughout.

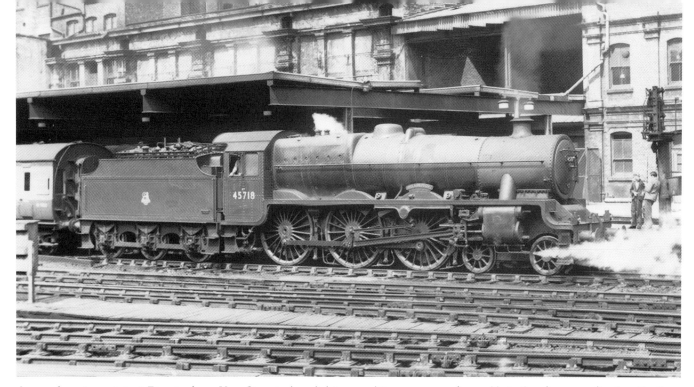

A popular viewpoint at Birmingham New Street where lighting conditions were now favourable in the afternoon after the attentions of the Luftwaffe. The London and North Western side of the station suffered severe damage during the Second World War and in 1948 temporary shelters were erected which lasted throughout the 1950's. With cylinder cocks open, No **45718 *Dreadnought*** stands in Platform 3 at the east end, having just arrived with a Manchester train.　　　　　**31ST JULY 1952** ◉ **AUTHOR'S COLLECTION**

BIRMINGHAM NEW STREET

Drifting slowly through the station between Platforms 3 and 4 is No **45556 *Nova Scotia*** after another arrival from Manchester.

20TH NOVEMBER 1950 ◉ **MILLBROOK HOUSE COLLECTION**

Departing for Manchester in the opposite direction, No 45587 *Baroda* gets away from the west end of Platform 6 with an afternoon express. The imposing building is the rear of the Queens Hotel.

1954 ◉ **AUTHOR'S COLLECTION**

MONUMENT LANE

Bursting forth from the short tunnel ▶ after departing from New Street Station, No **45723 *Fearless*** passes within the restricted confines of Monument Lane MPD. The train, the 4.45pm from Birmingham to Manchester via Stoke was recorded on the occasion of a shed visit by the *Manchester Locomotive Society* whose itinerary that day covered the Wolverhampton and Birmingham districts. A coal drencher unit, an appliance used to soak loco coal prior to it being discharged into the bunkers, is prominent on the right. This helped restrict dust pollution within the neighbourhood.

18TH MAY 1952 ◉ **JOHN SPENCER**

DUDLEY PORT

Leaving a dirty exhaust in its wake, No 45638 *Zanzibar* blasts her way through the ramshackle Dudley Port (High Level) Station with a morning Manchester to Birmingham train. Standing in the island platform is ex-LNWR No 2-4-2T No **46712** waiting to leave with the 'Dudley Dasher', a shuttle service which operated between here and Dudley. The Low Level station lines passed under both the high level lines and an aqueduct carrying the *Birmingham Canal* at this point. **JULY 1949** ● **MILLBROOK HOUSE COLLECTION**

PERRY BARR

Roaring through Perry Barr Station at 60mph is the southbound *Pines Express* with No **45644** *Howe* in charge. Being a Wednesday, the train would proceed by way of Bushbury Junction and Bescot to New Street, (where *Howe* was diagrammed to make way for a Derby loco), crossing from the Western to the Midland Division in the process. The route was somewhat different on a Summer Saturday when both Up and Down trains, together with two southbound reliefs, ran via Darlaston to Walsall, where the locomotive exchanges took place. From there the route was via the former Midland branch through Sutton Coldfield to Castle Bromwich, proceeding via Camp Hill and Kings Norton, thus avoiding the busy environs of Birmingham New Street. During the 1950s, Longsight's Caprotti Class Fives regularly featured on this train, supported by their Class 6P and 7P locos, whilst Derby tended to use Class Fives or the occasional Jubilee. **27TH JUNE 1956** ● **M. MENSING**

CHESTER

Passing the Great Western shed at Chester is No 45632 *Tonga*, easing the 9.45am Llandudno - Manchester Exchange into General Station. Chester was a hive of activity on a summer Saturday in the 1950's and a good number of Jubilees passed through the city. The loco is recently ex-works and may not yet have returned to its home depot, but to suggest that she would be next allocated to this very shed, Chester West, (four years later) was almost beyond comprehension. **10TH JULY 1954 ● B.W.L. BROOKSBANK**

No 45680 *Camperdown* heads a northbound express at Winwick on the West Coast main line. Earlier in the year, the Rugby League Cup Final at Wembley was played between fierce Cumbrian rivals Workington and Barrow on 30th April. This ensured a heavy excursion programme over the Furness line the previous evening and into the small hours which involved four Manchester Jubilees. *Camperdown* worked the 4.10am Barrow to St. Pancras whilst the 4.30am Barrow to Euston went forward behind another Longsight member, No 45689 *Ajax*. The 6.45am Barrow to Wembley Central had Patricroft's No 45668 *Madden,* assisted to Ulverston by 2-6-4T No 42395. The trains from Workington took the Barrow avoiding line, and on one of these another 9A engine, No 45578 *United Provinces* passed Dalton at 2.32am. **AUGUST1955 ● N.R. PREEDY**

BUXTON

Whilst going about their regular work, Jubilees usually displayed Class 1 headlamps which signified 'Express Passenger Train'. This standard locomotive code also indicated 'Breakdown Train going to clear the line' and was given priority en route by signalmen. No **45680 *Camperdown*** found herself at Buxton with the Longsight crane and vintage support vehicles - a job usually performed at that time by Class 2P 4-4-0 No 40674 which was kept in light steam for such duties. No 45680 has been sent to assist a Mold Junction WD 2-8-0 No 90242 which had come to grief descending the 1 in 66 from Buxton No 1 signal box to Buxton East Junction whilst marshalling loaded wagons. The larger Crewe crane was also summoned and duly arrived behind Warrington Class Five No 45354. There was no shortage of motive power as a pair of 8Fs and a 'Super D' 0-8-0 from the local depot were also on standby.

17TH JUNE 1953 ● E.R. MORTEN

COLWYN BAY

Longsight Jubilees were uncommon in North Wales and it may well be that No **5552** *Silver Jubilee* had been borrowed on this occasion. The Saturday excursion bowls along the picturesque shore of Colwyn Bay, the rear carriages passing the site of Old Colwyn Station. Although numerically first of class, it would appear that *Silver Jubilee* was the last member to carry LMS numerals. The engine emerged from Crewe with raised cab side numerals and standard BR Gill Sans front number plate week-ending 25th September 1951.

5TH JUNE 1948 ● AUTHOR'S COLLECTION

Prior to dieselisation, all Euston to Blackpool trains were handled by Camden Top Link who utilised Class 7 motive power, except for one working by Blackpool shed who used their Jubilees. Additionally, the Saturday 5.05pm Euston to Blackpool, which was a much lighter load than weekdays, engaged a Longsight engine - often a Jubilee. The loco had worked up to the Capital earlier in the day and was then diagrammed for this train, returning to London with the following day's 2.45pm from Blackpool Central via the coast route. Shortly after departure, No **45680** *Camperdown* cautiously brings this train 'bang road' near Gillett's Crossing on the approach to St. Annes.   **c1957 ● D.T. GREENWOOD**

THE FYLDE COAST

The same train making slightly better progress near St. Annes with No **45638** *Zanzibar.* Six years earlier, this loco had also been used for an interesting working, when on 19th August 1953 she handled an excursion from Sowerby Bridge to Morecambe (Promenade) via the ex-GN Halifax - Queensbury - Keighley branch. The train was piloted by Bradford Hammerton Street's N1 0-6-2T No 69449 between Halifax and Keighley in both directions.   **5TH APRIL 1959 ● PETER FITTON**

ROCHDALE

Caught within the environs of Rochdale is No **45623** *Palestine.* The loco and its train of empty stock off a London Euston to Oldham holiday extra, is descending the short bank from Milnrow Road overbridge to Rochdale East Junction. This was during *Palestine's* fourth and final short sojourn at Longsight but she was later to become a familiar sight in the area sporting a 26A and later 9D Newton Heath shedplate.

25TH JUNE 1960 ● R.S. GREENWOOD

DROYLSDEN

Photographs of No 45734 *Meteor* displaying a 9A plate in the BR period are rare. Having spent the greater part of the war at Longsight, *Meteor* returned for a further 15 months in April 1950 before becoming one of the Bushbury elite, moving on with No 45742 *Connaught* week-ending 7th July 1951. The 9.50am Newcastle to Liverpool express approaches Droylsden Station on the outskirts of Manchester with the pilot loco displaying commendably clean plates on the smokebox door. The train engine is an unidentified 'Royal Scot'

MAY 1951 ● JIM DAVENPORT

UPPERMILL

The Longsight Jubilees were regularly observed on the former LNWR line between Manchester and Leeds. A grubby **No 45633** *Aden* forges upgrade near Uppermill with the 2.20pm Liverpool Lime Street to Newcastle express, a train which appears to be composed entirely of Gresley stock. No 45633 will be relieved at Leeds City by ex-LNER motive power and was the first member to receive the 1946 black livery.

MARCH 1949 ● JIM DAVENPORT

DELPH JUNCTION

The final member of the class, double chimneyed No **45742 Connaught** makes a rousing appearance with the same train. The wooden platforms of Moorgate Halt are situated immediately behind Delph Junction Signal Cabin, shrouded in exhaust. The Delph Branch line is on the right and paralleled the main line for 440 yards before curving away towards Dobcross. **25TH APRIL 1953** ● **JIM DAVENPORT**

LINTHWAITE

No 45632 Tonga pilots a rebuilt Patriot (unidentified) ▷ through Linthwaite, west of Huddersfield, on the climb to Marsden and Standedge. Meanwhile, a Stourton 8F, No **48721** struggles along with a westbound excursion. The train, the 9.50am ex-Newcastle, was another duty which involved a Longsight loco. It firstly worked the 10.40pm ex-Liverpool parcels forward from Stockport, departing at 12.34am (Saturdays Excepted) throughout to York before returning to Leeds with the 7.30am 'all stations'. It then retired to Farnley Junction MPD for servicing and next piloted the 9.50am Newcastle to Liverpool as far as Manchester Exchange. The return working was the 4.12pm stopping train to Leeds before ending the day with yet another piloting job, this time the York - Shrewsbury and Liverpool forward from Leeds (depart 10.42pm). This train divided at Stalybridge, with the pilot loco taking the Shrewsbury portion on to Stockport before, presumably, returning light engine to Longsight. On Saturdays it was a Crewe North running-in turn.

1955 ● **AUTHOR'S COLLECTION**

HUDDERSFIELD

◁ **The immediate post-war period** presented a great many irregularities and it was not uncommon to find Class 5 4-6-0s working minor passenger services around the West Riding. No **5603 Solomon Islands** finds herself awaiting departure at the head of a three coach train to Bradford (Exchange) via Halifax in the No 2 bay at Huddersfield. Such a duty had previously been considered below the capabilities of such a powerful engine. This loco, which features prominently in earlier pages during the BR period, enjoyed an initial four year spell at Longsight from April 1943.

2ND OCTOBER 1946 ● **F. ALCOCK**

THE PEAK DISTRICT

When Trafford Park MPD was short of express passenger locomotives, Longsight usually stepped into the breach. Here are three examples of their Jubilees on loan, working over the former Midland main line with Manchester Central to London St Pancras services.

◄ **The enginemen of No 45553** *Canada* observe the mandatory speed restriction whilst passing through Rowsley Station with the 1.55pm Up express.

23RD JANUARY 1955 ● **E.R. MORTEN**

A loco very much at home over the route was No ► **45655** *Keith.* Having been a Trafford Park loco for many years, she returned after a year away at Longsight. The date of this photo is significant insofar as it was taken on the last day of May 1951. Official records show the loco as having moved back week-ending 2nd June 1951, but a 9A plate remains clearly affixed! The train is the 2.15pm ex-St.Pancras and is passing an 8F in the loop at Peak Forest.

31ST MAY 1951 ● **E.R. MORTEN**

An interesting vantage point made possible by renowned cameraman Ray Morten's possession of a lineside permit. He was also safe in the knowledge that Sundays saw little traffic over the Peak. No **45680** *Camperdown,* again with the 1.55pm Up express, catches the sun between the short Chee Tor Tunnels - situated between Millers Dale Junction and Station. She was one of ony three Jubilees whose liveries changed directly from Crimson Lake to Brunswick Green. (The others were Nos 45670 *Howard of Effingham* and 45720 *Indomitable*)

15TH JULY 1951 ● **E.R. MORTEN**
▼

ALTRINCHAM

During the rebuilding of Manchester London Road Station and the Crewe to Manchester electrification between 1957-60, many express trains were subjected to daily diversion - a popular route being that from Sandbach via Middlewich to Northwich and then via the MSJ&A, terminating at Manchester Central Station. No **45578 *United Provinces*** is caught passing through Altrincham Station on one such train.
AUGUST 1959 ● R. H. HUGHES

MANCHESTER (EXCHANGE) STATION

No 45555 *Quebec* is at Manchester (Exchange) Station with empty stock for Ordsall Lane.
10TH APRIL 1954 ● PETER HUTCHINSON

MONUMENT LANE

No 45631 *Tanganyika* 4TH AUGUST 1960 ● F.A. WYCHERLEY

 BLACKPOOL (NORTH)

No 45638 *Zanzibar* 26TH APRIL 1953 ● K. BOULTER

 BUSHBURY

No 5561 *Saskatchewan* 2ND AUGUST 1936 ● F.A. WYCHERLEY

NEWTON HEATH

No 45680 *Camperdown* 1955 ● N. PREEDY

 SHREWSBURY

No 45644 *Howe* 1954 ● G.W. SHARPE

CAMDEN

No 45680 *Camperdown* 20TH JULY 1958 ● R. BROUGH

WILLESDEN

No 5631 *Tanganyika* 13TH JUNE 1945 ● H.C. CASSERLEY

BLACKPOOL (CENTRAL)

No 45736 *Phoenix* 11TH JUNE 1952 ● AUTHOR'S COLLECTION

THE
STOCKPORT
(EDGELEY)
LOCOMOTIVES

By the time Stockport Edgeley became the recipient of members of the class, cascading had become commonplace and old favourites could now be found at the unlikeliest of places such as Canklow, Agecroft and even the ex-LNER stronghold of Sheffield (Darnall). A pair, Nos **45596 *Bahamas*** and 45632 *Tonga* arrived from Carlisle (Upperby) week-ending 21st July 1962, both in excellent condition, *Tonga* having been through Crewe Works for the last time three months earlier. Having been displaced from West Coast Main Line duties, they were immediately put to use on the overnight Aberystwyth to York mail train, worked by Farnley Junction men, as far as Leeds. Nicely illuminated here, is what was later to become the pride of Edgeley, *Bahamas* herself, passing down the yard in readiness for her next turn. This classic view shows the elegance of the Jubilee class to great advantage, although the purists would take issue about the double chimney!

3RD MARCH 1963 ● W.A. BROWN

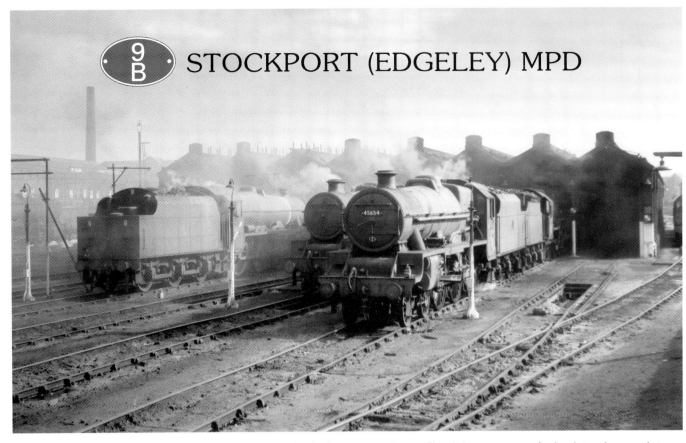

⬭ 9B STOCKPORT (EDGELEY) MPD

A trio of Jubilees, all in steam, grace the shed yard. This happy coincidence offered the opportunity for local signalman and steam enthusiast Tony Steele to record Nos **45632 *Tonga*, 45596 *Bahamas*** and **45654 *Hood*** all awaiting their next duties.

16TH MAY 1965 ● A. STEELE

Standing amidst deposits of ash and clinker on the shed arrival road is No **45678 *De Robeck*.** This loco and others became surplus to requirements at Carlisle Kingmoor MPD which was receiving increasing numbers of Britannia Pacifics by this time. She arrived week-ending 25th August 1962, by which time both *Bahamas* and *Hood* had found themselves popular with engine-men. Unfortunately this engine bucked the trend and soon became an early candidate for withdrawal after the discovery of a cracked frame. Subsequently, *De Robeck* was restricted to local work and during October was placed in store awaiting a decision. Shedmaster Terry Smith had submitted a shopping proposal which was rejected and was officially withdrawn w/e 8th December 1962 and banished to the Sand Sidings behind the shed. She was sold locally for scrap to Taylor Brothers, Trafford Park, being finally cut up during January 1964. This was unusual for the class and only two other members were similarly, locally dealt with - neither of which were ever Manchester locos. No 45695 *Minotaur,* after its ill-fated collision at Broadheath by J. S. Parker of Altrincham and No 45606 *Falkland Islands* in Wardleworth goods shed by Carrex Metals of Rochdale.

5TH OCTOBER 1962 ● A. STEELE

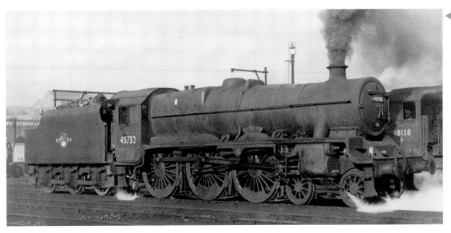

◀ **With the unexpected withdrawal of *De Robeck*,** a replacement arrived in early 1963 from Blackpool in the shape of No **45732 *Sanspareil*,** a loco which had spent nearly all its life at Carlisle Kingmoor. The cab side of this grubby member still displays the larger St Rollox numerals and retains the small bracket associated with tablet-catching apparatus, but her name-plates have been removed. With cylinder cocks open, No 45732 is about to reverse out of the shed yard. Locomen always called this engine *Sasperella*.

25TH JULY 1963 ● A. STEELE

No 45632 *Tonga* had been a familiar sight passing through Stockport as one of the Longsight contingent during the 1950's, but after regional boundary changes in February 1958, the loco rather surprisingly found herself at the former GWR depot at Chester West with Nos 45613 *Kenya* and 45624 *St Helena* for company. They featured on the Chester - Paddington services as far as Wolverhampton but were all transferred away within the year, after which time Shrewsbury MPD assumed control and ex-GWR engines were in evidence once more. No 45632 stands just clear of the shed building on the shortened No 8 road, having been prepared for an inter-regional working.
20TH JUNE 1963 ● G. HARROP

Another portrait of No 45596 *Bahamas*. Having arrived back on shed, the Jubilee awaits her turn for servicing on the reception road. During September 1963, *Bahamas's* tender had a slight altercation with a diesel shunter in Farnley Junction shed yard, which resulted in a visit to Horwich Works where she awaited her fate. The decision to withdraw the loco was met by a fierce rebuke from the Edgeley Shedmaster Terry Smith, who had developed a penchant for what he regarded as *his* engine. His powers of persuasion resulted in the decision being overturned. She eventually returned to Edgeley where it was apparent that the replacement tender (No 10750) was not only filthy but rusting in places, again to the consternation of Smith. He immediately ordered a quantity of Brunswick Green paint and a pair of totem transfers from Crewe Works. Shed labourer Eric Dunscombe then set to work on No 1 road, cleaning and then preparing the tender. He applied the paint using a brush called a 'Turk's Head' which had previously only been used for whitewashing the turntable pit! Unfortunately, the totem transfers were of the smaller size and looked slightly out of place on the larger, Stanier tender.
29TH FEBRUARY 1964 ● A.C. GILBERT

A loco long associated with the Midland Division was No 45654 *Hood.* Her arrival from nearby Newton Heath in March 1964 was unexpected and she duly returned there 18 months later. Even more unexpected was the arrival of a trio of Britannia Pacifics in June 1965, leaving No 45596 *Bahamas* as the sole Jubilee representative.　　　**3RD JULY 1965　●　N. FIELDS**

As a result of tests conducted on No 45722 *Defence* at the Rugby Stationary Plant in 1956, various modifications were made to 8 members, including No **45596** *Bahamas,* which received a double blastpipe. The double chimney was fitted during a Heavy General overhaul at Crewe in early 1961, at which time she received boiler No 8604 previously fitted to No 45580 *Burma.* No 45596 is stood at the end of No 7 road inside the depot, apparently receiving attention to the double blastpipe itself which had been removed and placed on the running plate above the buffer beam. A 'Not To Be Moved' disc is also evident. Standard Class 2 2-6-2T No **84026** stands in steam on the adjacent road.

18TH SEPTEMBER 1965　●　PETER FITTON

Receiving coal from the electrically-operated conveyor belt is No **45654** *Hood.* The servicing of locomotives was especially labour-intensive at Stockport Edgeley. Coal was shovelled manually from adjacent wagons on to the belt and hot ash and clinker similarly removed from the pit into the ash wagons, one of which stands to the right of *Hood.* The firedropper's cabin stands between the belt and the original LNWR coal stage with water tank over

4TH AUGUST 1964　●　A. BARNARD COLLECTION

Six Jubilees featured on the allocation list. Three were considered good engines whilst the others were indifferent, to say the least.

No 45670 *Howard of Effingham*. Arrived initially on loan from Derby w/e 26th September 1964, a move made permanent two weeks later. After a further fortnight and following a boiler washout, Foreman Fitter Charlie Cross declared the loco 'unfit for work' and she was withdrawn on the spot. Her Stanier tender was rescued before before being sent for scrap and attached to one of the sheds 8F 2-8-0's which had been previously paired with a Fowler version.

No 45678 *De Robeck*. Arrived from Carlisle (Kingmoor) in August 1962 in poor condition and was remembered as a rough rider. After storage, was officially withdrawn four months later with a suspected cracked frame.

No 45732 *Sanspareil*. The best of the others. Another Kingmoor import via Blackpool Central. Lasted 13 months.

◄ **Another view of No 45632 *Tonga*.** Officially, this loco had moved to Newton Heath during the previous month!

18TH SEPTEMBER 1965 ● PETER FITTON

No 45654 *Hood* drifts down the shed yard and is caught in the close company of Stanier 8F No **48503**, a visitor from nearby Heaton Mersey MPD. A cinder path leading from a gate on Booth Street to the building is to the left, which was the official entrance, although access could also be gained off the Sykes Bleachworks Branch behind the premises. 18TH SEPTEMBER 1965 ● PAUL CLAXTON

The former Sand Sidings behind the shed alongside the Cheadle line were used for storing withdrawn locos prior to disposal. Rather surprisingly, the front numberplate remains in situ here, but in her prime, No **45678 *De Robeck*** had always been a Western Division engine and during one of its many spells at Crewe North was loaned to Longsight as cover, whilst a succession of their own members received attention between January and June 1952. Her activities whilst at Edgeley were few but on 29th August 1962 she worked the 06.03 'Divi' shunt up the Buxton branch as did the other short lived loco, No 45670 *Howard of Effingham* on 5th October 1964.

20TH JUNE 1963 ● G. HARROP

STOCKPORT (EDGELEY) STATION

◀ **Making her way back to the depot, No 45654 *Hood*** awaits the road at the south end of Platform 2 on a rather dank summer's day.

4TH AUGUST 1965 ● **KEN TYLER**

No 45596 *Bahamas* going about her business at Stockport Edgeley Station marshalling parcels stock.

14TH MAY 1966 ● **JOHN CLARKE** ▼

HEATON NORRIS JUNCTION

An atmospheric winter action shot of No 45632 *Tonga* approaching Heaton Norris Junction with a northbound mixed freight. The main running lines are flanked here by Wellington Road Goods Depot (left) and the Signal and Telegraph Department Sidings (right). The view is from Bowerfold Lane bridge, a popular haunt for enthusiasts over the years. **17TH NOVEMBER 1964** ● **G. WHITEHEAD**

MONSAL DALE

The ex-Midland main line south of Millers Dale Junction was familiar territory for Heaton Mersey engines and men, but not for their counterparts at Edgeley. Having travelled by way of the Buxton Branch and Ashwood Dale, No **45632 *Tonga***, which has probably been borrowed, is passing Monsal Dale Signal Box with an express freight destined for Rowsley. The severe winter of 1963 recorded her deputising for 'Peak' diesels on no fewer than three occasions, working the same train - the 9.15am Nottingham Midland to Manchester Central. (5th, 15th and 18th February 1963). Later in the year (27th November 1963), *Tonga* ventured further afield when she arrived at Newcastle Central 35 minutes late with the 5.00pm from Liverpool (Lime Street), having worked through from Manchester (Exchange). She left with the return working next day at 8.42am, but ran short of steam and was replaced by an A3 Pacific at Darlington.

4TH JULY 1964 ● AUTHOR'S COLLECTION

TIPTON

Stockport Edgeley's engines regularly worked south to the Wolverhampton and Birmingham area on parcels traffic, No **45654 *Hood*** arrives at Tipton Station with a short Down train.

1964 ● M.S. WELCH

BIRMINGHAM NEW STREET

Blowing off steam within the confines of Birmingham New Street Station is No **45654 *Hood*** once more - this time having arrived with a holiday relief from Rhyl. During the year, *Hood* had been observed on several occasions off the beaten track. On 10th July, she substituted for a failed diesel at Leeds City on the 3.16pm Newcastle to Liverpool and despite leaving 24 minutes late, had recovered 4 minutes by Huddersfield. Although there was a strict embargo on the use of Jubilees south of Crewe, on 29th September No 45654 worked the 10.40am Healey Mills to Aston goods.

8TH AUGUST 1964 ● AUTHOR'S COLLECTION

MALTON

◀ **Threading its way through the Derwent Valley** on the approaches to Malton is No **45732** *Sanspareil* with a special bound for Scarborough. Newton Heath engines were regularly observed this far east during the summer season, but Edgeley engines far less so. *Sanspareil* appears to have been a popular engine during its year-long stint and, although a regular sight on the Buxton Branch with freight and Parcels duties - on 25th June 1963 she worked ECS from Longsight to Buxton, the train comprising 2 x 2-car DMU's.

8TH AUGUST 1963 ● N. SKINNER

SHAP WELLS

Light engines trundling up Shap weren't exactly a common sight, especially Stockport Edgeley ones. The exhaust nicely picks out the shapely outlines of No **45654** *Hood* as she makes for Carlisle. During the previous week commencing Monday 20th July, *Hood* had been borrowed by Blackpool MPD to work the 8.45am Blackpool Central to Lakeside (Mon, Wed and Fri) and Windermere (Tue and Thurs). On Saturday, 25th July, *Hood* had the 10.35am (SO) to Perth as far as Carlisle. Ray Farrell captured her the following Thursday, but was she still working out of Blackpool? **30TH JULY 1964 ● RAY FARRELL**

WINWICK JUNCTION

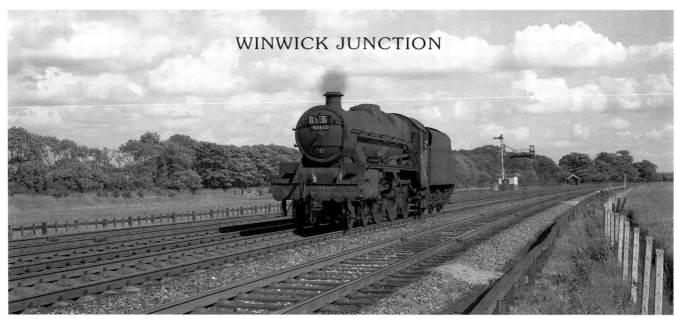

Another member caught running light engine northbound on the West Coast Main Line. In this case No **45632** *Tonga* makes for Wigan at Winwick Junction, showing an indecipherable reporting number (the second pasted digit having come adrift from its board). The photo is undated although *Tonga* is carrying her diagonal stripes. **c1964 ● GERALD DROUGHT**

QUEENS ROAD CARRIAGE SIDINGS

Further evidence of a borrowed locomotive. No 45596 *Bahamas* finds herself in the company of two Newton Heath Class Fives within Queens Road Carriage Sidings. All three are biding their time before drifting down Red Bank and into Manchester Victoria to head up respective 'residentials'. *Bahamas* is earmarked for the 4.55pm express to Blackpool North.   **15TH MAY 1964 ● R.S. GREENWOOD**

PRESTON

The likelihood of two photographers recording the same train on a normal weekday service at different stages of its journey was fairly remote. Nevertheless, Peter Fitton has managed to capture No **45596 *Bahamas*** again, this time getting away from Preston and about to pass the site of the ex-LNWR depot there. The previous month - on 23rd April, *Bahamas* had been borrowed by Trafford Park to work the 5.22pm commuter train to Buxton.   **15TH MAY 1964 ● PETER FITTON**

Just prior to Nationalisation, some Edgeley enginemen had experience working with Jubilees. Driver Jack Pickford was sent to Longsight to work the 2.25pm Manchester London Road to Euston express. 9A's No 5552 *Silver Jubilee* was his engine and it had a bad reputation for steam. After preparation and about to move off shed, he was approached by a Longsight man. *"Your'e a rum bugger Pickford. We've all refused to take it"*. His response was curt. *"You flaming well come and tell me when I've rung off the shed. I can't stop the job now"*. With that, Driver Pickford and his mate were on their mettle, but he advised his fireman as follows. *"They've got sloping fireboxes. When we leave Manchester, get your dart and spread the fire. Shift all this from under the door and fire her thin. If you put it under the door, it more or less rolls to the front on the blast of the engine"*. As a result they had a marvellous trip and arrived in Euston bang on time. They then went on to Camden shed where he soon discovered that the engine had a similar reputation. He was told in no uncertain terms *'You're having that bugger back'*. The return journey was also trouble free and when they got to Longsight shed to book off, the Foreman, 'Leonardo', who didn't like Edgeley men, sarcastically asked if they had run on time. Pickford had the last laugh. *"On time London, on time Manchester, no problem"*. His jaw dropped. The man was speechless.

KIRKHAM

Nos 45632 *Tonga* and 45596 *Bahamas* both handled Blackpool excursions on the same summer Sunday in 1963. *Tonga* brought 1Z38 from her home town Stockport *(top)* whilst *Bahamas* worked 1T61 from Pendleton (Broad Street) *(above)*. The trains are passing through Kirkham bound for North and Central Stations respectively.

4TH AUGUST 1963 ● PAUL CLAXTON

No 45632 *Tonga* returned the following March, although on this occasion the train was the 10.25am Manchester Victoria to Blackpool North. The loco is likely to have been borrowed by Newton Heath for the duty.

23RD MARCH 1964 ● DAVE HAMPSON

ST. ANNES

This was familiar territory for No 45732 *Sanspareil* having been a Blackpool engine for the last six months of 1962. The stopping train is the 7.05pm Blackpool Central to Rochdale, comprising 4 bogies, which, again, was a Newton Heath working. St Annes was the third of seventeen stations served en-route and, according to the timetable, arrival at Rochdale was 9.24pm

14TH AUGUST 1963 ● PETER FITTON

LLANDUDNO JUNCTION

In tandem with an unidentified Stanier Class 5, No **45632** *Tonga* awaits the signal within the platforms of Llandudno Junction Station before proceeding to the nearby engine shed, having brought an excursion to the North Wales resort. The 00.30 Birkenhead to Buxton freight often required banking assistance from Cheadle Village Junction and on 7th November 1963, York B1 No 61018 *Gnu* had *Tonga* coupled to the brake van for company. Other observations include a special from Whaley Bridge to Southport (1T63) on 30th June 1964, whilst the following Monday, 1st July, she worked the Mayfield to Buxton parcels before returning light engine back to Edgeley - a regular turn.

AUGUST 1962 ● JOHN SPENCER

NEW MILLS (NEWTOWN)

The 'Divi'-Shunt, was a name bestowed by Edgeley men on the daily local trip job up the Buxton Branch. After leaving Edgeley Sidings at 6.03am, four wagons of coal were left on the 'Block Road' at at the Stockport Co-op Sidings *(hence the nickname)*. After shunting, the loco would proceed on to Disley Goods, then to New Mills (Newtown) where the crew would have their breakfast after attending to whatever work was necessary. Next stop was Whaley Bridge which occasionally involved a short trip down to Shallcross Yard. A return to Edgeley Sidings was scheduled for 2.00pm, after which the loco retired to the shed. This, of course, was rather mundane work for 9B's flagship loco No **45596** *Bahamas,* but she continued to be regularly diagrammed for the duty during the first three years of her four year stay. With the tender just beyond the New Mills (Newtown) signalbox, a very presentable *Bahamas* rests between shunting duties.

MARCH 1963 ● BILL AVEYARD

BUXTON UP SIDINGS

By the end of 1964 the loco's external condition had deteriorated, but it wouldn't be long before she was spruced up again. Now running nameless, No **45596** *Bahamas* reverses its short train of oil tanker wagons into Buxton Up (or Lower) Sidings on New Year's Eve. When the diagonal yellow stripe was applied to the Edgeley trio (*Bahamas, Tonga* and *Hood*) by a painter seconded from Crewe, Passed Cleaner John Nixon requested that the band be kept within the cabside lining, which in his, (and many others) opinion was less obtrusive. The request was upheld.

31ST DECEMBER 1964 ● KEN TYLER

HELLIFIELD

By 1966, the unique double-chimneyed No 45596 *Bahamas* was the only Jubilee left at Edgeley and she became something of a celebrity in the first half of that year. Although bereft of nameplates, Shedmaster Smith kept the loco in immaculate condition and *Bahamas* was occasionally called out for a return to the main line. On a bitterly cold day in April, The *Stephenson Locomotive Society* organised a *Lakes and Fells Railtour* which departed from Manchester Exchange and ran via Bolton and Blackburn to Hellifield, encountering blizzards on the way. Here she was relieved by the celebrated ex-LNER Pacific already secured for preservation, No *4472 Flying Scotsman*. Later in the day, *Bahamas* retraced her steps back to Manchester.

2ND APRIL 1966 ● RAY FARRELL

SECURED AT LAST!

Despite the occasional railtour, by mid-July 1966 No 45596 *Bahamas* had been placed in store behind the shed with its double chimney sacked over. Rumours abounded and speculation was rife regarding the possibilities of preservation. In January 1967, a local press announcement stated that the locomotive had been bought from British Railways for £3,000 by the newly formed *Bahamas Locomotive Society*. After a further nine month period of storage, she was delivered to *The Hunslet Engine Company* at Leeds for overhaul back to main line standards, costing a further £6,500. On 11th March 1968, *Bahamas* re-emerged in this pseudo-LMS guise with numerals and a shade of red that hardly satisfied the purists.

16TH MARCH 1968 ● G. HARROP

OPEN DAY AT STOCKPORT (EDGELEY)

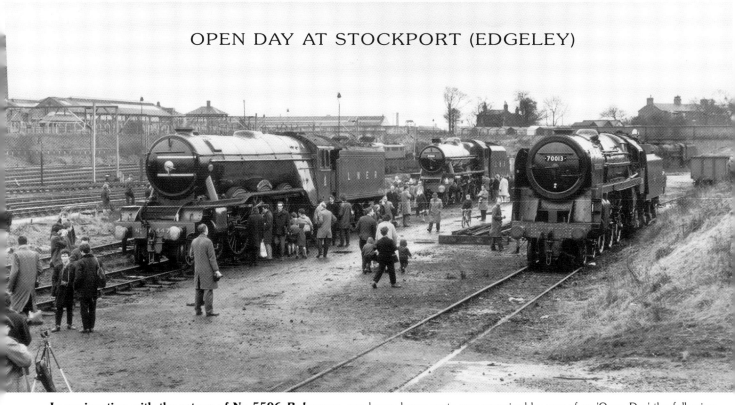

In conjunction with the return of No 5596 *Bahamas*, a welcome home party was organised by way of an 'Open Day' the following Saturday in the Sand Sidings behind the Depot. The event was well attended and visiting engines, Britannia Pacific No **70013** *Oliver Cromwell* and ex-LNER Pacific No **4472** *Flying Scotsman* were also present and were due to haul *Williams Deacons Bank Club* Specials to Carnforth the following day. Note the withdrawn steam locos and electric loco on standby duty. **16TH MARCH 1968** ● **M.S. WELCH**

THE BAHAMAS LOCOMOTIVE SOCIETY

Engine No 5596 was constructed at the Queen's Park works of the North British Locomotive Co in Glasgow toward the end of 1934. As one of the 191 examples of the 'Jubilee' class, the engine entered traffic with the LMS railway in January 1935 and was allocated to Crewe. It was named *Bahamas* during its first service repair at Crewe Works in June 1936. The engine subsequently operated from Preston, Camden, Willesden, Kentish Town and Derby, prior to the outbreak of the Second World War. Indeed, its highest annual mileage was during 1939 when it achieved in excess of 72,000 miles during that year. During the war period *Bahamas* worked from Grimesthorpe, Millhouses and Bristol. It was back at Crewe by 1947, and would see further operation from Edge Hill and Carlisle.

It was while the engine was based at Carlisle that it became the subject of, what subsequently became, the last attempt by the British Railways engineering team to improve steam locomotive performance. This was the fitting of a double blastpipe and exhaust system. The concept and design of this arrangement had evolved at the Rugby Locomotive Testing Station during 1956/57 during a series of trials on another member of the 'Jubilee' class, No.45722 *Defence*. The intention was to find ways of keeping these engines as effective forms of motive power for the duration of their remaining lifetime and until newer forms of traction could replace them.

The double exhaust system designed for the Jubilees was found to increase the steaming capacity of the boiler by some 30 per cent. Not only that, but further tests also proved the effectiveness of the design using poor quality coal - an important consideration with the anticipated reduction in the availability of high quality coal and the serious implications that could have for railway operation. It was in May 1961 that, during a works overhaul at Crewe, *Bahamas* was fitted with this double exhaust system. It was initially intended that five 'Jubilees' would have this modification in order to see how they performed under day-to-day service, however, *Bahamas* was the only example so fitted. All experiments on steam locomotives were terminated the following year, and thus precluded further the opportunity to establish any positive results.

The engine was allocated to Stockport Edgeley in 1962 and from where it was withdrawn from service in 1966. Following an appeal led by local enthusiast Alan Bidder, a group of individuals came together to form the *Stockport (Bahamas) Locomotive Society* with a view to purchasing the engine and to operate it on excursion trains. With limited funds available, the success of the venture appeared doomed until Geoffrey Potter, a local businessman, offered to loan the Society the sum of £3000 to purchase the engine from British Railways. The offer was gratefully accepted and *Bahamas* was purchased during 1967. With enthusiasm and funds growing, the engine was sent to the Hunslet Engine Co. in Leeds for repair and a repaint into its former LMS livery in anticipation of the Society's achieving its desired aims. However, the ban by British Rail of operating privately owned steam locomotives over their rail network prevented these ideas coming to fruition.

Meanwhile a home was required in which the engine could be kept safe. The Society, now renamed the *Bahamas Locomotive Society*, found such a home at the former Great Central Railway steam shed at Dinting, near Glossop. Here the Society volunteer members subsequently created the *Dinting Railway Centre*. This not only provided an operational base for *Bahamas*, but also a home to a growing collection of other locomotives, which included such notable examples as *Scots Guardsman*, *Leander*, *Blue Peter* and *Bittern*.

During 1972, and following a 'Return to Steam' campaign by the Association of Railway Preservation Societies, *Bahamas* was chosen by BR to be amongst the first group of steam locomotives to operate enthusiast special trains on designated routes over the national rail network. *Bahamas* ran its first revenue-earning trip in October 1972 from Shrewsbury to Hereford. The success of such early forays created a market for mainline steam operation, one that continues today and in greater abundance than anyone could then have imagined.

Expiry of the engine's boiler certificate in 1973 saw *Bahamas* withdrawn from service until, following a seven-year overhaul by Society volunteers, it steamed once more on the occasion of the Society's 21st birthday celebration in 1988. Then followed numerous successful railtours on the main line and visits to various heritage railways, before, once more, the expiry of its boiler certificate in 1997 resulted in its withdrawal from operation. Since then the engine has been displayed in the museum of the *Keighley & Worth Valley Railway* at Oxenhope.

In 2010, the **STEAM'S LAST BLAST** appeal was instigated with the intention of re-invigorating interest in the engine and to provide funds to have the engine overhauled and for it to return to working trains over the national rail network.

For further details regarding the ongoing future of Bahamas visit: **www.bahamas45596.co.uk**

Ingrow Loco, the *Bahamas Locomotive Society's* museum on the *Keighley and Worth Valley Railway* on the occasion of the opening ceremony in 2003. Those present are just a few of the volunteer members involved with its creation - some 13 years after the move from Dinting. Following the ceremony, *Bahamas* went to Oxenhope, where she remained until May 2012 at which time she moved to the National Railway Museum, York to take part in *Railfest 2012*.

Top left: Rhoda Adamson *Middle left to right:* Graham Allen, Mike Stephens, Gary Davison, Matt Fennel *Lower left to right:* Pete Skellon, Steve Allsop, Steve Peach, Gary Howard, George Bowler, Martin Harper, Mark Winderbank, John Smith. **2003 ● PETE SKELLON**

The view from Heaton Mersey West Signal Box looking in the Cheadle direction. No **45732** *Sanspareil* is about to come on shed and is standing on the headshunt within the shadow of the girder bridge which carries the ex-Midland main line to Cheadle Heath. In later years, this headshunt had to be slightly lengthened when Standard 9F 2-10-0's became regular visitors. Beyond the loco, the CLC crosses the River Mersey and onwards to Cheadle Junction.　　　　　　　　　　　　**2ND NOVEMBER 1963** ● **A. STEELE**

26A NEWTON HEATH

No 45596 *Bahamas*　　　　1966 ● AUTHOR'S COLLECTION

55A LEEDS (HOLBECK)

No 45654 *Hood*　　　　12TH JULY 1964 ● AUTHOR'S COLLECTION

55C FARNLEY JUNCTION

No 45632 *Tonga*　　　　1964 ● AUTHOR'S COLLECTION

24C LOSTOCK HALL

No 45732 *Sanspareil*　　　　23RD JUNE 1963 ● D. BURDON

THE
TRAFFORD
PARK
LOCOMOTIVES

Winding its way through Kingsterndale on the approaches to Buxton is the 5.22pm Manchester Central to Buxton commuter train behind a rather grubby No **45628 *Somaliland.*** The cab side number had received a cursory wipe over but she had just been through the shops for a Light Intermediate repair. The completion of over 67,000 miles during this calendar year was above average for a Trafford Park Jubilee which was obviously held in high regard. **22ND JUNE 1953 ● E.R. MORTEN**

TRAFFORD PARK MPD

The fireman of No 45705 _Seahorse_ positions the lamps in readiness to move off shed to work the 5.22pm Buxton. She had arrived at Newton Heath in June 1964 with the impending closure of Blackpool Central and although _Seahorse_ found regular work throughout the summer season, the winter timetable was a different matter. A request in October for her transfer across the city, specifically to work the morning Buxton to Manchester Central commuter train and evening return was granted, resulting in _Seahorse_ becoming something of a celebrity engine (see page 185).

12TH MARCH 1965 ● J.A. OLDFIELD

Britain took control of the island of Mauritius in 1810 and Longsight took the Jubilee of the same name 140 years later. Standing in splendid isolation in the shed yard, No **45617 _Mauritius_** has been borrowed on this occasion for excursion work, but had a short loan period at Trafford Park the following year.   **11TH JULY 1952 ● B.K.B. GREEN**

The shed was situated on the north side of the CLC line to Liverpool east of Trafford Park Station and alongside the Bridgewater Canal. Historically the premises were shared, and, after the Grouping, LMS and LNER locos made up an interesting allocation of roughly equal numbers. Well into the BR period, Jubilees rubbed shoulders with ex-LNER 'Original' and 'Large' Director 4-4-0s, but by now there was always an air of desolation about the place. The large 20 road building, which had lost a great part of its roof, easily accommodated whatever locos were on shed. Despite this, their 5XPs were always kept in fine mechanical order, as were the Britannia Pacifics and Royal Scots that followed. Long-standing No **45628 _Somaliland_** rests between duties, fittingly alongside Midland Compound No **41112**, one of a class which had graced the shed since 1909.

14TH JUNE 1953 ● AUTHOR'S COLLECTION

No 45705 *Seahorse* awaits departure with the 5.22pm train to Buxton. This was the last surviving Jubilee engaged on regular passenger work in the Manchester area and her activities are examined in detail on page 185. **25TH AUGUST 1965** ● G. WHITEHEAD

MANCHESTER CENTRAL STATION

The Jubilees were allocated to work the St. Pancras services and whilst on occasions they performed heroics, in later years were more often prone to be indifferent, to say the least. There is, however, no record of them having worked over the CLC line to Liverpool Central. Caught amidst dramatic light, No **5572 *Eire*** is ready for departure from Manchester Central's Platform 5 with an express. Originally named *Irish Free State*, she was renamed *Eire* on 19th July 1938 after the formation of a new sovereign state - seven months before arriving at Trafford Park. Records show that this engine completed 1,576,431 miles in service, but during the year of 1946 recorded a mere 21,976 - well below half the annual average - which remains something of a mystery, especially as there is no record of repair during the period.

APRIL 1946 ● J.W. NEVE

The extended wooden section of Platform 8 beyond the station canopies was an ideal vantage point to record departures from No 6, the platform used by the majority of St Pancras expresses. No **45652 *Hawke*** appears to be in fine fettle as she draws her train away. Platforms 8 and 9 were outside the magnificent train shed caught in the background, and monopolised the Chester trains. Behind the photographer at this point were locomotive servicing facilities, comprising a water tower and 65ft turntable with stabling roads. For a time, Kentish Town's Jubilees made use of these when engaged on filling-in duties, as did members from Millhouses which were regularly used on the services to and from Sheffield Midland via the Hope Valley.

1956 ● W.A. BROWN

The Buxton Commuter train gets away behind No 45705 *Seahorse* in this unusual view, looking almost due east. The land in the left foreground, now given over to the inevitable car park, once carried the approach lines serving the former Great Northern Railway Goods Warehouse, adjacent to Deansgate, which became an early casualty in 1956 when goods traffic was being rationalised in the city. The unmistakeable arched roof Manchester Central Station is of course prominent, but there are other points of reference of local interest which feature within the cityscape. The chimney belongs to the Electricity Station, alongside the Rochdale Canal, whilst the tower of the St James Building, head office of the Calico Printers Association on Oxford Street, is prominent. The clock of the Refuge Building correctly shows 5.25pm (kestrels apparently once nested there), and is also clearly visible. Having passed beneath the signal box, *Seahorse* is about to cross Bridgewater Street, beyond which on the extreme right, is a glimpse of Gaythorn Gas Works.   **17TH AUGUST 1965 ● HAROLD D. BOWTELL**

CHORLTON-CUM-HARDY

Gathering speed through the south Manchester suburbs. A sun-drenched but deserted Chorlton-cum-Hardy Station witnesses the passage of No **45561** *Saskatchewan* with the 2.25pm Up 'Palatine'. The engine carries a headboard on this occasion which, unfortunately, was not always the case. After an 18-month spell at Trafford Park, this Jubilee moved to the other end of the line, taking up residence at Kentish Town on 30th June 1958. As such she continued to work over the route but, somewhat surprisingly, returned north in July 1959 for another 4 months, officially on loan, but once again wearing a 9E shedplate. By this time the shed had 6 Britannia Pacifics to call on which had displaced the Jubilee allocation. In 1960, Nos 45614 *Leeward Islands* and 45616 *Malta G.C.* had very short spells on loan which proved to be Trafford Park's last association with the class … until the arrival of No 45705 *Seahorse*!   **22ND AUGUST 1959 ● W.A. BROWN**

CHORLTON JUNCTION

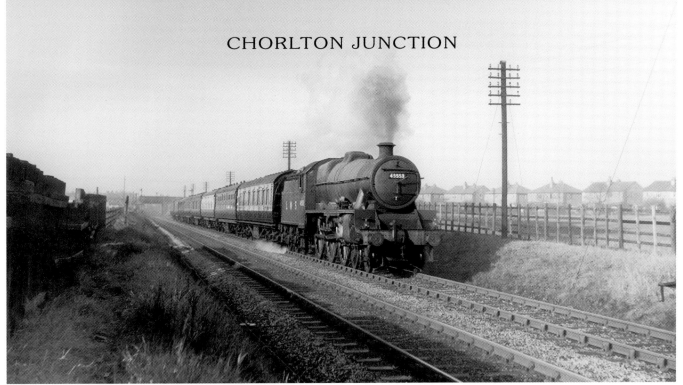

No 45553 *Canada* and its train, comprising 8 coaches, all of which appear to be different, is clear of Chorlton Junction and heading towards Didsbury. St. Werburgh's Road overbridge is in the distance and at this point the former Great Central line from Fairfield Junction (commonly referred to as the Fallowfield Loop) trails in to meet the Midland's South District line. A low sun nicely highlights the LMS letters on the tender and despite the loco recently receiving its BR number, she carries the 1946 lined black livery. After a two-year interlude at Trafford Park, this much travelled loco moved across the city in June 1951 to Longsight for a further five years and later returned for a loan period in September 1956 *(see page 52)*   **1950 ● G.M. SHOULTS**

DIDSBURY

When Trafford Park's Jubilees were away for major overhaul, the shed would occasionally receive another member on temporary loan. Such was the case here. No **45604 *Ceylon*** was a Crewe North engine throughout the 1950's and appeared to be a favourite choice for cover. It worked out of Trafford Park between w/e 9th May 1953 and w/e 4th July 1953 covering for No 45655 *Keith* which was indisposed at the time. The following May, *Ceylon* helped out at Patricroft for a mere week whilst No 45645 *Collingwood* was away and a final sortie placed it at Bushbury in 1958. No 45604 eventually became a Manchester engine, retiring from Newton Heath in 1965 but is seen here working the 9.00am Manchester Central to London St. Pancras express. Didsbury Goods Yard and adjacent allotments are prominent as is Class Five 4-6-0 No **44664.** The Sheffield (Millhouses) loco has clear signals, working the 8.05am stopping train from Sheffield Midland via Stockport Tiviot Dale.   **25TH MAY 1953 ● B.K.B.GREEN**

PARR'S WOOD

The view from Didsbury Road overbridge looking back towards Manchester. No **45629** *Straits Settlements* has the customary 9 bogies behind the tender which form the 5.50pm Manchester Central to London St. Pancras express. The rear coaches are passing under Kingsway road bridge. Just visible in the distance is another bridge carrying the Slade Lane Junction to Wilmslow line, commonly referred to as the Styal Loop. A public footpath ran by the main line at this point and was a regular haunt for both the author and fellow enthusiast David Young who lived close by. The added attraction was the yard of the Manchester Corporation Bus Depot at Parr's Wood which lay directly opposite. A wonderful collection of motley vehicles could often be found there. **3RD MAY 1952** ● **B.K.B.GREEN**

HEATON MERSEY STATION JUNCTION

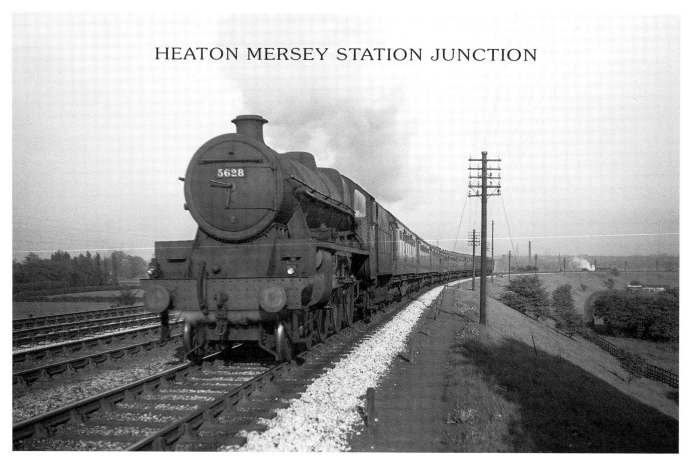

No 5628 *Somaliland* tearing towards Heaton Mersey Station with the 2.15pm from London St Pancras. This loco was to retain her original Crimson Lake livery until January 1951. The tracks to the left form the 'South District' chord to the CLC's Glazebrook to Godley line (note the wisp of steam) at Heaton Mersey East Junction. **27TH APRIL 1948** ● **J.D. DARBY**

Soaring high above the Mersey and about to cross the CLC line is No **45628 *Somaliland*** once more. The view is looking upstream towards Stockport and further down the towpath, just out of view, was the official entrance to Heaton Mersey MPD. A footbridge spanned the river to Gorsey Bank Road at this point. **MARCH 1957 ● PETER REEVES**

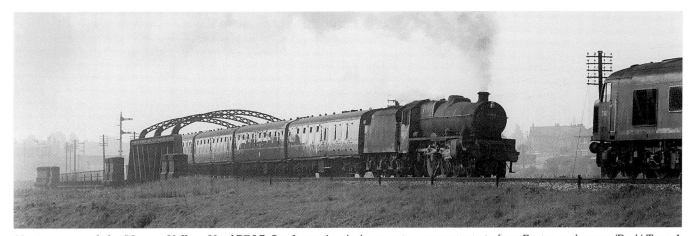

Having crossed the Mersey Valley, No 45705 *Seahorse* heads the morning commuter train from Buxton and passes 'Peak' Type 4 diesel No **D117** working the 8.25am Manchester Central to London St Pancras express. **MARCH 1965 ● JOHN CLARKE**

CROSSING THE RIVER MERSEY

◄ **This dramatic low level view** again features a loco crossing the river. No **45628 *Somaliland*** makes a fine sight working a southbound excursion. At this point, the knowledgeable enthusiast travelling on the train would be keeping a sharp eye out for the Heaton Mersey Coal Stage, situated to the east, down in the valley and well within view. Any locos on shed, however, were too far away to identify.

22ND MARCH 1951 ● TOM LEWIS

BREDBURY JUNCTION

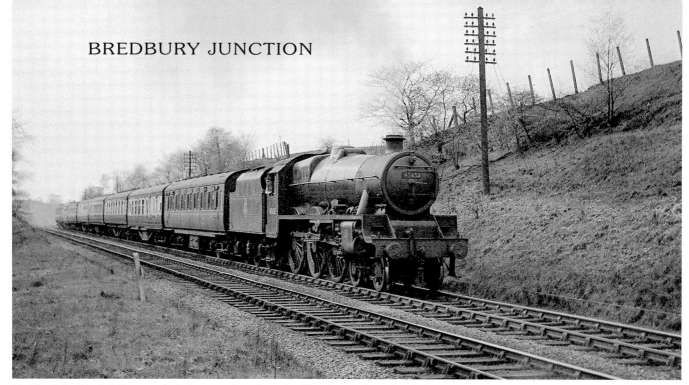

Trafford Park's Jubilees worked almost exclusively on the Manchester Central to St Pancras services and photographs of them straying off this beaten track are very rare. The only regular exception was the original route diverging at Heaton Mersey Station Junction, through Stockport Tiviot Dale, Bredbury Junction and rejoining at New Mills South Junction. No **45652 *Hawke*,** fitted with BR standard chimney, climbs the 1-in-82 between Brinnington and Bredbury Junction with a stopping passenger train for Sheffield Midland.   **1955 ● JOHN SPENCER**

STRINES

◀ **In addition to the Sheffield services,** it was used as a diversionary route for the St Pancras expresses, particularly on Sundays when Disley Tunnel and its environs would often be in 'possession'. On other occasions trains went by way of the 'Fallowfield Loop', Guide Bridge and Hyde Junction, then on to Romiley. Photographic evidence exists of such a train passing through Woodley Station, but unfortunately for this book, was in the hands of a Kentish Town Jubilee! No **45652 *Hawke*,** again on a Sheffield stopping train, arrives at Strines Station. The loco was subjected to a Heavy Intermediate Overhaul a fortnight later.

30TH JUNE 1951 ● R.D. POLLARD

CHEADLE HEATH STATION

It would appear that fewer photographs ▶ were taken of trains in the Down direction over this section of line. One theory is the very high speeds attained through the outer suburbs, which have become almost legendary, may have deterred certain cameramen who preferred to record locos working hard upgrade. No **45629 *Straits Settlements*** brings a Manchester bound express under Stockport Road bridge leaving Cheadle Heath Station in its wake. The tracks in the foreground form the connection with the CLC at Cheadle Junction, which offered a useful path to the west and a route taken by many a rare Jubilee from the Midlands to Blackpool or Llandudno over the years.

29TH MAY 1952 ● TOM LEWIS

Yes, it's that engine again! No one could accuse No **45628 *Somaliland*** of being camera shy and on this occasion she is passing through the Manchester platforms at Cheadle Heath Station. The train is the 12.20pm St Pancras express and the hard work is about to begin in earnest for the loco crew. Cheadle Heath offered a convenient facility for passengers residing in the Stockport district and certain expresses called en-route. Platforms 3 and 4 are out of view to the left and were always referred to as the Liverpool platforms, despite no timetabled trains leaving for that destination. Much freight passed through but they were exclusively used by the outer suburban services starting out and arriving from Manchester Central, although many seasonal excursion trains, travelling by way of the CLC, also called there.

7TH AUGUST 1954 ● B.K.B. GREEN

CHEADLE HEATH
SOUTH JUNCTION

The same train has cleared the station and the rear coaches are passing under Edgeley Road overbridge. This was a Trafford Park working but with Nos 45622 *Nyasaland* and 45628 *Somaliland* away for overhaul and Nos 45629 *Straits Settlements* and 45655 *Keith* due for shopping, the motive power situation was acute. Although not officially recorded as such, there is good reason to believe that Kentish Town's No **5665 *Lord Rutherford of Nelson*** was on temporary loan to help relieve the situation. The engine had a previous three year spell on the books but is more recently remembered as a rare bird which migrated to Corkerhill (Glasgow) in September 1952.

SEPTEMBER 1948 ● AUTHOR'S COLLECTION

BRAMHALL
MOOR LANE

A powerful image of a Jubilee in full cry. No **5572 *Eire*** brings another Up express climbing the 1-in-40 past Bramhall Moor Lane and onwards towards Hazel Grove and Disley Tunnel. The gentle incline through Manchester's South District now gives way to the more arduous gradients on the climb to Peak Forest, nearly 1,000 feet above sea level and 25 miles south of the city. *Eire* was an engine allocated only during LMS days, but then stayed on the Midland, spending the greater part of the BR period based at Bristol (Barrow Road) MPD.

1946 ● PETER WARD

NEW MILLS SOUTH JUNCTION

◀ **No 45618 *New Hebrides,*** in all her glory, has just passed over Newtown Viaduct off the 'new' or 'cut-off' line with a 10 coach St Pancras train. Trailing in from the right are the 'old lines' via Romiley and New Mills Central. Having now crossed over the county boundary, the gradient steepens to 1-in-90 for the continual climb through the Derbyshire Peak District. Arriving just one month before Nationalisation, *New Hebrides* worked out of 9E for a decade or so, and, after running-in as new, was another engine to spend its lifetime on the Midland Division.

1946 ● R.D. POLLARD

Another impressive picture of a Jubilee in full cry. No **45614 *Leeward Islands*** had been a short term loan, late in the day, to Trafford Park from Kentish Town MPD, but whether the engine remained on this turn covering the Up *Palatine* must be debatable. Britannia Pacifics were now in residence and the 'Peak' Type 4 diesels were also in operation. According to records, she arrived on Tuesday, March 1st and was caught three days later, just beyond New Mills South Junction complete with headboard. Although *Leeward Islands* isn't in the best of condition externally and is hardly steam tight, the newly fitted 9E shedplate is a redeeming feature, but this photograph may well be a unique record of the final occasion a Trafford Park member worked this prestige train, as *No 45614* was also the last Jubilee to be officially allocated to the shed, returning to Kentish Town on 14th March 1960.

4TH MARCH 1960 ● N. FIELDS

CHINLEY

The 6.19pm express for Manchester glides into Platform 5 at Chinley Station behind No **45629 *Straits Settlements.*** Despite her appearance, photographer Doug Darby made a note that the engine is now 'green', and records confirm it as being one of the first to receive a coat of Brunswick Green paint. Chinley was an important interchange station, boasting six platforms, and whilst the gas lamps and Midland style station nameboards survive, the lettering has been somewhat 'toned down' from days of old. **4TH JUNE 1950 ● J.D. DARBY**

▲
No **45629** *Straits Settlements* once more, restarting the 9.00am Manchester to London from Chinley. In the background, Fowler 2-6-4T No **42367** stands in Platform 1 with the 9.43am to Sheffield Midland.
22ND MARCH 1953 ● **E.R. MORTEN**

Another regular on the route, No 45652 *Hawke* brings her train under the Chinley Road overbridge *(from where the above picture has been taken)* and into the station for its penultimate stop.
22ND MARCH 1953 ● **R.D. POLLARD**

Super power for a Sheffield slow. Canklow's 2P 4-4-0 No **40491** pilots No **45628** *Somaliland* away from Chinley. Double heading was unusual and it may be a case of saving a path for the pilot engine off an unbalanced working. **21ST MAY 1949** ● **R.D. POLLARD**
▼

CHINLEY NORTH JUNCTION

The beautiful Peak District. One of the classic photographs on this stretch of line. In perfect light and with the rods down, old favourite, No **45628 _Somaliland_** approaches Chinley North Junction with a London express. Chinley Churn forms an impressive backdrop.

16TH JUNE 1951 ● **B.K.B. GREEN**

HOPE STATION

◀ **Jubilees were a fairly common sight** traversing the Hope Valley route with stopping passenger trains to Sheffield Midland. No **45561 _Saskatchewan_** has the attention of two schoolboys as she awaits departure at Hope Station with the 4.30pm from Sheffield. Evidence that this engine was a 'good un' is borne out by two published performance logs. Both runs had loads of 400 tons behind the tender and on each occasion, the 91 mile section between Leicester and St Pancras was monitored. The Up _Palatine_ went south without a pilot to which the driver was entitled and achieved an actual time of 98mins 48secs despite a signal check at Millbrook. The other was in the company of 4-4-0 No 40682 when a maximum speed of 86½ mph was reached at Sharnbrook and the run completed in 91 mins.

12TH APRIL 1957 ● **H.C. CASSERLEY**

CHAPEL-EN-LE-FRITH

A goods train has been put 'inside' whilst No **5629 _Straits Settlements_** passes by with the 1.50pm Manchester Central to St Pancras express. The engine and 11 coaches are approaching Chapel-en-le-Frith Station and loops were in situ between here and Chinley South Junction. ▶

12TH JUNE 1948 ● **R.D. POLLARD**

Coasting downgrade towards Chapel-en-le-Frith Central is No 45622 Nyasaland. Spring has given way to summer and the beauties of the Derbyshire landscape are there for all to see. The rear coaches are still within the 104-yard tunnel, over which lies the former LNWR route to Buxton. High on the hill, the Down Home signal is off for Chapel-en-le-Frith South Station. **19TH JUNE 1953 ● E.R. MORTEN**

DOVE HOLES TUNNEL

◄ **Emerging from the south end of Dove Holes Tunnel** and into the deep and rugged limestone cutting is another member paired with a Fowler tender, in this case her third. No **45712 Victory** had previously spent the greater period on the Central Division in LMS days, after which a loan from Newton Heath became permanent in March 1957. The stay was relatively short lived but she remained a Midland Division engine, aquiring a Stanier tender (ex-No 48752) in the meantime. *Victory* eventually became one of the mass exodus of Jubilees to Burton MPD in January 1962.

13TH APRIL 1958 ● TOM LEWIS

PEAK FOREST

A second view of No 45553 *Canada* at Peak Forest shortly before her transfer to Longsight, week-ending 2nd June 1951. It was unusual to find a Trafford Park Jubilee coupled to a Fowler tender, but this was a well travelled engine which had operated predominantly over the Western Division. Despite the problems of 1953, there was a further chronic shortage of Jubilees three years later, when between September and November 1956, Nos 45629 *Straits Settlements,* 45652 *Hawke* and 45655 *Keith* were all indisposed at Crewe. This resulted in a two month return on loan for *Canada,* by now a Crewe North engine, and it was joined by Camden's No 45591 *Udaipur.*

8TH MAY 1951 ● E.R. MORTEN

Having worked 'bang road' through Dove Holes Tunnel, No 45652 *Hawke* regains the Up line by Peak Forest North signal box with another St. Pancras express. Certain sets of stock working over the route were roofboarded, but on this occasion only the leading carriage appears to be carrying one. They were designated LONDON - MANCHESTER irrespective of direction of travel. It is perhaps also fitting that one of the ICI hopper wagons is featured as part of a train of empties having returned from Northwich, Cheshire. The intensive limestone traffic from Tunstead Quarry to Oakleigh Sidings, Northwich, which survives to this day, was largely in the hands of Stanier 8F 2-8-0's during the period when Jubilees reigned supreme over the Peak.

6TH JULY 1952 ● E.R. MORTEN

GREAT ROCKS

Trying to obtain a photograph of a Trafford Park Jubilee on freight duties has proved nigh on impossible, but on 28th May 1953 two 9E engines took trains out of Toton. Class Five 4-6-0 No 44938 was on the 1.20pm to Rowsley and No 45618 *New Hebrides* the 5.15pm to Trafford Park. The previous summer this Jubilee was observed in Blackpool when on 6th August it worked the 7.30pm from North Station to Manchester Central returning excursion (Reporting No W665). One assumes that it also worked outwards with this train, which travelled via the Whelley Loop and Lowton St Mary's. The train was composed of 11 ex-LNER coaches, being one of the sets kept at Cornbrook Sidings for trains leaving Central for Eastern Region destinations. Five days later, No **45618 *New Hebrides,*** having resumed normal duties, is working the 2.15pm St. Pancras to Manchester Central through Great Rocks.

11TH AUGUST 1952 ● E.R. MORTEN

ASHWOOD DALE

It was unusual to find a Trafford Park engine on the 5.22pm commuter train to Buxton at this time. It was a Kentish Town filling-in turn, with the loco having worked the 10.25am St. Pancras express Down to Manchester Central earlier in the day. After stabling overnight at Buxton MPD, it worked the following morning's 7.05am to Manchester before returning home with the 10.25am Up express. This was a Jubilee turn, but on occasions Stanier Class Fives deputised. Perhaps resulting from a failure, A grubby No **45622** *Nyasaland* threads its way though the picturesque Ashwood Dale on the final leg of its journey. Beyond the gate from the spur in the foreground were the sidings of the Buxton Gas Works which fell into disuse shortly after this time. **19TH JUNE 1951** ● E.R. MORTEN

CHEE TOR TUNNELS

The mile-long section between Millers Dale Junction and Station encounters a succession of short tunnels interspersed with viaducts. The Fireman of No **45622 *Nyasaland*** casts a wary eye in the direction of photographer Ray Morten who has positioned himself just within the entrance to the 401 yard long Chee Tor Tunnel No 1. The rear carriages are still within the shorter Chee Tor Tunnel No 2, whilst the engine and leading carriages are passing over Viaduct No 76. The cliffs here tower over 300ft above the valley floor - altogether a most impressive feat of railway engineering. The train is the Sunday 9.00am service from Manchester Central to London St Pancras.

25TH MAY 1952 ● E.R. MORTEN

MILLERS DALE

Under the watchful eye of the signalman, a Down semi-fast moves away from Millers Dale with a pair of Midland clerestory carriages behind the tender. The engine is No **5665 *Lord Rutherford of Nelson*** which, together with No 5570 *New Zealand*, were the first arrivals at Trafford Park in July 1938, a situation brought about by the rebuilding of a weight restrictive bridge in the Chapel-en-le-Frith area. The London services had previously been in the hands of Stanier Class Fives. The following 22 year period saw 32 Jubilees either allocated or officially loaned to the depot. Doubtless there were unofficial others.

3RD JUNE 1939 ● E.R. MORTEN

LITTON DALE

It was unusual to find Jubilees carrying stopping passenger lamps over the Peak. The train is the 4.15pm Derby Midland to Chinley service which then formed the 6.09pm to Manchester Central via Stockport Tiviot Dale. The day is Whit Monday 1956 and No **45655 *Keith*** is recorded as passing at 5.49pm - running rather late! The location is less than 1 mile south of Millers Dale Station with the River Wye flowing in the valley below. The train has latterly called at Monsal Dale before passing through Litton and Cressbrook Tunnels.

21ST MAY 1956 ● M. MENSING

HASSOP

▲

Hassop Station, situated some 2 miles north of Bakewell, was a similar distance from the village it served. Hardly surprising, then, that closure came about as early as 17th August 1942, but in its heyday, the Midland Railway had provided rather opulent facilities here for the Duke of Devonshire whose Chatsworth Estate lay nearby. A similar situation existed at Bakewell Station for the Duke of Rutland's benefit at Haddon Hall. No **45629 Straits Settlements** passes the site with the 2.15pm ex-St Pancras Down express. Goods facilities lasted until 5th October 1964.

17TH MAY 1952 ● E.R. MORTEN

ROWSLEY

A southbound excursion comprising six non-corridor coaches is cautiously passing Rowsley North Junction signal box. The driver of No **5572 Eire** will have observed the permanent 50mph speed restriction in force in both Up and Down directions at this point. Above the engine stands Rowsley Station, another glorified Midland Railway edifice, again provided for the Duke of Devonshire's benefit. The recently built premises of the Express Dairy are adjacent, served by sidings behind the signal box.

12TH AUGUST 1939 ● E.R. MORTEN

MATLOCK

◀ **A pleasant change** from the regular engines working over the route is this fine portrait of No **45617 Mauritius.** Her stay at 9E lasted barely a month, having arrived from Crewe North week-ending 9th May 1953. It was officially another engine on short term loan but, once again, a shed plate had been affixed in the meantime. Other than this short sortie, *Mauritius* spent her entire lifetime on the Western Division. The fireman appears to be pointing towards something of interest, perhaps a vehicle on the nearby A6 at this point, as his St Pancras-bound express gets away downgrade between Matlock and Matlock Bath between the High Tor Tunnels.

24TH MAY 1953 ● **J. CUPIT**

CROMFORD

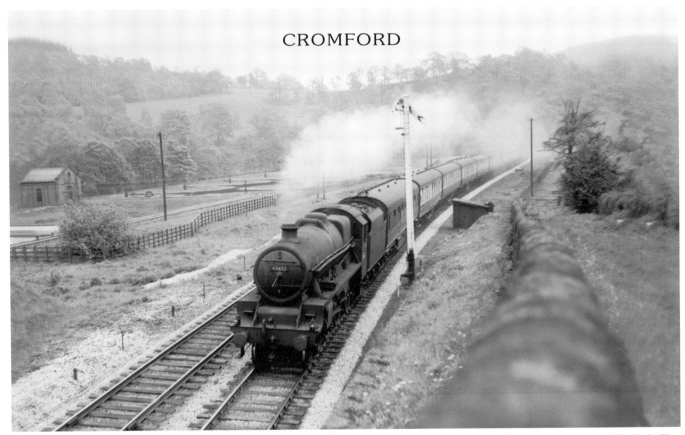

With the Cromford Down Distant signal in her favour, No **45652 Hawke** is only 2 miles away from the next stop at Matlock. The River Derwent, never far away, passes under the line immediately after Leawood Tunnel, whose northern portal is shrouded in exhaust - just beyond the rear of the train. A stone aqueduct within a cast iron trough allows the Cromford Canal to pass under at the same point and a pumping house nearby, dating from 1849, to transfer water from river to canal, is a local attraction. **1954** ● **AUTHOR'S COLLECTION**

BREADSALL CROSSING

In the immediate post-war and early Nationalisation period, Jubilees appeared in a variety of different guises. Photographic evidence shows No **45622 Nyasaland** carrying a BR Block 1948 front numberplate, and whilst the engine is in the BR version of the 1946 black livery and running with blank tender, the cab side reveals an M prefix over its former LMS Number 5622. This combination lasted a further three months. Having just passed Little Eaton Junction, the 9.00am Manchester to London train is approaching Breadsall Crossing (or Ford Lane Crossing as it was locally referred to) on the northern outskirts of Derby.

3RD JUNE 1951 ● **R.J. BUCKLEY**

DERBY
SOUTH JUNCTION

No **45622** *Nyasaland* yet again. This is seven months after Nationalisation yet nearly three years before the preceding photograph. She appears to be in the 1946 black livery with BR cab side number and wording BRITISH RAILWAYS on the tender. Engine and train are approaching Derby Midland Station and passing the shed yard, where a 'Crab' 2-6-0 and a Compound 4-4-0 are identifiable.

10TH JULY 1948 ● H.C. CASSERLEY

SPONDON

The 9.00am Manchester Central to London St Pancras ran via Nottingham. After a stop at Didsbury in the Manchester suburbs to pick up only, the train called at Chinley, Millers Dale and Matlock to Derby where arrival was scheduled for 10.43am. No **45629** *Straits Settlements* is approaching Spondon on her way to Trent Junction, the next port of call.

15TH APRIL 1956 ● R.J. BUCKLEY

Next Station - Nottingham (Midland). Departure was at 11.15pm from Platform 3 and eventual arrival in London was at 2.00pm, having called at Kettering, Wellingborough and Luton en-route. No **45629** *Straits Settlements* gets away past Nottingham Station East signal box, beyond which an unidentified Ivatt 2-6-0 is on pilot duty. The Jubilee would hardly have been a stranger to many of the gricers gathered opposite at the end of Platform 4.

1956 ● AUTHOR'S COLLECTION

NOTTINGHAM (MIDLAND)

LOUGHBOROUGH

Bursting under the ex-Great Central main line and approaching Loughborough Station at speed is No **45622 *Nyasaland*.** This engine was was accredited with the fastest pre-war run over the Midland main line, reaching 95mph between Leicester and St Pancras, covering the 99.1 miles in just 84½ minutes and was allocated to Holbeck at the time,. This was eclipsed after the war when Kentish Town's No 45579 *Punjab* achieved 97½ mph on the descent from Luton to Bedford, but many enginemen maintain that unofficial speeds of over 100mph had been reached. After a Heavy General at Crewe - on 12th May 1949, she was pilot loco on the 7.10pm Manchester to Cardiff express, a Crewe North running-in turn as far as Stockport, and then went on Edgeley MPD.

AUGUST 1957 ● D.J. MONTGOMERY

BRAYBROOK

Some three miles south of Market Harborough and into Northamptonshire lies Braybrook. On Easter Monday 1957, No **45618 *New Hebrides*** passes by, returning home with the 2. 25pm from St Pancras. At the end of her days, she became one of the large contingent based at Burton MPD, from where withdrawal took place in February 1964 after a lifetime of almost 30 years.

22ND APRIL 1957 ● M. MENSING

SHARNBROOK

Derby Works were responsible for the building of only 10 members of the class during 1934/5. Their first example, No **45655 *Keith*,** passes through Sharnbrook, some 8 miles south of Wellingborough with yet another London-bound express. According to records, *Keith* and Nos 45656 *Cochrane* and 45657 *Tyrwhitt* all 'ran in' from Crewe North before returning to the Midland at Nottingham two months later. Records also reveal that on 19th November 1946, No 45655 entered Derby Works to receive a light overhaul lasting 16 days, the result of collision damage, rather than be dealt with at Crewe.

c1954 ● REAL PHOTOS

BEDFORD

The power of the Jubilees. A statement nicely encapsulated here with this dramatic lineside view of No **45652** *Hawke* getting to grips with a London-bound express near Bedford. Many Jubilees remained fitted to their original tenders throughout their lifetimes and this was one such example (No 4635). Stablemate No 45622 *Nyasaland* was another. **6TH SEPTEMBER 1952 ● AUTHOR'S COLLECTION**

NAPSBURY

Certain Jubilees spent their entire lives as Midland-based engines. No **45628** *Somaliland* was one such example which, after a running-in period at Longsight, was allocated exclusively to either Kentish Town or Trafford Park, save for short loan periods at Longsight (re-visited), Neasden and Newton Heath *(see page 140)*. On 14th April 1949, whilst working the 2.15pm St. Pancras - Manchester Central and travelling at 70mph, 1.5 miles south of Loughborough, she collided with a stray horse. After a 55 minute delay, 0-6-0 No 44182 was summoned to assist as far as Derby, where their own Jubilee, No M5602 *British Honduras* took over. This loco also apparently struggled over the Peak and Manchester was reached at 8.15pm, as against the booked time of 6.34pm. Whether *Somaliland* suffered any damage is unknown, but she had a Light Intermediate Overhaul shortly afterwards. She is back at work here with the 6.40pm St Pancras - Manchester Central passing Napsbury on the approach to St. Albans. **AUGUST 1949 ● R.K. BLENCOWE COLLECTION**

RADLETT

The introduction of the XL timetable in the summer of 1957 was an attempt to return to the revolutionary winter schedules of the LMS on this route in 1937. Jubilees still ruled the roost but were now 20 years older and the results were inconsistent. A typical run on a Down express with 9 bogies (300 tons) behind the tender would record speeds increasing to 75mph by Radlett, some 15 miles out of London and up to 90mph on the descent to Bedford. Trains made similar, if not better, progress in the Up direction. Before the accelerated service, No **45629 *Straits Settlements,*** wearing her new 9E shedplate, brings a northbound Manchester train through Radlett at a more sedate pace.

24TH JULY 1950 ● AUTHOR'S COLLECTION

KENTISH TOWN

Treading a cautious path through the Kentish Town complex is No 45628 *Somaliland* with the 12.30pm Sunday service to Manchester. The driver has the Junction's home signal in his favour on the approaches to Belsize Tunnels. The architecturally distinctive bottling stores belonging to Read Brothers, which features in so many loco portraits on Kentish Town MPD, is prominent in the background, as are the coaling and ash lifting plants. Rolling stock stabled within the City Carriage Sidings frustratingly often denied the enthusiast glimpses of the shed yard from passing trains.

4TH JULY 1954 ● H.C. CASSERLEY

LONDON ST PANCRAS STATION

◀ **A trio of Jubilees,** all in LMS livery, grace the Midland Railway terminus at London St Pancras. No **5572 *Eire*** arrives with the 10.00am from Manchester Central and passes Johnson 3F No **7241** on Station Pilot duties. This was one of six 0-6-0 tanks working out of Kentish Town at the time, all fitted with condensing apparatus for the London area. *Irish Free State* had been renamed *Eire* the previous July whilst still at Millhouses but is best remembered during the BR period as a Bristol (Barrow Road) engine. Also prominent behind the locos are the gas holders belonging to the Imperial Gas Company - a local landmark.

24TH JUNE 1939 ● H.C. CASSERLEY

Just within the cavernous interior of the great train hall stands No **5628 *Somaliland***. Kentish Town are making use of her on a filling-in turn to Bedford, whilst lurking in the shadows is former Midland Railway '1P' 0-4-4T No **1423**.   **10TH JUNE 1947 ● H.C. CASSERLEY**

Awaiting departure with the 2.15pm express for ▶ Manchester is No **5652 *Hawke*.** The 19G shedplate confirms that she is a Trafford Park engine, as in 1935 the depot had become a 'garage' of Sheffield (Grimesthorpe - 19A), a situation that was to remain until 1950. Trafford Park then endured a rather nomadic life, as firstly, early BR reorganisation brought about an extremely short lived period as 13A. This officially constituted its own district with responsibility for those former MR and CLC depots in the Greater Manchester area, but by June of that year it was re-coded 9E, continuing under the juristiction of Longsight (9A) who had supervised since 1935. It later entered the Derby District in a further short-lived change between January 1957 and April 1958 (shed code 17F) before finally reverting to 9E.

9TH SEPTEMBER 1948 ● J.H. ASTON

BERKHAMSTED

The only logical reason for a Trafford Park Jubilee to be working on the West Coast Main Line was a running-in turn - and so it proved to be. At 10.00am on Wednesday, 19th October 1949, No **45618** *New Hebrides* is north of Berkhamsted Station on the Down Slow line with a van train. She had been through Crewe Works for a Heavy General Overhaul a matter of days before. **19TH OCTOBER 1949** ● **H.C. CASSERLEY**

KENTISH TOWN MPD

The only shed that Trafford Park Jubilees visited with any regularity was Kentish Town. Here are two members on shed on the same occasion, still officially in wartime, but hostilities are all but over. The familiar backdrop mentioned in a previous caption features behind the unique No **5655** *Keith* (above), awaiting her turn on the ash pit road, whilst further down the yard stands No **5572** *Eire* (right).

21ST APRIL 1945 ● **H.C. CASSERLEY**

THE
PATRICROFT
LOCOMOTIVES

The East to West passenger services over the Pennines were the principal turns for Patricroft's Jubilees. The Liverpool Lime Street to Hull and Newcastle trains were worked as far as Leeds in conjunction with Farnley Junction and Edge Hill engines. The Liverpool shed also provided Rebuilt Patriots and Royal Scots. Arriving in 1950, No **45558** *Manitoba* spent a decade on such duties and is about to pass through the platforms at Saddleworth with an eastbound excursion. The bulk of the train is on Saddleworth Viaduct, beneath which the *Huddersfield Narrow Canal* crosses the *River Tame* - a source of the *River Mersey*. Beyond the station nameboard, the branch line to Delph curves away towards Dobcross.   c.1958 ● JIM DAVENPORT

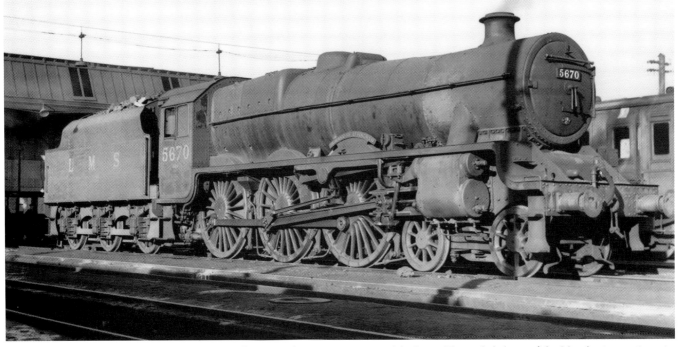

Thirteen Jubilees survived Nationalisation still carrying their pre-war crimson lake livery. This included two of the Manchester contingent - Longsight's No 5680 *Camperdown* and Patricroft's No **5670 *Howard of Effingham*.** The surviving portion of the original LNWR 'Old' shed is behind the engine. A further 10 years were to elapse before BR set about replacing the shed roof.   **22ND AUGUST 1946** ● W.D. COOPER

Patricroft shed has always been strongly associated with Jubilees. Members which were allocated during the LMS period were: Nos 5562/6/7/8/84/99, 5613/7/31/2/7/48/50/1/2/3, 5670/4/92, 5708/20/1/2/3/4/6. In addition, Nos 5672/89 were on loan from Crewe North between 30th April 1938 and 14th May 1938. Of these, two are particularly noteworthy. No 5637 *Windward Islands* was a high profile casualty of the Harrow disaster in 1952 which also involved Princess Royal Pacific No 46202 *Princess Anne,* and No 5692 *Cyclops* became a Scottish loco in December 1940, never to return. These Jubilees, some of which arrived un-named, replaced ex-LNWR 'Claughtons' at the same time as Stanier Class Fives were replacing the 'Prince of Wales' 4-6-0's. During the early BR period, transfer activity subsided and the shed was left with six members on its books:

45558 *Manitoba*	2nd December 1950 - 19th April 1964
45559 *British Columbia*	10th May 1947 - 2nd July 1960
45563 *Australia*	28th May 1949 - 14th September 1963
45600 *Bermuda*	10th June 1950 - 2nd January 1965
45645 *Collingwood*	7th September 1952 - 3rd August 1963
45668 *Madden*	26th April 1947 - 24th October 1959

No 45645 came from Corkerhill, Glasgow in exchange for No 45720 in September 1952. No 45668 departed for Derby in October 1959 and No 45663 Jervis arrived in exchange - initially on loan.

◄ **No 45668 *Madden*** drifts past the coal hopper towards the turntable. The 'New' shed building is in the background.

1952 ● W.D. COOPER

The nameplate and leading driving wheel of No **45559 *British Columbia*.** 1952 ● W.D. COOPER

No 5650, as yet un-named, graces the 'Old' shed yard. In her early years she was very much a Western Division engine and like many others, never settled at any particular depot. The nameplates **Blake** were affixed during a short spell at Patricroft, but probably at Crewe coinciding with an overhaul. Nos 5568 and 5617 also received their plates *Western Australia* and *Mauritius* respectively whilst at 10C - but the recorded dates did not coincide with works visits. Were these sent from Crewe for the attention of the Patricroft Shedmaster, I wonder? Just before the war, *Blake* transferred on to the Midland Division where she was to remain throughout the BR period (*other than a loan to Newton Heath - see page 140*). Notice the original shed roof, which is in a dire state by this time and would shortly be demolished.

DECEMBER 1936 ● AUTHOR'S COLLECTION

After the initial five Crewe-built locos (Nos 5552 - 6), the next numerical batch of 50 were built by the North British Locomotive Company, Glasgow with 25 each emerging from the Hyde Park and Queens Park Works. Meanwhile Crewe started work on a further 48, commencing with No 5607 to satisfy the demand for new locos. The second NBL engine into traffic was No 5558 in July 1934, destined to stay in service for 30 years - the second half of which were almost entirely at Patricroft. No **45558 *Manitoba*** stands over the ash pits between duties. Records indicate that she moved on to Leeds (Holbeck) in April 1964, then to Newton Heath on 9th August before withdrawal the following week. In reality, No 45558 spent the final six months at Crewe Works, being observed on 10th May (yard) and 14th June (stripping roads) before being finally cut up week-ending 14th November 1964.

22ND OCTOBER 1962 ● PAUL CLAXTON

Standing at the throat of the 'Old' shed yard are Nos 45559 *British Columbia* and 45553 *Canada* which is a Crewe (North) visitor. The footbridge behind the engines was the official entrance to the shed, reviving memories of great trepidation on crossing for multitudes of trainspotters. Fortunately the shed offices were at the back of the buildings and instant ejection wasn't usually the case here - but often happened at Longsight, Manchester's other ex-LNWR depot.　　　　**4TH MAY 1959 ● AUTHOR'S COLLECTION**

A directive to remove nameplates to prevent theft coincided with the arrival of No **45657 *Tyrwhitt*** from Bank Hall. One of the plates found its way into Patricroft's mess room for a while before finding a safer haven at the nearby Monkshill Museum, Eccles. She remained in service a mere four months before withdrawal, during which time No 45657 was mainly engaged on freight work in the Tyldesley area. Just the one observation to hand was on 15th May 1964 at Huddersfield when she relieved a failed Class Five, No 44763 (5A) on the 3.30pm ex-Manchester. Having spent her earlier years on the Midland Lines, including a wartime spell at Gloucester (Barnwood), she moved north to Perth in August 1952 as part of an exchange to standardise boiler types which involved 16 engines in each direction. *Tyrwhitt* then spent 9 years at Carlisle Kingmoor and continued to receive attention at St Rollox after moving south. Was the unusual positioning of the electrification warning flashes on the running plate a Scottish trait?

AUGUST 1964 ● J.A. OLDFIELD

Shortly before her transfer to Derby, No 45668 *Madden* has the company of visiting Stanier 2-6-0 No **42954** from Crewe (North) in the Old shed yard. During her 12 years in residence, the only notable recorded movement was on 7th July 1952 when she passed through Bedford on a Down afternoon milk train.

1959 ● AUTHOR'S COLLECTION

No 45645 *Collingwood* was the 'black sheep' amongst the flock of Jubilees at Patricroft. Her last recorded annual mileage in 1960 was 23,253, which tells its own story. She is seen here five years earlier as a 10C engine in the shed yard.

6TH APRIL 1955 ● THE COLTAS TRUST

No 45600 *Bermuda*, on the other hand, was the pride of the shed and was usually kept in this tidy condition, a facility which was hardly extended to the other members. Here she passes beyond the throat of the New Shed yard under the watchful eye of Signalman Tony Oldfield whilst working in Patricroft Sidings signal box. Another engine awaits its turn to come off shed beyond which are the faint outlines of the second building and original coal stage with tank over. The line from Eccles Junction to Springs Branch curves away towards Monton beyond which are the 'Engineer's Sidings'. *Bermuda* was the longest serving Jubilee and last to depart - leaving for Newton Heath during December 1964. After withdrawal a year later, she was observed en-route to Cashmores, Great Bridge, in store at Chelford (6th March 1966) and at Crewe South. Cashmores dealt with 1,233 engines, including 33 Jubilees.

AUGUST 1964 ● J.A. OLDFIELD

MANCHESTER VICTORIA EAST JUNCTION

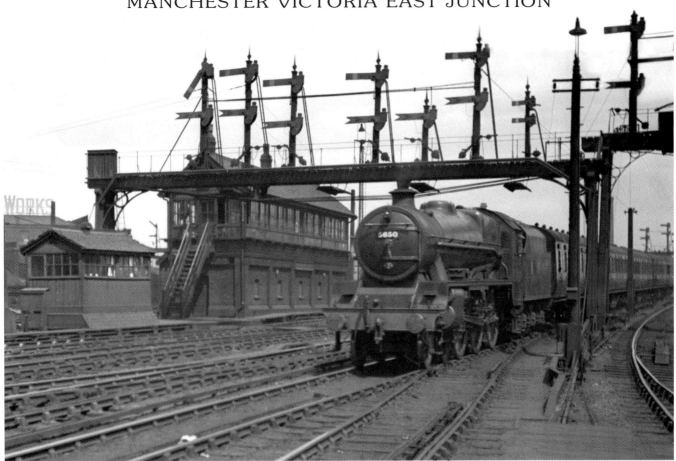

A familiar view from the east end of Manchester Victoria's Platform 11, just beyond Cheetham Hill Road bridge. Red liveried No **5650** must have looked impressive making a cautious descent of Miles Platting bank with a stopping train. She arrived at Patricroft on 4th January 1936 and stayed for a further 16 months. **4TH APRIL 1936 ● W. POTTER**

MANCHESTER VICTORIA
WEST JUNCTION

The roof of Manchester Exchange Station, Victoria West Junction Signal Box and Threlfall's Brewery form the familiar backdrop in the view looking west from a deserted Manchester Victoria Platform 12. No **45668** *Madden* gets away from Exchange through the middle roads with an eastbound excursion. Passengers wait on the lengthy Platform 11, extending to 11 Middle, becoming Exchange No 3. **AUGUST 1959 ● AUTHOR'S COLLECTION**

MANCHESTER EXCHANGE

◄ **All manner of parcels and newspaper** trains made use of Manchester Victoria's Platform 11 Middle. No **45558 *Manitoba*** awaits departure under the gaze of a pair of admiring schoolboys. 'Namers' always held a special fascination and a great many would enter into the notebooks of Jack Lord, Jack Hartshorne, Arthur Haynes, Alan Bidder and a multitude of others over the years. On a summer Saturday, they would have to jostle for position at the end of Exchange's Platform 3, the best spot to observe through trains and those in and out of neighbouring Victoria. The magnitude of traffic often resulted in a trek down to the east end of Platform 11 to discover what had 'slipped in round the back'. The chalked reporting number 3X22 on *Manitoba's* smoke-box door relates to a previous working.

1963 ● **JOHN CLARKE**

No **45558 *Manitoba*** is on the through line between Platforms 3 and 4. As well as a release road, trains off Victoria's 11 Middle and westerly bound freight made use of this path through Exchange Station. **8TH SEPTEMBER 1960** ● **PETER FITTON**

No **45600 *Bermuda*** stands facing east in 11 Middle. The glazed screen served to protect both parcels and bundles of newspapers, not forgetting the odd passenger, from those squally showers which appeared to be rather frequent in the Manchester area!

1963 ● **A. DEVONPORT**

A similar viewpoint records the arrival of more parcels vans behind No **45663 *Jervis*.** The Patricroft Jubilees regularly worked to Chester and beyond, often with heavily loaded trains. A typical example was on 14th July 1962 when *Jervis* worked the 4.20pm Holyhead to Manchester Exchange with 13 bogies. **1963** ● **BRIAN MAGILTON**

DIGGLE

Class 2P 4-4-0 No 40691 lends a hand to No **45668** *Madden* on a special climbing towards Diggle Junction. The eastbound excursion has just emerged from Butterhouse Tunnel, having been routed via the Micklehurst Loop from Stalybridge. In the early 1950's, 2P's were common assisting heavier trains over the Pennines. The leading carriage appears to be a 'strengthener', but the photograph is undated. No 40691 was at Farnley Junction for a short spell from August 1952, so it's safe to assume it was shortly after this.   **AUGUST 1952 ● ARTHUR BENDELL**

DIGGLE JUNCTION

No **45645** *Collingwood* brings a Manchester to Newcastle relief, again, off the Micklehurst Loop, past Diggle Junction Signal Box.

1ST SEPTEMBER 1962 ● DON CASH

Taking the direct line is another Farnley Junction engine, Class Five No **45211** piloting No **45559** *British Columbia* on a Hull to Liverpool express.

1959 ● JIM DAVENPORT

GOLCAR

Approaching the eastern end of Linthwaite Goods at Low Westwood is immaculate No **45600** **Bermuda** shortly after her transfer from Longsight with a Newcastle to Liverpool express. Golcar is a former weavers' village some 3½ miles south of Huddersfield, situated on a hillside crest in the Colne Valley north of the River Colne and the Huddersfield Narrow Canal. The station, visible in the distance whose platforms served all four lines, closed in 1968.

AUGUST 1950 ● **JIM DAVENPORT**

HUDDERSFIELD

From an elevated position above Paddock Cutting, west of Huddersfield, No **45600** **Bermuda** once more gets to grips towards Longwood and Milnsbridge on the climb to Standedge with a Manchester/Liverpool express. Immediately west of the Station lie the 695 yard Huddersfield Tunnel followed by the shorter Paddock Tunnel, whose portal is shrouded in steam at the rear of the train. The Penistone line branches off at Springwood Junction, situated between the tunnels.   **4TH JULY 1959** ● **G.W. MORRISON**

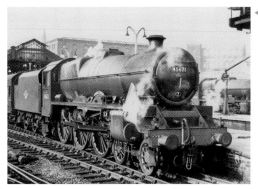

Two for the price of one! Awaiting departure from Huddersfield Station are Longsight's No **45671** **Prince Rupert** and No **45600** **Bermuda.**

1959 ● **AUTHOR'S COLLECTION**

Approaching Huddersfield from the east and passing Hillhouse MPD is No **45558** **Manitoba.**

1961 ● **G.W. SHARPE**

THORNHILL

No 45668 *Madden* brings an excursion from the Leeds area through the West Riding towards Mirfield. From Thornhill LNW Junction to Heaton Lodge Junction, the Leeds to Manchester route via Huddersfield is shared with the ex-Lancashire and Yorkshire Railway (tracks on the left) as a section of the Calder Valley Main Line. **1958 ● JIM DAVENPORT**

ALTRINCHAM

The Patricroft Shunt, as it was referred to, left the local Sidings before 6.00am and travelled via Ordsall Lane to Castlefield Junction. There, the engine ran around its train before proceeding along the MSJ&A line to Stretford, then to Sale and finally Altrincham, dealing with whatever traffic was necessary within the goods yards. This weekday turn had always been a job for a 'Super D' 0-8-0, but by 1964, Patricroft could afford to use No **45600 Bermuda,** seen here in Altrincham Goods Yard before returning home, late morning, running round once more at Castlefield.

12TH MAY 1964 ● AUTHOR'S COLLECTION

STOCKPORT (EDGELEY)

The 5.05pm Garston to Newcastle van train loaded with bananas is held at Edgeley Junction beside No 2 signal box. No **45663 Jervis** has travelled over the CLC route to Northenden Junction, then via Cheadle Village Junction to this point. Stockport Edgeley MPD is on the right and just in view are engines on the arrival road.

14TH AUGUST 1963 ● A. STEELE

WIGAN
(NORTH WESTERN)

Photographs taken during wartime are rare ▶
enough without being shrouded in mystery.
Information provided on the reverse states: No
5617 *Mauritius*, Wigan (North Western)
Station, 20th June 1942. Observation reveals the
loco as being on a stopping train and carrying a
10C shedplate. She received her nameplates on
7th September 1937, fitted at Patricroft after
Derby Works had failed to do so the previous
March and according to the Engine History Card,
she left for Carlisle Upperby week-ending 6th
December 1941!

20TH JUNE 1942 ⬤ **AUTHOR'S COLLECTION**

LIVERPOOL
(LIME STREET)

◀ **Standing in dramatic light** at Liverpool
Lime Street Station and awaiting departure
with a stopping train is No **45668**
Madden. Jubilees averaged 8 successive
days in service before examination and
subsequent attention, completed 40,000
miles between piston and valve exams and
covered 70,000 miles before wheel and
axlebox examination. During its spell at
Patricroft, *Madden* averaged 48,500 miles
per year.

1955 ⬤ **R. BLENCOWE COLLECTION**

KENYON JUNCTION

No 45645 *Collingwood* passes through Kenyon Junction with a Liverpool express. The branch towards Pennington curves away on the
left where a freight train appears to be 'wrong road' through the platforms.

1961 ⬤ **TOM LEWIS**

CHESTER

One of the Jubilees involved in the Scottish exchanges of 1952 was No **45720** *Indomitable*. This photograph of the engine leaving Chester in the North Wales direction was taken between September 1948, when she gained her BR block style number, and April 1950 when No 45720 received a repaint in Brunswick Green and 8" Gill Sans cab side numerals. The former Great Western depot at Chester (West) is above the tender, whilst the shed building between engine and Chester No 4 signal box is that of the former LNWR, abandoned when that company opened new premises at the Manchester end of the station in 1870. In later years, as can be seen, it was used by the GWR for extra accommodation.

c1949 ● AUTHOR'S COLLECTION

DEGANWY

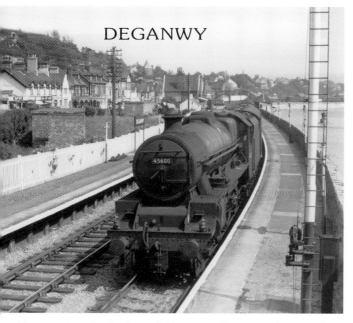

Progressing slowly through Deganwy Station and approaching Llandudno with a train from Manchester is No **45600** *Bermuda*.

5TH AUGUST 1963 ● G. HARROP

LLANDUDNO

The 5.30pm to Manchester Exchange (1C94) awaits departure from Llandudno Station behind No **45563** *Australia*.

5TH AUGUST 1963 ● G. HARROP

BANGOR

A crew change in the Bangor platforms might involve Patricroft men, but the working is unknown. The train, with stopping lamp, has arrived from the Chester direction and the engine is No **45663** *Jervis*. The onset of the 1963 Winter Timetable brought about her transfer to Warrington, then Speke Junction, working out mileage on freight and parcels before withdrawal a year later. She was in trouble on 21st October 1960 having 'dropped a plug' at Dewsbury while working the 8.18am Leeds to Liverpool Lime Street and was declared a failure before being hauled to Hillhouse shed by WD No 90680.

AUGUST 1963 ● I. TRAVERS

BIRMINGHAM NEW STREET

A dramatic, low level view of a football supporters excursion departing from Birmingham New Street. The occasion was the 1949 FA Cup Final at Wembley Stadium between Leicester City and Wolverhampton Wanderers and this would be one of many trains taking Wolves fans to the Capital. The newly painted smokebox of No **45668 Madden** has been defaced by a Leicester fan who wrongly predicted a 4-0 scoreline (the outcome was a Wolves victory 3-1). The engine, a mere 3 days out of shops, remained coupled to her first tender which showed LMS for a further 18 months.

30TH APRIL 1949 ● D.J. MONTGOMERY

WATFORD JUNCTION

A northbound express makes haste through Watford Junction Station behind No **45559 British Columbia.** The photograph is undated but with the engine in cleaner than usual condition, it may be on another running-in turn. Using his knee as a rest, one youngster is eagerly entering the number in his 'grice' book - perhaps he knows its a 'cop', as Patricroft Jubilees were something of a rarity in these parts. *British Columbia,* however, came this way on 7th April 1953 with the 12.40pm Euston to Wolverhampton - normally a job for one of the Bushbury 'elite'.

1955 ● R.S. CARPENTER COLLECTION

LONDON EUSTON

Extra traffic on the Saturday before Christmas 1962 on the West Coast main line was considerable. Standing in Platform 15 at London Euston is No **45558 Manitoba,** awaiting departure with the 10.30am relief to Liverpool Lime Street (1X17). Euston Station was in the midst of redevelopment at the time - an air of gloom and neglect had pervaded here for many years, especially on the departure side (Platforms 12 to 15), as can be witnessed here. Despite public outcry, the old building, including the historic Euston Arch and Great Hall, had recently been demolished, rather than integrated into future plans. Surely an official act of early vandalism.

**22ND DECEMBER 1962 ●
B.W.L. BROOKSBANK**

WALSALL

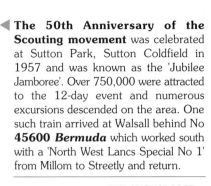

The 50th Anniversary of the Scouting movement was celebrated at Sutton Park, Sutton Coldfield in 1957 and was known as the 'Jubilee Jamboree'. Over 750,000 were attracted to the 12-day event and numerous excursions descended on the area. One such train arrived at Walsall behind No **45600** *Bermuda* which worked south with a 'North West Lancs Special No 1' from Millom to Streetly and return.

7TH AUGUST 1957 ● **AUTHOR'S COLLECTION**

ASTON

The 4.10pm Birmingham New Street to London Euston has unlikely motive power in the form of No **45645** *Collingwood*. With a Permanent Way gang 'In Possession' between Stechford and New Street, the train left facing west and took the Soho curve to Perry Barr, thence via Aston (passing time: 4.41pm) to Stechford to reach the normal route. 30 minutes earlier, the same loco and empty stock had passed by after leaving the carriage sidings. **15TH MARCH 1959** ● **M. MENSING**

MADELEY

Not long out of shops and now fitted with Automatic Warning System as betrayed by the protective shield under the buffer beam, No **45559** *British Columbia* is at Madeley with an unidentified express. Other notable observations were at Bath on 27th December 1951 when she arrived with the Down *Pines Express* and on 19th September 1955, the engine passed through Luton with the 10.05am Edinburgh Waverley to London St. Pancras.

1960 ● **TOM LEWIS**

NEWTON

Rugby League Challenge Cup Finals at Wembley in May inevitably brought large numbers of unusual engines to the capital. The 1961/62 season saw Huddersfield drawn against local rivals Wakefield, so Leeds (Holbeck) Jubilees were naturally to the fore. Patricroft's No **45663** *Jervis,* however, was borrowed for a trip down the former Great Central main line and is seen at Newton, north of Rugby. Four trains originated from the Wigan/St Helens area, but the only other Manchester Jubilee involved on the day was Newton Heath's No 45737 *Atlas,* which worked a Shaw to Wembley excursion over the ex-LNWR route. The full list is as follows:

12TH MAY 1962 ● **PETER FITTON**

No 46165	1Z45 Wigan - Wembley via West Coast Main Line		No 45562	1X62 Huddersfield - Wembley via Great Central Line
No 45189	1Z64 Relief via West Coast Main Line		No 45694	1X63 Wakefield - Wembley via Great Central Line
No 46161	1Z30 St Helens - Wembley via West Coast Main Line		No 45663	1X65 Huddersfield - Wembley via Great Central Line
No 45737	1T65 Shaw - Wembley via West Coast Main Line		No 45605	1X66 Huddersfield - Wembley via Great Central Line
No 45398	1Z40 Wigan - Wembley via West Coast Main Line		No 45581	1X67 Huddersfield - Wembley via Great Central Line
No 44746	1Z61 Wakefield - Wembley via Great Central Line		No 45597	1X62 Wakefield - Wembley via Great Central Line

CREWE

No **45563** *Australia* has just come off ▶ an Up express in the original Platform 3 at Crewe Station. If the chalked reporting number 1V58 is correct, it may well be a Manchester to West of England train originating at Victoria or Exchange Station whilst Piccadilly Station was under reconstruction. Both Patricroft and Newton Heath Jubilees were regular visitors during this period, otherwise their presence usually coincided with works visits. Another unidentified member lurks in the background.

1960 ● **M.S. WELCH**

SKEW BRIDGE

◀ **Those Jubilees still carrying original domeless boilers** were gradually married to the domed variety, but five original specimens remained in circulation. One of the last, if not the last, to carry one was No **45645** *Collingwood*. Boiler No 8748 was fitted at Crewe as part of a last Heavy General Overhaul in October 1957 and stayed with her until withdrawal. During the BR period it had previously been attached to Longsight's No 45578 *United Provinces*, Leicester's 45615 *Malay States* and 45592 *Indore* (Carlisle Upperby, Edge Hill and Longsight). A rather grubby *Collingwood* passes Skew Bridge Signal Box, 1 mile south of Preston with a Manchester express.

9TH JUNE 1962 1961 ● **PAUL CLAXTON**

PRESTON

◄ **Passing Fylde Junction, Preston** with the Heysham vans is No **45645 *Collingwood*.** She had been through Crewe the previous month as the condition of her smokebox will testify. According to enginemen, she did little work in 1963, and was transferred away to Carnforth in August, from where she lasted a further two months in service. The only Jubilee withdawn as a Patricroft engine was No 45657 *Tyrwhitt*, although No 45569 *Tasmania* had been the subject of a 'paper transfer'.

17TH MARCH 1962 ● PAUL CLAXTON

TREALES

No **45563 *Australia*** was one of a select ► band of Manchester Jubilees chosen for Royal Train duty. Specially cleaned for the occasion - as all Royal engines and standbys had to be - she brought H.M. The Queen from Newton-le-Willows to Manchester as part of a north-west tour on 31st May 1951. Almost ten years later and now in a workaday condition, the engine is bowling along in fine style at Treales, near Kirkham, with 1N79, a Blackpool Central to Newcastle excursion.

1ST JULY 1961 ● PETER FITTON

DOWBRIDGE

◄ **Another holiday special** bound for Blackpool North, 1P28 from Crewe, has No **45600 *Bermuda*** in customary clean condition. Observations of interest that summer include: 16th May - Engine standing in a bay at Birmingham New Street at 8.30am. 26th June - Worked the 11.00am Liverpool to Newcastle owing to a shortage of diesel locos at Edge Hill. 6th August - Was the only Jubilee on Kentish Town MPD.

6TH AUGUST 1962 ● PAUL CLAXTON

WEETON

No **45600 *Bermuda*,** borrowed yet again, ► is seen here working a returning excursion from Blackpool (North) to Leeds (1X85). The location is Weeton Cutting, situated between Poulton and Kirkham. Further sightings of this popular engine were on 9th May 1960, when she was noted at Sheffield Midland working the Up 'Condor' express container freight (Gushetfaulds to Hendon), usually powered by a pair of Metrovick Co-Bo diesels. She returned north the following day with the Down working - whilst on 8th September 1963, *Bermuda* was receiving attention at Annesley MPD.

23RD JULY 1961 ● PETER FITTON

LANCASTER

Piloting a Polmadie Royal Scot 4-6-0 No 46102 *Black Watch* may have been a case of operational convenience for No **45563** *Australia*. The pair are recorded with a Glasgow to Manchester express near Lancaster but three years previously, this same combination had worked together, when on 20th September 1958 they had the 5.00pm Liverpool Lime Street to Newcastle as far as Leeds via the Spen Valley line from Huddersfield.   **16TH NOVEMBER 1961** ● **N. MACHELL**

One of the best ever runs recorded by a Jubilee on the former LNWR main line between Carlisle and Euston was by this engine. On 15th December 1954, No **45558** *Manitoba* was paired with Britannia Pacific No 70023 *Venus* (81A) which was running in after repair at Crewe. The train was the 1.00pm Barrow to Euston which *Manitoba* worked as far as Preston. 82mph was recorded over Brock Troughs and timings were 4 minutes inside that of the 'Coronation Scot' schedule which had Class 8 power. Ten years later the engine is passing over the next set of troughs further north - those at Hest Bank - with an Up freight, but it's doubtful whether the speed here would be even half of that previously mentioned.

5TH NOVEMBER 1963 ● **RAY FARRELL**

HEST BANK

SHAP WELLS

Patricroft's premier duty for many years was the 11.15pm newspaper train to Glasgow St Enoch, running express via Preston and Carlisle. The loco went as far as Carlisle, from where it was often made use of during the day on a stopping passenger filling-in turn to Glasgow Central and return. It came home on the night fast fish from Aberdeen to Manchester Victoria. No **45563** *Australia* is heading south over Shap Wells in mid-afternoon with a van train, but on 20th August 1955 she worked the 2.33pm Edinburgh Waverley to Carlisle, an exceptional visitor over the Waverley route.   **30TH JULY 1963** ● **RAY FARRELL**

THRIMBY GRANGE

◄ **W270, the 7.30am Aberdeen to Manchester Victoria** has the luxury of 2 engines with No **45600 Bermuda** piloting No **45723 Fearless,** one time Longsight stalwart but now of Carlisle Upperby. The location is Thrimby Grange, south of Penrith on the Northern climb to Shap. It was *Bermuda's* turn to convey Welsh rugby supporters to Edinburgh and on 2nd February 1957 she was one of five Jubilees on Dalry Road MPD. No 45644 *Howe* arrived once more, having worked forward from Crewe on a train which originated from Neath the previous evening at 8.27pm.

18TH JULY 1959 ● A.C. GILBERT

CARLISLE

Restarting a Glasgow to Manchester train away from Carlisle Citadel is No **45645 Collingwood.** The previous year she was involved in the biennial Rugby International between Scotland and Wales at Murrayfield. The fixture entailed the running of 27 special trains from Wales involving several Jubilees, the only Manchester representatives were *Collingwood* and Longsight's No 45644 *Howe*, both being serviced at Dalry Road MPD.

13TH AUGUST 1954 ● NORMAN PREEDY ARCHIVE

BEATTOCK

Purposefully climbing Beattock with ▶ the 2.00pm Manchester Victoria to Glasgow Central is No **45663 Jervis** and has the support of No 42214 from the rear. Later in the day, another Manchester engine, No 45710 *Irresistible* was also in Glasgow, coinciding with the return day for Fair traffic. *Jervis* had been on Polmadie earlier in the year on 14th April but this was possibly her last visit over the border as she was transferred to Warrington (Dallam) after the Summer Timetable.

27TH JULY 1963 ● A.C. GILBERT

BEATTOCK

No 45600 *Bermuda* stops at Beattock with a lightweight stopping train from Glasgow to Carlisle. During her time at Patricroft, *Bermuda* was the favourite Jubilee and was probably selected for the 'Glasgow News' more than the others. The number of sightings north and south of the border would substantiate that theory and even as late as 22nd February 1964, she was observed on main line duty. In tandem with Newton Heath Class Five No 45220, No 45600 arrived at Carlisle with the 4.15pm Manchester Victoria to Glasgow 4 minutes early, the pair having substituted for a Type 4 diesel. The two 4-6-0's were replaced by Duchess Pacific No 46255 *City of Hereford*.

22ND JULY 1958 ● **J.J. CUNNINGHAM**

SYMINGTON

Carlisle Kingmoor regularly made use of the Patricroft Jubilee which had arrived with the newspaper train for Glasgow St Enoch. Returning to Carlisle from Glasgow Central and calling at Symington Station with another filling-in turn is No **45559 *British Columbia.*** Four years previously, she had been used on a different job, when on 30th June 1954 the engine worked north from Carstairs to Perth with a special, put on in place of trains re-routed via the Waverley route because of local floods and landslips. The following day, No 45559 was in charge of the 7.15am Glasgow Buchanan Street to Aberdeen, eventually returning south with the 3.30pm 'Postal'.

17TH OCTOBER 1959 ● **J.J. CUNNINGHAM**

The afternoon stopping train is within the vicinity of Polmadie MPD. No **45558 *Manitoba*** has a tender full of coal in readiness for the fast fish train from Carlisle later in the day.　　**14TH APRIL 1959** ● **J.J. CUNNINGHAM**

SUNDERLAND

On Good Friday 1955, No 45645 *Collingwood* was the subject of conflicting football excursions. Whilst Sunderland entertained Manchester United in a First Division fixture, the engine awaited the signal before collecting its empty stock for the return journey. Meanwhile, Accrington Stanley had travelled to York for their Third Division (North) clash and it was later reported that *Collingwood* had brought the Accrington fans into the Minster City. Probably a case of mistaken identity at York Station!

8TH APRIL 1955 ● R. BLENCOWE COLLECTION

POLMADIE

◄ **No 45645** *Collingwood* once more, about to move off the shed yard at Polmadie. As well as her excursions to Sunderland - on 26th May 1958, she worked a Whit Monday excursion from Manchester Exchange to Newcastle and was serviced on Gateshead MPD.

**14TH APRIL 1956 ●
AUTHOR'S COLLECTION**

With '1T14' Reporting Number in place and with a tender full of coal, No **45563** *Australia* is ready to move off Trafford Park MPD. The cab side number has received a cursory wipe, but smokebox char remains on the running plate.

1961 ● AUTHOR'S COLLECTION

▼

TRAFFORD PARK

BLACKPOOL (CENTRAL)

No 45593 *Kolhapur*   10TH OCTOBER 1964 ● PETER FITTON

CHESTER (MIDLAND)

No 45645 *Collingwood*   26TH APRIL 1953 ● K. BOULTER

LONGSIGHT

No 45600 *Bermuda*   JUNE 1963 ● AUTHOR'S COLLECTION

 NEWTON HEATH

No 5566 *Queensland*   1937 ● F.A. WYCHERLEY

CARSTAIRS

No 45563 *Australia*   1958 ● BRIAN HILTON

FARNLEY JUNCTION

No 45663 *Jervis*   14TH JULY 1963 ● A.G. ELLIS

MONUMENT LANE

No 45558 *Manitoba*   4TH NOVEMBER 1951 ● H.C. CASSERLEY

POLMADIE (GLASGOW)

No 45668 *Madden*   21ST JUNE 1952 ● AUTHOR'S COLLECTION

THE
AGECROFT
LOCOMOTIVES

No 45654 *Hood* makes good progress past Greenfield Junction with a Manchester Victoria to Filey excursion (1N75). The holiday-makers were en-route to Butlins Holiday Camp which had its own station to receive them. The Agecroft engine worked throughout with a crew change at Wakefield. The disused platform at Greenfield is visible, as is the Oldham line which it served - above the leading carriage. Passenger services ceased over this line in May 1955.   **4TH AUGUST 1962 ● DON CASH**

26B AGECROFT MPD

By 1962, displaced Jubilees were being cascaded to the most unlikely of places. One such recipient was the ex-L&Y depot at Agecroft which received eight members, but all had disappeared by June 1963. First to arrive was No 45590 *Travancore* on 25th February, which had been in store at Staveley (Barrow Hill) MPD after the closure of Millhouses in December 1961. This was followed by three more next month from the same source, namely Nos 45607 *Fiji*, 45654 *Hood* (Staveley GC MPD) and 45664 *Nelson*. Evidence that these ex-Midland engines were in good condition and used by the shed is shown in the following pages, but a further quartet which came four months later tell a different story. Nos 45716 *Swiftsure*, 45718 *Dreadnought*, 45728 *Defiance* and 45729 *Furious* came officially on loan from Carlisle Kingmoor, a move made permanent the following month. Other than No **45716 Swiftsure**, there is little evidence that the other three saw much work before their withdrawal a mere two months later. *Swiftsure* stands in the shed yard shortly before her transfer to Newton Heath. **6TH JUNE 1963 ● A. STEELE**

A class more readily associated with the shed were the diminutive 0-4-0ST 'Pug' engines. Here No **51232,** still in use, stands alongside No **45728 Defiance** out in the open. Whereas No 45718 *Dreadnought* had been a Longsight engine for short periods, *Defiance* and *Furious* were very much Scottish Jubilees during the BR period. This migration south came as a surprise, especially as they were evidently in poor condition. After withdrawal, all three returned to Scotland and after storage at St Rollox, were cut up at Cowlairs Works, prompting speculation that they completed more mileage in transit than they had done in service! Also, a little known fact is that No 45728 was the only member to have reverted from a Stanier to a Fowler tender in January 1959.

23RD SEPTEMBER 1962 ● J. SCHATZ

◁ **The ex-Sheffield contingent,** together with No 45716 *Swiftsure* were officially transferred away to Newton Heath week-ending Saturday 22nd June 1963 - other than No 45607 *Fiji* which had been withdrawn the previous November. No **45590 Travancore** stands on the open Road 5 alongside the wooden wall in the southerly half of the shed. During LMS days the original shed roof was removed and because of subsidence problems, only four of the eight roads were re-roofed. This picture was taken on the Sunday after transfer date and the Reporting Number shows that she was possibly earmarked for excursion traffic earlier in the week.

23RD JUNE 1963 ● D. BURDON

MANCHESTER VICTORIA STATION

No **45664** *Nelson* was fondly remembered during the late 1940's as being a regular on the 5.10pm Manchester Victoria to York. This had been an ex-Midland working with the Sheffield (Millhouses) engine spending the afternoon on Agecroft MPD, having arrived from York with the morning train. Ironic then, that she should find her way back after being made surplus to requirements over the Midland lines. *Nelson* brings empty stock into Platform 12 at Manchester Victoria Station which will form an afternoon stopping train to Southport.

5TH MAY 1963 ● BRIAN MAGILTON

PENDLEBURY BANK

◄ **A rare view of an Agecroft Jubilee** on freight duty - even though that constituted the bulk of what little work they did. No **45716** *Swiftsure* drifts down Pendlebury Bank tender first.

18TH SEPTEMBER 1962 ● W.D. COOPER

No **45607** *Fiji* reaches Pendlebury Junction with the 4.10pm Manchester to Southport express. **4TH AUGUST 1962 ● DAVE HAMPSON**

RYLANDS SIDING

Passing Rylands Siding with a Wigan to Preston stopping train is No 45654 _Hood_. The engine has evidently been borrowed by Springs Branch who normally provided a Stanier 2-6-4T for the service. Although this series of photographs might suggest otherwise, Agecroft's Jubilees were mainly used for freight duties and often into Yorkshire. On one such occasion, Driver Harry Dean and Fireman John King of Sowerby Bridge MPD booked on to relieve Wakefield men working an evening Mytholmroyd to Brindle Heath mixed goods. An Austerity 2-8-0 was normally provided for the job, but on this occasion _Hood_ appeared out of the gloom. With five to six hundred tons behind the tender, all seemed to be going well. It was a good, clear night and after 'going round the corner' at Castleton East Junction, Fireman King suggested pinning a few brakes down. His request wasn't granted but the confident driver soon regretted the decision as, after passing through Heywood, despite the application of all brakes, he lost control. Speed increased down the gradient through Broadfield and Heap Bridge Junction and although the speedometer wasn't working (which wasn't uncommon on Jubilees by this time), the road remained clear. Sensing imminent danger, Driver Dean issued an instruction to open both doors and be prepared to jump. Fortunately they were met by more green signals at Bury Loco Junction and after passing through Knowsley Street Station at a great rate of knots, they negotiated Bury Hollow and Gas Works Junction but it wasn't until they reached Bradley Fold before control was regained. The men eventually put the engine on Agecroft shed before working home with an Austerity at a more leisurely pace. They heard no more about the incident. **11TH JUNE 1963 ● AUTHOR'S COLLECTION**

BURSCOUGH BRIDGE

No **45607** _Fiji_ was one of the arrivals from the Midland Division in March 1962 but didn't see the year out, being withdrawn week-ending 1st December. The reasons are unclear but she would have completed little mileage - unlike 1938 when _Fiji_ achieved an astounding 89,224 miles, and this despite 5 weeks away at Crewe. She was one of only three Jubilees cut up locally at Horwich Works. A stopping train leaves Burscough Bridge Station, signalled for the Wigan line. The other arms were for Ormskirk and Preston respectively.

28TH MAY 1962 ● B. HOPER

SOUTHPORT

No **45590** _Travancore_ was another Midland Division engine denied the fitting of an Automatic Warning System, but was one of 47 members which had a driver's name bracket on both cab sides above the numerals. The idea, introduced in 1959 as a PR initiative, was to inform passengers of the driver's name. It proved unpopular and the idea was quickly shelved. The engine reverses out of Southport Chapel Street Station, having arrived with an excursion train.

AUGUST 1962 ● AUTHOR'S COLLECTION

SKEW BRIDGE

A three coach local from Wigan approaches Skew Bridge Signal Box and once again, the engine appears to have been borrowed by Springs Branch. Running 'neck and neck' on the Down Fast, passengers cast a sideways glance from within a recently delivered Metropolitan Cammell Diesel Multiple Unit. They will get good views of the cabside number and nameplate of No **45664 Nelson,** a pleasure which may well have been denied to the three enthusiasts high upon the embankment.

14TH APRIL 1962 ● **PAUL CLAXTON**

PRESTON

Two more enthusiasts get in on the act. Whilst a low sun nicely portrays No **45654 Hood** with her rods down, the youngster nearest the oncoming engine has to shield his eyes to get the number. The train is 1X13 - Blackpool to Low Moor, leaving Preston on the Up Fast line.

3RD JUNE 1963 ● **PAUL CLAXTON**

SALWICK TROUGHS

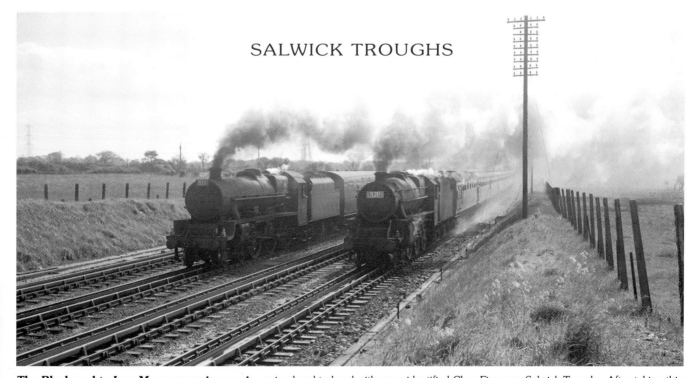

The Blackpool to Low Moor excursion again, going head to head with an unidentified Class Five over Salwick Troughs. After taking this shot, Paul Claxton quickly cycled through the country lanes to gain position to record No **45654 Hood** *(above)* once more.

3RD JUNE 1963 ● **PAUL CLAXTON**

ANSDELL & FAIRHAVEN

The 4.40pm Liverpool to Blackpool Central makes progress towards St Annes, leaving Ansdell station in the distance. This popular location, adjacent to Arundel Road and near the Royal Lytham St. Annes golf course, offered classic views such as this. No **45716 *Swiftsure*** and her short train are very much the focus of attention, unspoilt by anything else of significance. **9TH MAY 1963 ● PAUL CLAXTON**

BLACKPOOL NORTH

The abundance of holiday traffic brought multitudes of Jubilees into the town. The Central Division locos were commonplace, but examples of the Midland and the rarer Western Division engines made welcome appearances. The 'Glasgow Wakes' weeks were eagerly anticipated with the possibility of Corkerhill engines working through. Gladdening the hearts of the local spotting fraternity on Saturday 24th September 1960 were the arrival of Nos 45692 *Cyclops* and 45720 *Indomitable*. The following year brought Nos 45673 *Keppel* and 45727 *Inflexible*, but the Scottish 'Jubs' were all withdrawn in December 1962. The locals then had to make do with the likes of No **45716 *Swiftsure*,** still carrying 10" St Rollox cab side numerals and 26B shedplate, on Blackpool North MPD later in the year.

29TH JUNE 1963 ● PAUL CLAXTON

BLACKPOOL CENTRAL

Reversing her stock out of Central Station and away to Bloomfield Road Carriage Sidings is No **45664 *Nelson*.** Agecroft and Patricroft engines were fairly regularly observed but Longsight and certainly Trafford Park locos much less so. The Corkerhill engines mentioned above used the North Station and MPD for servicing, but a highlight at Central must surely have been the arrival on 28th September 1963 of Bristol Barrow Road's No 45685 *Barfleur*, complete with GWR smokebox reporting number X36.

7TH JUNE 1963 ● FRANK DEAN

GREENFIELD JUNCTION

A mystery surrounds this photograph. Reporting number 1N73 was allocated for the 8.30am Manchester Victoria to Scarborough (7th - 28th July 1962) and from Stalybridge to Scarborough (4th/11th August). All trains were booked to take the Micklehurst Loop. On 4th August, No **45716 *Swiftsure*** was recorded as working the 8.50am Stalybridge to Scarborough, but not only has she taken the direct route via Saddleworth, but is showing empty stock lamps and Reporting Number 3N73. One assumes these were set at Irlam Carriage Sidings, and it was simply a case of the Driver overlooking the re-setting of lamps and headcode at Stalybridge - it wouldn't be the first time! *Swiftsure* worked the train throughout with a crew change at York. The following Monday, 6th August 1962, was a Public Holiday and *Swiftsure* was observed light engine within York Station ready to relieve a southbound train. Did she spend the weekend in Yorkshire or work another day excursion?

4TH AUGUST 1962 ● DON CASH

BRADLEY WOOD JUNCTION

The Manchester Victoria to Filey Holiday Centre (Butlins Camp) Summer Saturdays Only service is in the hands of No **45716 *Swiftsure***. The Agecroft enginemen had reached Bradley Wood Junction, beyond Huddersfield with their filthy steed whose 10" high cab side numbers had been revealed by a wipe over. Other than the lamps and reporting number, she presented a sorry sight with char on the running plate and signs of priming on the smokebox. At least front number and nameplates were in situ at the time. *Swiftsure* spent 25 years at Carlisle Kingmoor and continued to recieve attention at St Rollox after transfer.

JULY 1962 ● R.K. BLENCOWE

SHREWSBURY

Before her return to Agecroft, No **45654 *Hood*** is caught on a running-in turn in time honoured fashion. The Crewe to Shrewsbury line was a favourite path and *Hood* may well have firstly worked light engine to Shrewsbury. After turning on the triangle south of the station, she is reversing on to the stock of an excursion at the north end, probably relieving a GWR engine off the North and West route.

APRIL 1962 ● DEREK PENNEY

 HEATON MERSEY

No 45664 *Nelson*   12TH JUNE 1963 ● R. BLENCOWE

 LOW MOOR

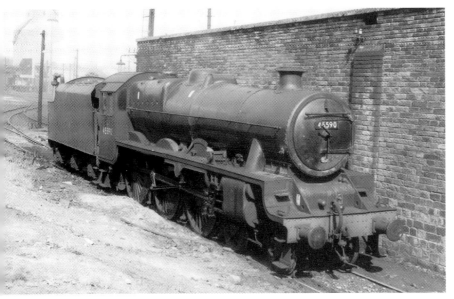

No 45590 *Travancore*   1962 ● AUTHOR'S COLLECTION

No 45716 *Swiftsure*   1962 ● AUTHOR'S COLLECTION

 BLACKPOOL (NORTH)

No 45590 *Travancore*   18TH AUGUST 1962 ● FRANK DEAN

THE
NEWTON HEATH
LOCOMOTIVES

No 45679 *Armada* **passes Treales signal box, Kirkham,** on 1X12, a Blackpool Central to Huddersfield relief. This was a Jubilee with an interesting history. Her LMS days were spent in equal part between the Western and Midland Divisions, before becoming a Carlisle Kingmoor engine in 1952. She arrived initially on loan to Newton Heath week-ending 25th June 1960 after short spells at Crewe (North) and then Longsight, a move made permanent the following month. What may be unique is the fact that she passed through four different workshops for attention: Crewe, Derby, Cowlairs and St Rollox, the latter for her last overhaul between July and September 1961, whilst a 26A engine. One of *Armada's* last jobs was the 2.50pm (Sundays Only) Manchester Victoria to Blackpool North during November 1962, which was a regular 5X job. She 'sat down' before Bolton for no apparent reason, but later that week was seen standing on the scrap lines behind Newton Heath Station - probably as a result of the driver's report and subsequent investigation. **18TH AUGUST 1962 ● PETER FITTON**

The shed was associated with no fewer than 52 members of the class, but No **5711** *Courageous* was not one of those readily associated. After spending the war years at 26A, she was away to Farnley Junction before taking up residence north of the border in Glasgow, alternating between Polmadie and Corkerhill MPD's - never to return. No 45711 subsequently became a much sought after engine by the local spotting fraternity, but paid at least one visit to Manchester, on 17th November 1960. An unidentified ex-L&Y 'A' Class 0-6-0 and a pair of Class Fives, Nos **5079** and **5105** keep her company at the south end of the shed.

4TH APRIL 1948 ● HAROLD D. BOWTELL

A regular for many years was No 45661 *Vernon.* With the vacuum pipe safely attached. she has nearly completed a revolution of the St Mary's Road turntable, situated at the north eastern end of the yard.

23RD MARCH 1963 ● G.W. MORRISON

The last member in traffic, No **45654** *Hood* is ready to move off shed for the 11pm Manchester Victoria to Oldham Mumps parcels train.

29TH APRIL 1966 ● R. CORT

Another long-standing member was No 45706 Express, unique insofar as it carried distinctive nameplates which incorporated a plaque beneath the raised plate, which depicted Mercury, the winged messenger, adorning the front splashers. She could also be described as a true Lancashire & Yorkshire locomotive, going new to Farnley Junction in May 1936 before crossing the border during the war years to Newton Heath where she remained until withdrawal in September 1963. As did many other Jubilees, *Express* exchanged a 3,500 gallon Fowler tender for a Stanier version in 1958.

31ST MARCH 1962 ● AUTHOR'S COLLECTION

Standing just off the St Mary's Road Turntable is No 45700 Amethyst which was originally the sixth of eight Jubilees delivered into traffic from Crewe Works as No 5700 *Britannia* between 23rd March and 5th May 1936 (Nos 5695 - 5702). The first to arrive had been during the previous March when No 5591, barely four months old and as yet un-named, came on loan for three weeks followed by No 5552 *Silver Jubilee* herself, recently named and resplendent in high gloss black livery. She had been loaned for a three week period from Camden in June 1935 for a tour of the Central Lines system before the delivery of further members. A further 31 year period of association culminated in the withdrawal of No 45654 *Hood* in June 1966.

c.1953 ● ARTHUR BENDELL

That eminent railway author and photographer, Raymond Keeley, considered this to be his best shed portrait and it subsequently became the subject of the front cover of his book 'Memories of Steam Sheds'. I make no apologies for repeating it here as Raymond also had a penchant for Jubilees and this portrait of a clean No **45642 Boscawen** certainly shows them off to good advantage. The two 'Crabs' are the shed's own No **42705** and a visitor from Crewe (South), No **42856**. 5TH OCTOBER 1958 ● RAYMOND KEELEY

An evocative shot as ex-LMS and LNER named engines share the shed yard. Newton Heath's last Jubilee, No **45654** *Hood* drifts by making for the turntable and passing York B1 4-6-0 No **61035** *Pronghorn* stabled on shed. It was unusual to find nameplates on any locomotive as by this time they were becoming sought after items of railwayana. APRIL 1966 ● PAUL JORDAN

Hood spent two periods on allocation, interspersed with a period at Stockport (Edgeley). The following is extracted from the engine history card:

22nd June 1963 - Transfer to Newton Heath (from Agecroft)	9th March 1964 - Returned to Traffic
2nd September 1963 - Stored	14th March 1964 - Transfer to Stockport
16th December 1963 - Returned to traffic	16th October 1965 - Transfer to Newton Heath
6th January 1964 - Stored	25th June 1966 - Taken out of stock

One of the Midland contingent on loan for the summer of 1961, No **45585** *Hyderabad.* JULY 1961 ● N.R. PREEDY COLLECTION

Large and small locomotives stand behind the 'Parlour' awaiting routine examination. The shed's own No **45635** *Tobago* has the company of 0-4-0ST No **51230** from nearby Agecroft MPD. 1957 ● JIM DAVENPORT

THE PARLOUR

In February 1956, Chief Mechanical Foreman Burgess was instructed to select and prepare a Class 6P locomotive in readiness for Royal Train duty. No **45671** *Prince Rupert* was chosen, probably because she had just been outshopped at Crewe. After being berthed in the Parlour, the engine was stripped down for further examination but Burgess was unhappy with the paintwork and his District Motive Power Superintendent agreed. He had good connections with the Horwich hierarchy which resulted in the swift arrival of a team of painters, supervised by the Paint Shop Foreman. Kept under lock and key were a set of specially burnished buffers, drawbar hooks and screw couplings to further enhance No 45671's appearance *(see also page 172)*. The previous August, she was caught in the Parlour undergoing routine examination.

24TH AUGUST 1955 ● B. MORRISON

During the 1950's, over 300 engines were allocated to the Newton Heath District, all of which regularly visited the 'Parlour' for Valve and Piston Examinations and various other repair work. During the 1935 modernisation plan, Roads 1 to 4 had been retained, as had the original Ramsbottom high pitched roof of 1876 vintage. The lack of smoke troughs made for ideal working conditions and ten fitters and their mates were employed in a workshop which was fully equipped with a wheel-drop table and weighing machine capable of dealing with a ten-wheel locomotive. The original beams, so prominent in these interior views, exist to this day as part of the diesel maintenance depot. In April 1958, a phase of reorganisation brought the ex-LNWR establishment at Patricroft under Newton Heath's jurisdiction. This coincided with an influx of Diesel Multiple Units on commuter services and their subsequent maintenance. As a result, certain Valve and Piston exams were transferred to Patricroft, but that was not without its problems. Receiving attention in splendid light is No **45719** *Glorious,* unkindly referred to as 'Gormless' by certain Newton Heath men. This loco is best remembered for passing the shed rather than being on it, as in 1953 she became one of the Bank Hall trio. Together with Nos 45698 *Mars* and 45717 *Dauntless* (both former 26A locos), not forgetting Unrebuilt Patriot No 45517 - this quartet handled the Liverpool Exchange to Newcastle trains to York on a daily basis for nearly a decade. Just identifiable at the far end of the shop is Class Five No **45105**.

JUNE 1950 ● W.M. LEES

With her centre driving wheels removed for attention and standing just within the new doorway of the Parlour is No **45653** *Barham* - now lacking nameplates and probably the last Jubilee to make use of the wheel-drop table here. Judging by the condition of the smokebox, it would appear she has already had a certain amount of work done, but by this time it was unusual to find a member receiving this degree of overhaul. Standing alongside is a Diesel Multiple Unit and beyond *Barham* is one of the shed's Crosti boiled 9F 2-10-0's, No **92022**.

JANUARY 1965 ● AUTHOR'S COLLECTION

Standing resplendent in the shed yard is No 5701 *Conqueror* with No 5702 *Colossus* immediately behind. Cleaner Wilf Titley recalled an occasion one morning when, instead of dealing with the locos chalked up on the slate by the Chargehand Cleaner, as was usual, things were slightly different. The gang were met by the curt message 'see me in office'. Fearing the worst, the young lads were relieved but puzzled when told to hang on and go and have a brew. Shortly after this, brand new engines, Nos 5697 *Achilles* and 5698 *Mars* arrived from Crewe on shed coupled together, one engine in steam, and the lads were promptly told to get to work and clean the pair - despite them being in ex-works condition!

1935 ● W. POTTER

In common with other locomotive classes, various
Jubilees were subjected to all manner of modifications and experiments. A perennial problem with all steam engines had been the build up of ash in the smokebox and in October 1938, No **5698** *Mars* was fitted with a patented device, a chute enabling ash to be 'flushed out' whilst over a pit without opening the smokebox door, by way of diverting water from the live steam injector, which was ultimately unsuccessful. *Mars* had left for the Midland Division the previous year, only to return in August 1940 and spend the rest of her days working on the ex-L&Y system.

1940 ● AUTHOR'S COLLECTION

◄ **The device fitted to No 5698** *Mars* *(above)* had been experimental, but during 1943, Nos **5671** *Prince Rupert,* 5702 *Colossus* and 5708 *Resolution* were similarly fitted with ash ejectors, modified in detail. This view of *Prince Rupert* shows the detachable tubes carried on the running plate, supported by brackets, ahead of the blastpipe on the Fireman's side. When coupled together and attached to an outlet at the base of the smokebox, the ash could be discharged directly into the pit. The trials were unsuccessful and all three engines had the apparatus removed by 1951.

1946 ● AUTHOR'S COLLECTION

No 5699 *Galatea* **is barely** ►
one month old. Despite arriving in 1935, it was a further 7 years before Jubilees worked on the Glasgow route. Unrebuilt Patriots Nos 5546/7/8, supported by Polmadie's Nos 5550/1, held sway up until then.

MAY 1936 ●
AUTHOR'S COLLECTION

THE NORTH YARD

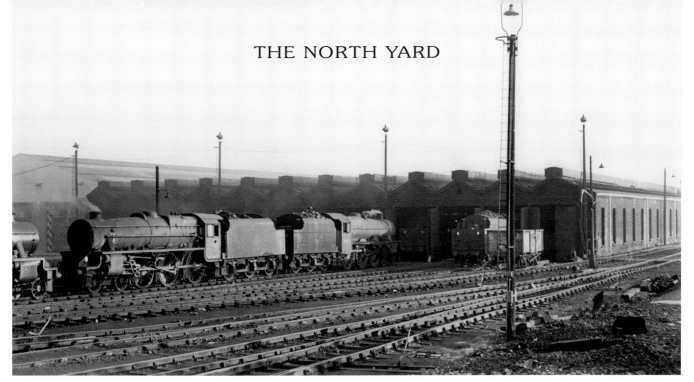

A 24-road through running shed, capable of housing 180 locomotives under cover, was erected in 1876 by the Lancashire and Yorkshire Railway - one of the largest depots in the country. The LMS modernisation plan of 1935 coincided with the arrival of the Jubilees, at which time five of the six original hipped sections of roof were replaced in single pitch style. By 1960, the southernmost 8 roads of the depot had been demolished to make way for a diesel maintenance depot between the surviving 12-road section and the 'Parlour'. One of the shed's numerous Class Five 4-6-0's, No **44934** keeps No **45635** *Tobago* company on the original road No 4 in this view taken off the end of the Newton Heath Station platform.   **AUGUST 1962** ● **I.G. HOLT**

Of all the photographs in the book, this is the one which strikes a particular chord with the author. Many happy hours were spent sitting on a wall by the 'Railway' public house enjoying this view and watching a seemingly endless procession of engines drift down past the shed to St Mary's Road turntable, as well as observing traffic on the main line. The spice of course was the visiting Jubilees, many of which resulted in 'cops'. A Sunday 'bunk' around the shed was considered fair game but there was always respect for officialdom and it was strictly taboo to clamber down the bank on a weekday. Lightbowne Carriage Sidings and associated buildings feature strongly in the background as does the coaling plant, something of a local landmark. Amongst the sea of Stanier locomotives, all out of steam, stands No **45600** *Bermuda.*   **MAY 1965** ● **R. CORT**

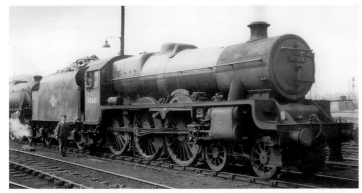

Driver John Cassell and his fireman pose before moving off shed with No **45601** *British Guiana.*   **15TH APRIL 1961** ● **DON CASH**

Between duties and once more standing in the east yard is No **45604** *Ceylon.*   **3RD MAY 1965** ● **CHRIS BANKS COLLECTION**

Withdrawn locomotives tended to congregate in sidings behind the station. Ahead of No **45601** *British Guiana* stand 0-6-0T's Nos **47284** and **47640** whilst alongside are No **45592** *Indore*, Stanier 2-6-4T No **42640** and Fowler 2-6-4T No **42379** which had been a surprising transfer from Buxton and the only member allocated during the BR period. Did she retain her 9D shedplate I wonder? This elevated view from the station footbridge reveals plenty of coal left in the tenders, all of which had to be manually removed prior to despatch to the scrap yard - and not via the firebox!　　　　　**NOVEMBER 1964** ● **AUTHOR'S COLLECTION**

An earlier withdrawal had been No **45679** *Armada,* one of the few members which retained a Fowler tender and the larger St Rollox 10" cab side numerals until the very end. Taken out of service during December 1962, she languished in store for almost a year before meeting her end at an unlikely destination - Darlington Works! As many as 21 Jubilees were officially withdrawn off the shed, but that included Nos 45558 *Manitoba,* 45564 *New South Wales* and 45568 *Western Australia,* which by all accounts were 'paper transfers', as was the renowned No 45705 *Seahorse* from Trafford Park.

MARCH 1963 ● **BRIAN CRAMER**

The withdrawal of No 45654 *Hood* week-ending 25th June 1966 ended both Newton Heath's and Manchester's association with the Jubilee class which had lasted over 30 years (other than No 45596 *Bahamas*). One of her last regular duties had been the 'Blackpool Papers', but she occasionally appeared as a 'Wallside Pilot' engine at Manchester Victoria. She was also utilised on various railtour duties and was mechanically sound up to the end. Many enthusiasts considered her as potential preservation material, but alas it was not to be. With coupling rods in the tender, *Hood* awaits her fate in splendid isolation.

JULY 1966 ● **BERNARD CRICK**

Class 1 lamps over the buffers defy the fact that No **5719** *Glorious* is drawing empty stock into Manchester Victoria Station from Queens Road Carriage Sidings. This will form a residential express from Platform 12 but the Fowler tender is sporting more than a generous amount of dubious looking coal for the journey - a fireman's nightmare! Victoria East Junction signal box is in view as is one of the three 4-4-0 Lancaster Compounds, No **931,** moving empty stock away towards Red Bank. *Glorious* left for Bank Hall in 1953, before which there were three recorded observations. On 13th May 1950, two specials left Edinburgh for Gourock - a works outing to connect with the cruise steamers *Duchess of Montrose* and *Jeannie Deans* - each consisting of 13 ex-LNER coaches, one hauled by a local Class Five and the other by No 45719. On 12th July 1952 she arrived at Stockport (Edgeley) with the 8.00am ex-Colne, piloted by Ivatt 2-6-0 No 43009 (12D) ex-Horwich Works. The pair were replaced by No 45529 *Stephenson* (1B). Two months later, *Glorious* was on Leicester (GC) MPD having worked in on an excursion (21st September 1952).   **18TH OCTOBER 1946** ● **H.C. CASSERLEY**

The same location six months later, looking across the tracks from the end of Platform 11, sees No **5642** *Boscawen,* the original No 5552 *Silver Jubilee,* getting its train of empty stock away and signalled for the loop line. Newton Heath enjoyed, many would say suffered, the services of the prototype Jubilee from May 1940 until its eventual withdrawal week-ending 9th January 1965. It was replaced by No 45600 *Bermuda* from Patricroft, which lost its last Jubilees at this time.   **24TH APRIL 1947** ● **H.C. CASSERLEY**

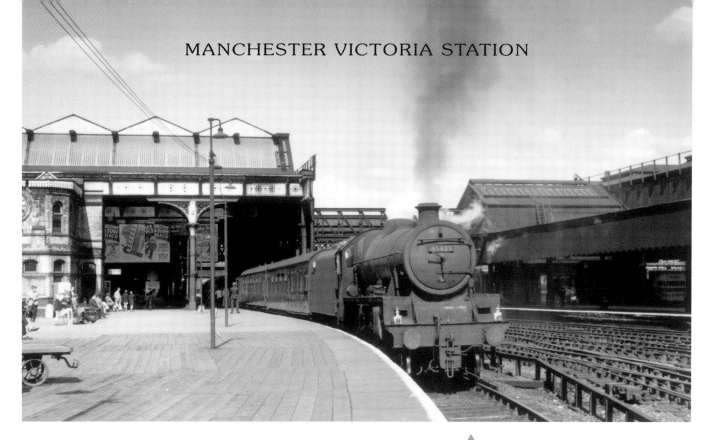

The station is hardly a hive of activity as No **45623 *Palestine*** brings empty stock into Platform 12 from Queens Road Carriage Sidings. This will form the 4.25pm residential to Blackpool Central but, strictly speaking, the engine should be showing the appropriate lamps at this point. This oversight seemed to be a regular practice here and one assumes that the local 'Bobbys' turned a blind eye. No 45623 was remembered by some men as being a 'rough rider' - the fact that it arrived from Crewe (South) in March 1962 may have a bearing on this, having worked almost exclusively on freight duties since December 1960. She soldiered on for a further two years or so before her final demise in week-ending 25th July 1964, thus becoming the eighth member to be withdrawn from the shed. After languishing behind Newton Heath Station for almost a year, she was cut up at the Central Wagon Company, Wigan, by 25th September 1965.

22ND JUNE 1963 ● A.C. GILBERT

A member with a much better reputation was No **45671 *Prince Rupert,*** seen standing in Platform 14 and awaiting departure with C100, a Leeds - Morecambe excursion, a train comprising of non-corridor stock.

3RD MARCH 1952 ● JIM DAVENPORT

Rumbling its way through Manchester Victoria middle and on through Exchange with a westbound mixed freight is a somewhat less than steamtight No **45623 *Palestine*.**

JULY 1962 ● IAN COCKROFT

SALFORD STATION

Deputising for a failed English Electric Type 4 diesel, No 45600 *Bermuda* gets into her stride through a deserted Salford Station with the morning Manchester to Glasgow express. This train went via the Down Slow line, through Pendleton (Broad Street) and the connecting line from Brindle Heath Junction to Agecroft Junction. *Bermuda* covered this turn for a further 3 days because of continuing problems. One of her last recorded workings fell on Saturday, 19th June 1965, when she worked 1D01, a Middleton to Llandudno Excursion throughout. The older hands at Newton Heath couldn't recall another occasion when a Jubilee had worked over the Middleton Branch, which, incidentally, closed to passengers three months later.　　**OCTOBER 1965 ● J.A. OLDFIELD**

AGECROFT JUNCTION

The direct route was via Pendleton (Old) Station. A most presentable No **45701 *Conqueror*** approaches Agecroft Junction with an unidentified express. The Down exit line from Brindle Heath Sidings occupies the foreground.　　**AUGUST 1957 ● PETER REEVES**

FARNWORTH TUNNEL

A dramatic track level view of No 45585 *Hyderabad* emerging from the original double track bore of Farnworth Tunnel with empty stock from Lightbowne Sidings to form a midweek excursion. This was one of seven members transferred from the Midland Division during the summer of 1961 to supplement the depot's chronic shortage of Class 6P motive power *(see page 142)*. Ironically, this loco had been stopped four days earlier at Lees (Oldham) MPD whilst the fitters attended to a faulty piston bush and sander.

30TH AUGUST 1961 ● JOHN MARSHALL

BOLTON

A train which used to travel by way of the former LNWR route via Eccles Junction, Tyldesley and Springs Branch to Wigan (NW) was the 3.59pm Manchester Victoria - Barrow. Poor patronage brought about a switch to the L&Y route at the commencement of the Winter 1960 timetable, and, to further bolster numbers, there was a rear portion for Blackpool, detached at Preston. The travelling enthusiast who had previously noted locos in the shed yards at Patricroft and Springs Branch, now had to be content with those at Bolton. No **45706** *Express* passes that shed with the re-timed 4.03pm to Blackpool and Barrow.

7TH APRIL 1962 ● DAVE HAMPSON

A rather grubby No 45652 *Hawke* passes the 145 lever frame Bolton East signal box, situated between the fast lines, on the approaches to Bolton Trinity Street Station. Immediately beyond is the lightweight lattice Lever Street footbridge, also built in 1902, which afforded splendid views for enthusiasts. The floodlights of Bolton Wanderers football ground at Burnden Park creep into view. **MAY 1961 ● IAN COCKCROFT**

Clattering over the diamond crossings at the west end of Bolton Station is No **45716 *Swiftsure*.** The non-corridor stock behind the Fowler tender forms the 11.48am SO Manchester Victoria to Blackburn stopping service. This member was one of those Jubilees that remained exclusively coupled to the narrower variety throughout their lifetimes. *Swiftsure* had three different Fowler tenders whilst No 45713 *Renown*, although never a Manchester engine, enjoyed the company of no fewer than 9 different tenders over 13 exchanges. Both had been Kingmoor locos virtually all their lives. Away in the distance, the Town Hall clock shows 12.10pm and a large percentage of the workforce will have just 'clocked off' after their Saturday morning shifts. **3RD AUGUST 1963 ● DAVE HAMPSON**

TONGE VIADUCT

The 8.00am Colne to London Euston train rumbles over the Tonge Viaduct on the approaches to Astley Junction within the Bolton suburbs. The engine is No **45623 *Palestine*** and the previous week it had been No 45706 *Express*. The end of the Summer Timetable heralded the cessation of this through service and on the 8th September, *Express*, once more, had the honour of hauling the last ever train. **25TH AUGUST 1962 ● DAVE HAMPSON**

SOUGH TUNNEL

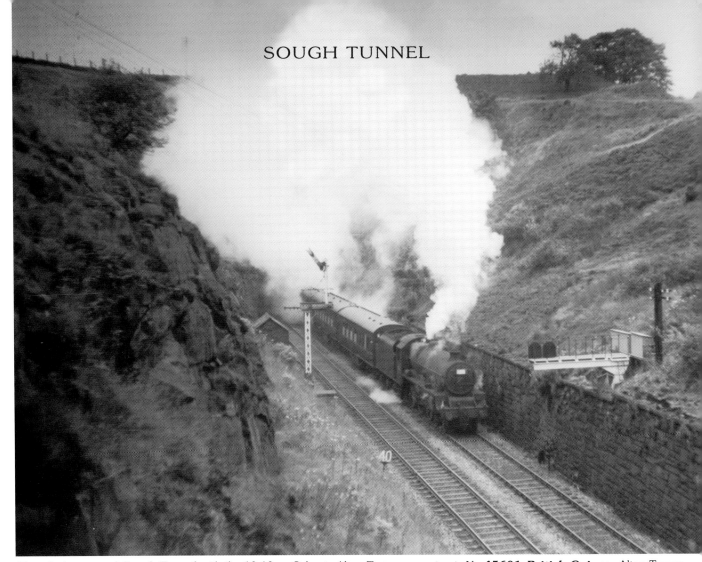

Thundering out of Sough Tunnel with the 10.10am Colne to Alton Towers excursion is No **45601** *British Guiana*. Alton Towers became a public resort in the 1920s, from which time specials ran regularly from the Lancashire mill towns. These usually involved Newton Heath engines and men, many of whom had route knowledge over the Churnet Valley line. 'Crab' 2-6-0's were the usual choice of motive power but by 1962, Jubilees were available for such jobs. After arrival from the north, locomotives ran light to Uttoxeter and made use of the triangular layout situated there, the empty stock being stabled at a convenient siding en-route.   **18TH AUGUST 1962 ● DAVE HAMPSON**

An unlikely combination departs from Bolton (Trinity Street) Station with Metropolitan-Vickers diesel No **D5713** piloting No **45642** *Boscawen*. Clocks are in unison at 10.15am and the morning Manchester to Glasgow leaves on time. The Jubilee is in attendance to provide steam heating for the carriages, the Type 2 not being equipped to do so. One assumes that the pair were substituting for a Type 4 diesel locomotive which was usually provided by this time.   **7TH MARCH 1964 ● RAY FARRELL**

DEANE CLOUGH

Carnforth's No 45592 Indore pilots No 45661 *Vernon* at Deane Clough, Bolton, with the 1.30pm(SO) Manchester Victoria to Glasgow.
29TH SEPTEMBER 1962 ● **DAVE HAMPSON**

LOSTOCK TROUGHS

The Easter of 1954 was blessed with good weather, and on Good Friday, No **45700 *Amethyst*** accelerates away from Bolton and over Lostock Troughs with a typical excursion train comprised of non-corridor stock. Reporting Number C900 indicates it to be a Diggle - Blackpool excursion. The following weekend, *Amethyst* was engaged on Rugby League duty to Wembley *(see page 150).*
16TH APRIL 1954 ● **JIM DAVENPORT**

LOSTOCK JUNCTION

◀ **No 45706 *Express*** once more, this time returning to Manchester and showing Class 1 lamps but on the Up slow line with an unidentified train. She has just cleared Lostock Junction with the home signal in her favour. The imposing overbridge carries Beaumont Road.

c1960 ● **JIM DAVENPORT**

BRINDLE HEATH

◄ **A dramatic low level view of No 45661 *Vernon*** taking the Fast (or top) line and crossing the low level lines at Brindle Heath Junction with a Blackpool express. Irlam Carriage shed was situated between Fast and Slow lines at this point, beyond which were Agecroft MPD and Brindle Heath Sidings, part of which are in view.
28TH MAY 1963 ● **W.D. COOPER**

PENDLEBURY BANK

Nearing the top of Pendlebury Bank and once more on the Fast line is No **45642 *Boscawen,*** recently outshopped and handling yet another express bound for the Fylde coast. The first two coaches are ex-LMS articulated stock which was built to run in the pre-war 'Coronation Scot' express but during the 1950's appeared in the formation of the Manchester residential trains, such as the one illustrated here. Agecroft Road is prominent on the left, beyond which can be seen the winding house of the local colliery, amidst all other manner of local industry, looking east towards Lower Kersal.
FEBRUARY 1958 ● **PETER REEVES**

The 3.12pm SO Manchester Victoria to Southport stopping passenger comes up the Slow Line and is approaching Pendlebury Junction behind No **45578 *United Provinces*.** Traffic could transfer from slow to fast at this point but not vice versa. The stations at Pendlebury, Swinton, Moorside & Wardley and Walkden had island platforms serving the slow lines only. The concrete structures looming on the horizon are part of the Agecroft Colliery complex, reopened in 1960 principally to serve the Central Electricity Generating Board's Agecroft Power Station.
18TH AUGUST 1962 ● **DAVE HAMPSON**

MOORSIDE AND WARDLEY

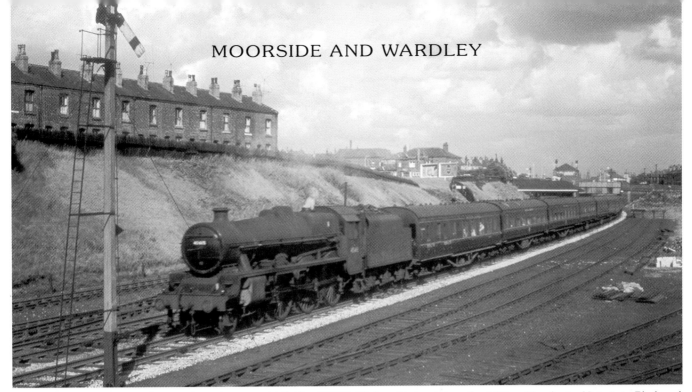

One of the Leicester Jubilees on loan *(see page 142),* **No 45615** *Malay States,* brings the 4.55pm Manchester Victoria to Blackpool 'Residential' through Moorside and Wardley. Having arrived on Saturday 1st July 1961, she was immediately outstationed to Bury MPD for a week, working excursions mainly to the Lancashire coast. Wartime observations were rare, but on 19th March 1944, No 45671 *Prince Rupert* arrived at Bury (Bolton Street) from the Manchester direction over the electrified line, before reversing round the loop to Knowsley Street and was reported as being the first Jubilee to be seen there. **8TH AUGUST 1961 ● PETER REEVES**

WALKDEN TROUGHS

Leaving its mark over Walkden Troughs with another 'Residential' for Blackpool is No **45623** *Palestine*. When Swinton Rugby League Club entertained local rivals Oldham on 12th April 1963, a supporters' excursion was provided. Newton Heath prevailed upon *Palestine* for the duty. A train comprising nine non-corridor coaches left Lightbowne Sidings, working empty stock via Rochdale and around the Oldham Loop. Pick-ups were made at Royton Junction, Oldham Mumps, Central and Werneth before passing through Manchester Victoria Middle en-route to Swinton Station, which was conveniently situated adjacent to the rugby ground. After discharging her passengers, No 45623 then worked ECS forward, again over the troughs but on the slow line, via Dobbs Brow and Horwich Fork Junctions, before turning the entire train on the Blackrod Triangle. There was little layover time before *Palestine* retraced her steps to pick up the disgruntled fans for the trip home. Ironically, the ECS mileage outweighed that of the journey.

JUNE 1962 ● W.D. COOPER

DOBBS BROW JUNCTION

A Signalman's view as the 4.25pm Manchester Victoria to Blackpool Central passes by. The spur from here to Blackrod was a convenient bypass avoiding Bolton. The engine once more is No **45623** *Palestine*. **22ND JUNE 1963 ● DAVE HAMPSON**

HINDLEY NORTH

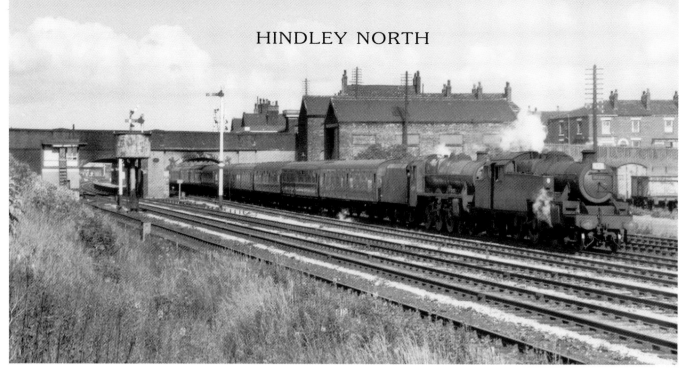

Double-headed trains were a rarity on the Southport route but Agecroft Stanier 2-6-4T No **42474** is offering assistance to No **45590** *Travancore* as the pair leave Hindley North for the Lancashire coast.   **13TH JULY 1963 ● TOM HEAVYSIDE**

BLACKROD

A typical Blackpool-bound excursion made up of non-corridor stock is nearing Blackrod on the Bolton to Preston line. No **45706** *Express* had passed this way many times before but on 17th November 1956, she stood in at late notice for Britannia Pacific No 70050 (66A) which had been 'stopped' at Newton Heath MPD. The 9.30am to Glasgow arrived at Carlisle only 11 minutes late with 14 bogies behind the tender, representing 465 tons net. Four years earlier, *Express* spent some time in Scotland, having arrived at Perth with the 9.25am from Crewe on 15th November 1952. Two days later she reached Aberdeen with the 9.18am, after which she returned to Perth piloted by Class Five No 45459 on the Up 'Postal'. Her return south remained unrecorded.

AUGUST 1956 ● JIM DAVENPORT

An award for the shabbiest of all the Manchester Jubilees must surely go to No **45604** *Ceylon* during her final three months in service. It's hard to believe that she was one of three Leeds Holbeck Jubilees selected to carry the experimental livery of light green, fully lined in red, grey and black with pale straw insignia, in May 1948. *(The other two were Nos 45565 Victoria and 45694 Bellerophon which were never Manchester engines)*. This photograph was taken during her first week as a Newton Heath engine, by which time she had lost her front number, name and shedplates. Previous codes have been obliterated and closer inspection reveals 9D applied just below the lower smokebox door hinge. Hauling a lone van of Gresley vintage, *Ceylon* struggles north past the Leyland motor factory with a morning parcels for Preston. Despite her condition, she reached Holyhead on 19th June 1965, and a fortnight before withdrawal visited the east coast with an excursion from Bury to Scarborough on 3rd July 1965.

24TH APRIL 1965 ● RAY FARRELL

LEYLAND

ROE GREEN JUNCTION

The ex-LNWR line from Eccles Junction to Springs Branch (Wigan) provided yet another alternative route for traffic from the Manchester area heading towards Preston. No **45710** *Irresistible* has just cleared Roe Green Junction and passed under Greenleach Lane Bridge with the afternoon train to Barrow. The 4.15pm Manchester Victoria to Glasgow also made use of this line and, as such, was part of the Polmadie men's route knowledge. An unusual duty for the engine occurred on 3rd March 1952 when she arrived at Southport (Lord Street) - then closed - with a train of new BR Standard stock (later called Mark 1) for storage. **JULY 1958 ● PETER REEVES**

TYLDESLEY

It also offered a convenient diversionary route via Manchester when engineering work was taking place on the West Coast Main Line north of Crewe. Approaching Tyldesley Station, again with the afternoon Barrow train, is No **45661** *Vernon*. On 23rd September 1961, she was noted on Bury MPD.

1957 ● DON GREENWOOD

WIGAN (NORTH WESTERN)

Newton Heath Driver Bob Hamilton casts a backward glance down his train from the cab of No **45635** *Tobago* at Wigan (North Western) Station. The Liverpool portion of the 4.15pm Glasgow was attached here. After the war, this engine, together with Nos 45661 *Vernon* and 45671 *Prince Rupert,* were the Jubilees primarily considered for the Glasgow turns because of their larger tenders. The 1.30pm Manchester Victoria to Carlisle was extended to Glasgow on Fridays Only and the engine did not return south until late on Sunday night with the 11.55pm Glasgow Central to Manchester Exchange. On Sunday, 27th November 1955, Polmadie made full use of *Tobago's* availability and she worked the 7.15am Glasgow Central to Perth before being used on trains between Perth and Dundee, returning to Glasgow with the 8.08pm from Perth.

23RD DECEMBER 1958 ● A. HAYNES COLLECTION

STANDISH JUNCTION

No 45712 *Victory* approaches Standish Junction and is signalled for the Down Fast beyond the closed station at Standish. The Whelley route joins here and the line is quadrupled as far as Preston. The train appears to be the Manchester portion of a Glasgow train. *Victory* was allocated for 15 years (1942 to 1957) and in May 1945 she reputedly acted as Station Pilot at Manchester Victoria for a number of days during the 'Victory in Europe' celebrations - no doubt spotless and perhaps as a gesture of pride. She returned in the summer of 1961 as one of the Midland Division contingent *(see below)*.

1954 ● JIM DAVENPORT

The BR summer timetables invariably placed a great strain on Newton Heath's resources, especially with all the extra excursion traffic in connection with annual holidays from towns around the northern fringes of Manchester. Over the years the Operating Department had gained a notorious reputation for stopping larger visiting locomotives which arrived on shed during the week preceding a 'Wakes Weekend'. Whatever the reason given, they were miraculously available come Saturday! The situation would become even more desperate with the onset of the 1961 timetable because of the non-availability of several of their own Jubilees.

Of the eleven allocated, No 45661 *Vernon*, probably the best performer at the time, was already away at Crewe receiving a Heavy General Overhaul. No 45679 *Armada* (a former Carlisle Kingmoor engine) was about to be despatched to St. Rollox for a Light Intermediate followed by Nos 45601 *British Guiana* (Heavy General - Crewe) and 45700 *Amethyst* (Light Intermediate - Crewe). No 45635 *Tobago* was running rough and due for overhaul whilst No 45642 *Boscawen* had always been poorly regarded. On the plus side, Nos 45652 *Hawke*, 45701 *Conqueror*, 45702 *Colossus*, 45706 *Express* and 45710 *Irresistible* had all been through shops earlier in the year and were in fine working order. Control deemed that certain members of the class from the Midland Division could be made temporarily available to cover over the holiday period. The recent introduction of large numbers of 'Peak' Type 4 diesels on the ex-Midland main lines resulted in some being surplus to requirements. The transfer to the Central Division involved the following seven locomotives:

	ARRIVED	HOME DEPOT	RETURNED
No **45585** *Hyderabad*	1st July 1961	Leicester (Midland)	23rd September 1961
No **45615** *Malay States*	1st July 1961	Leicester (Midland)	23rd September 1961
No **45622** *Nyasaland*	1st July 1961	Kentish Town	15th July 1961
No **45628** *Somaliland*	15th July 1961	Kentish Town	23rd September 1961
No **45636** *Uganda*	1st July 1961	Leicester (Midland)	23rd September 1961
No **45650** *Blake*	1st July 1961	Leicester (Midland)	26th August 1961
No **45712** *Victory*	1st July 1961	Kentish Town	23rd September 1961

Note: No 45622 *Nyasaland* was due for shopping on 24th July and was replaced by No 45628 *Somaliland*

FARINGTON JUNCTION

A familiar panoramic view overlooking Farington Junction from Fowler Lane Bridge. No **45700** *Amethyst* brings a Manchester train along the Up Fast - a stretch of line which was formerly jointly owned by the LNW and L&Y. The ex-L&Y lines diverging to the right are for Lostock Hall and Blackburn. Mineral wagons and brake vans stand within the exchange sidings serving that route. **AUGUST 1963 ● AUTHOR'S COLLECTION**

FARINGTON CURVE JUNCTION

Another elevated view from Bee Lane Bridge showing three different approach routes into Preston from the south at Farington Curve Junction. No **45642 *Boscawen*** is on the Down Fast with W563 special to Blackpool whilst the Liverpool lines fork away to the right. Branching further left off these tracks is the route to Lostock Hall which turns eastwards before crossing over the West Coast Main Line. A further approach was by way of Whitehouse and Todd Lane Junctions, which served the platforms on the former East Lancs side of the station. On 17th March 1956, *Boscawen* reached London Euston with the Up 'Northern Irishman' - normally a Class 7P duty. **29TH MAY 1961 ● B.K.B. GREEN**

SKEW BRIDGE

The 9.20am Manchester to Glasgow is running as a relief to the 9.30am which by this time was in the hands of an English Electric Type 4 diesel. Still carrying a 26B shedplate, No **45654 *Hood*** has just passed Skew Bridge Signal Box having recently transferred from Agecroft where she had been in store from 22nd October 1962 until 8th April 1963, prior to which she had received a Heavy General Overhaul. This somewhat bucked the trend and the enginemen welcomed a loco in such fine condition. A fortnight later, Newton Heath borrowed, Stockport Edgeley's No 45596 *Bahamas* for this train.

6TH JULY 1963 ● PAUL CLAXTON

Making spirited progress south from Preston with a Heysham to Manchester empty van train is No **45578 *United Provinces***. This is on the Up Fast nearing Farington Curve Junction which offered no connection with the Liverpool and Lostock Hall routes. No 45578 had always been a Western Division engine and featured earlier within the Longsight chapter. She retired from Aston in March 1962 to work out her mileage at 26A but wasn't remembered with much affection by the enginemen who didn't take kindly to their old stalwarts being replaced by engines such as this. On Monday 9th March 1964, *United Provinces* was utilised along with Class Five No 45101 and No 45654 *Hood* to take Manchester United fans to Sunderland for an FA Cup replay.

4TH APRIL 1964 ● PETER FITTON

PRESTON STATION

A returning Oldham Wakes Week excursion passes through Preston station behind No **45701** *Conqueror.* Each Lancashire mill town had its allotted weeks and Oldham began the holiday season in mid-June. During the 1950's, Newton Heath would have to provide 12 extra locos for departures to the south coast on Friday night and a further 40 for east coast, west coast and North Wales trains, but by 1961, enginemen reported many trains as running half empty and less. **25TH JUNE 1960 ● JIM DAVENPORT**

The Liverpool Exchange carriages have been combined with those from Manchester Victoria to form a Glasgow train due to depart at 5.31pm. Whilst the driver will be watching for the 'right away' from the former LNWR signals protecting Platform 4, his fireman seems concerned about something - perhaps the positioning of the photographer! The impressive signals were removed during the following month, coinciding with the commencement of the winter timetable. In June 1961, No **45661** *Vernon* was fitted with a speedometer which was driven off the left-hand trailing crankpin and she also received the BR standard Automatic Warning System. Whilst the vast majority of Jubilees received 'speedos', those engines working from Midland Division depots did not have AWS fitted - accounting for about one third of the class.

29TH AUGUST 1960 ● PETER FITTON

Newton Heath's finest Jubilees, according to many enginemen, were Nos 45661 *Vernon* and **45710** *Irresistible,* and it was no coincidence that these two outlived the other long standing members - apart from No 45642 *Boscawen,* which was something of an enigma. *Irresistible* arrives with the 4.25pm Manchester to Blackpool in unison with Bank Hall's No **45713** *Renown* working the Liverpool Exchange to Glasgow at 5.14pm. On 11th August 1951, No 45710 reached Scarborough as did Farnley Junction's No 45708 *Resolution* and Millhouses' No 45664 *Nelson.* She returned on Easter Monday, 1958 with a train from Marsden and a final sighting was on 5th October 1957 at Leeds when, with Longsight Royal Scot No 46111 *Royal Fusilier,* they went forward with the 4.15pm Newcastle to Liverpool.

24TH AUGUST 1962 ● PETER FITTON

FISHERGATE BRIDGE

Under the watchful eye of two signalmen within the large Preston No 4 Signal Box, a remarkably clean No **45712** *Victory* heads north with a Glasgow express. *Victory* had her share of problems north of the border when, on 7th July 1953, working the 4.05pm Glasgow Central to Manchester and Liverpool combined, she needed the assistance of Crewe (South) Class Five No 45028 as far as Preston. The following year, (31st July 1954), Polmadie's No 45485 came to the rescue, acting as pilot on the 10.50am ex-Glasgow Central before being replaced by 4-4-0 No 40419 (5A) at Carlisle. There were happier times on 15th April 1950, when No 45712 was one of 10 visiting engines on Polmadie MPD on the occasion of the Scotland versus England football match at Hampden Park. Three other Jubilees were present: Holbeck's No 45565 *Victoria,* Longsight's No 45593 *Kolhapur* and Bank Hall's No 45717 *Dauntless.*   **JULY 1953** ● **D.T. GREENWOOD**

MAUDLAND JUNCTION

Another late arrival off the Western Division was No 45737 *Atlas,* scorned by the Newton Heath men, but in better condition than No 45578 *United Provinces.* She is in charge of one of the tightly timed 'Residentials' - the 4.25pm from Manchester Victoria to Blackpool Central and is passing Preston No 5 Signal Box at Maudland Junction before taking the Fylde line. This, however, was an engine that had been used to fast running as one of the Bushbury 'elite' which worked the intensive Wolverhampton (High Level), then Birmingham (New Street) to London Euston two hour expresses during the 1950's.   **15TH MAY 1964** ● **PETER FITTON**

SALWICK

Another of the Leicester contingent on loan for the summer season of 1961 was No **45615 *Malay States*.** A typical Saturday job was the working of the 7.25am Cleethorpes - Blackpool North (1M05) forward from Midland Junction, Manchester. Earlier in the day, motive power from the east coast may well have been an ex-LNER B1 or K3 locomotive as far as Sheffield from where electric traction would take over for the journey through Woodhead. *Malay States* is about to pass under Clifton Lane bridge and through the island platform at Salwick on the slow line towards Kirkham.

29TH JULY 1961 ● PETER FITTON

Shortly after the grouping in 1921, the lines between Preston, Blackpool and Fleetwood were relaid and reballasted with thousands of tons of Penmaenmawr stone as a matter of urgency. The L&Y had previously used clinker over their system, but the new Permanent Way made for both the safe and very fast running of express trains over this section. No **45710 *Irresistible*** bowls along in fine style just west of Salwick with 1T64 Blackburn to Blackpool Central.

18TH MAY 1964 ● PETER FITTON

DOWBRIDGE

The tender of No 45661 *Vernon* still sports the original BR totem in this view of a returning excursion composed of decidedly mixed stock on the Up Fast at Dowbridge. The Down Home signals are both off but notice the 'T' plates affixed midway up the posts, indicating the close proximity of telephone contact with Treales signal box, just visible in the distance within Wesham Park, on the outskirts of Kirkham.

20TH AUGUST 1960 ● PETER FITTON

KIRKHAM

C298 - The Saturdays Only Manchester Victoria to Fleetwood express passes through Kirkham on the Down Fast. Sightings of No **45701** *Conqueror* were frequent but perhaps the most unusual was on 24th February 1954 when she passed through Stamford on the Peterborough to Leicester line with a westbound freight, double headed with a Saltley 4F 0-6-0, No 43941.　　**9TH JULY 1960 ● PETER FITTON**

ST ANNES

◀ **A low sun picks out the shapely outlines** of No **45700** *Amethyst* and nicely illuminates the rolling stock, the first three carriages being of Gresley origin. The 7.00pm Blackpool Central to Rochdale stopping train is leaving St Annes.

28TH JULY 1959 ● PETER FITTON

Bradkirk signalbox, just out of view, stood between the line from Kirkham to Weeton and the direct route to Blackpool via Marton. Under clear signals, a pair of Newton Heath engines make haste with a mixture of non-corridor stock. The eight coaches comprise the 10.25am Manchester Victoria to Blackpool North and Fleetwood and will split at Poulton. No **45623** *Palestine* is piloting Class Five No **45336** which, rather confusingly, is carrying a reporting number.

6TH OCTOBER 1962 ● PETER FITTON
▼

BRADKIRK

MARTON

The Marton signalman's view of the approaching IT82 Pendleton Broad Street to Blackpool Central excursion. No **45642 Boscawen** is the engine and contrary to reputation, she did achieve the occasional creditable performance. An early 1950's log records Driver McMahon and Fireman Thompson of the 'Scotch Link' on the footplate working the 4.55pm Manchester to Blackpool 'Club Train'. This was 9 corridor coaches of about 300 tons gross which ran non stop to Poulton-le-Fylde via Dobbs Brow and Horwich Fork Junctions. 74mph was reached in the Atherton dip, but signal checks at Hilton House and the Preston approaches, caused by the 4.35pm Rochdale to Blackpool running just ahead, resulted in a ½ minute delay through the platforms. With 69mph between Kirkham and Poulton, recovery was such that Blackpool North was reached slightly ahead of schedule.

12TH APRIL 1963 ● PETER FITTON

ANSDELL AND FAIRHAVEN

Leaving Ansdell & Fairhaven Station with the 11.45am Blackpool Central to Manchester Victoria is No **45602 British Honduras.** As late as 22nd September 1963 she was noted on Polmadie MPD and was one of the last Newton Heath engines to have worked north of Carlisle.

11TH MAY 1963 ● PETER FITTON

No 45702 Colossus appears to be one of the Jubilees that ran in unlined green livery before her relatively early withdrawal in April 1963. There was no totem on her tender either when recorded bringing the 5.50pm Manchester Victoria to Blackpool Central away from Ansdell and Fairhaven Station.

31ST MAY 1962 ● PAUL CLAXTON

BLACKPOOL SOUTH

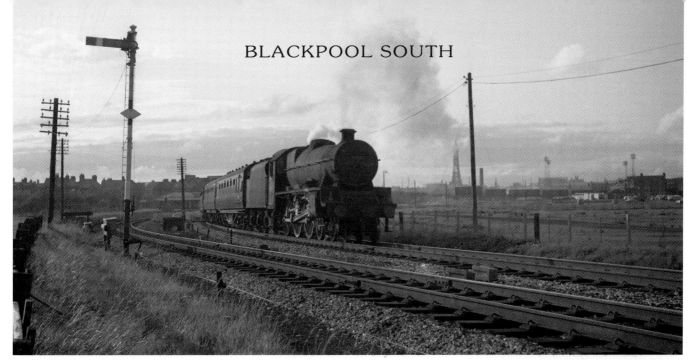

Curving away on to the Marton line with the 7.20am Blackpool Central to Manchester Victoria is No **45602 _British Honduras._** Blackpool South's station canopy protecting the coast line platforms is visible, as are the well known landmarks of the Tower and the floodlights at Bloomfield Road - the home of Blackpool Football Club. _British Honduras_ arrived on 25th February 1962 to replace unrebuilt Patriot No 45515 _Caernarvon._ According to '5X Charlie', _she was as filthy from the day she arrived till the day she left_ - which was just over 2 years later for Wakefield. Not long before departure - on Easter Monday, 1964 - No 45602 had charge of a Knottingley to Belle Vue excursion. It took 30 minutes to reach Slaithwaite from Huddersfield, from where she was uncoupled to allow her to run light engine to Marsden to take water. **25TH JULY 1963 ● PAUL CLAXTON**

BLOOMFIELD ROAD

A popular vantage point to witness the constant procession of excursion traffic on a summer Saturday. This, though, is a regular service - the 3.10pm stopping train from Manchester Victoria. Approaching Central Station on the Down Slow line is No **45652 _Hawke._** The empty stock in view is stabled within Bloomfield Road Carriage Sidings.

1ST JUNE 1963 ● PAUL CLAXTON

The view in the opposite direction overlooking Spen Dyke Carriage Sidings, which extend well beyond Bloomfield Road bridge. No **45601 _British Guiana_** gets under way with yet another Manchester-bound train.

11TH AUGUST 1962 ● PETER FITTON

A seagull is caught in mid flight within the locomotive's exhaust. This could only be Blackpool and this could only be a Newton Heath Jubilee in typical, some might say, workaday condition. A wisp is escaping from the tube cleaner steam cock as No **45710** *Irreststible* awaits departure. Later in the month (22nd August), she worked in tandem with a Doncaster B1, No 61125 south of York on the celebrated Heaton to Red Bank empty stock train, which was a regular job, but on 14th February 1953, an FA Cup fixture between Luton Town and Bolton Wanderers resulted in at least two excursions, worked south by *Irresistible* and No 45712 *Victory.* Both went to Kentish Town MPD for servicing, but *Victory* was declared a failure and replaced by the shed's own No 45616 *Malta GC.*   **11TH AUGUST 1963** ● **PAUL CLAXTON**

No 45700 *Amethyst* **departs from Blackpool Central** with the 7.00pm stopping train to Rochdale. Observations of this engine off the beaten track include: On 23rd April 1954 she was loaned to Low Moor MPD to transport Halifax supporters to Wembley for the Rugby League Cup Final against Warrington. Other Jubilees on Neasden MPD that day were Blackpool's Nos 45584 *North West Frontier* and 45588 *Kashmir*, Bank Hall's No 45698 *Mars* and Farnley Junction's Nos 45646 *Napier*, 45705 *Seahorse* and 45708 *Resolution*. On 25th April 1957, Polmadie did not have a 'Clan' available for the 5.55pm Dumfries to Aberdeen fast freight and borrowed *Amethyst,* which spent the next day on Ferryhill MPD before returning with the 10.10pm Aberdeen (Guild Street) to Dumfries. Finally - and again in Scotland, on 26th October 1958, the concreting train used for the Helensburgh line electrification was at Shields Junction, Glasgow behind No 45700.   **24TH SEPTEMBER 1960** ● **DAVE HAMPSON**

MAUDLAND JUNCTION

The 4.55pm Manchester Victoria to Blackpool North once more leaving Preston. The locomotive diagram was 'Turn 4' which involved a pair of Jubilee 4-6-0's. No **45642** *Boscawen* will later spend the night on Farnley Junction MPD.

19TH JUNE 1964 ● PETER FITTON

PASSENGER ENGINE WORKINGS commencing 15th June 1959. Turn 4 - TWO CLASS 6P/5F (Ex LMS 4-6-0)

'A'

	Shed	4. 5pm	LE	SX	
4.15pm	Queens Road	4.36	ES	SX	
4.40	Manchester Vic.	4.55	Pass	SX	(228)
6. 9	Blackpool Nth.	9.20	Pcls.	SX	(228) (55C/18)
1.14am	Leeds C.S.		LE	MX	
1.26	Farnley Shed			MX	
	Shed	10,25am	LE	SO	(246)
10.42am	Rochdale	11. 0	Pass	SO	
1. 1pm	Liverpool	1.14pm	LE	SO	
1.23	Kirkdale	1.51	ES	SO	
1.59	Liverpool	4. 0	Pass	SO	
5.17	Rochdale	5.32	LE	SO	
5.49	Shed				
	Shed	10.42pm	LE	SO	(55E/12)
10.52pm	Manchester Vic.	11.22	News	SO	
1.10	York		LE	Sun	
1.16	York Shed				
	York Shed	2.45pm	LE	Sun	
	York (Old)	3.10	ES	Sun	(50A/6L) (55C/7)
6.17	Red Bank	6.33	ES	Sun	
6.43	Ordsall Lane	7.10	LE	Sun	
7.25	Newton Heath Shed				

NEWTON HEATH LOCO to acknowledge receipt by wire to "TRAINS 'P' MANCHESTER"

'B'

	Farnley Shed	6.03am	LE	SX	
	Leeds C. S.	6.30	Pass	SX	(26F/30)
8.42am	Manchester Ex.	8.46	ES	SX	
8.51	Ordsall Lane			SX	
	TURN ENGINE				
	Ordsall Lane	12.15pm	ES	SX	
12.20pm	Manchester Ex.	12.55	Pass	SX	
2.59	Leeds C.S.				
	Leeds C.S.	6.20pm	Pass	SX	(55C/18)
8.31pm	Manchester Ex.	8.45	ES	SX	
8.50	Ordsall Lane	10.20	ES	SX	
10.25	Manchester Ex.	12.20am	News	MX	(302)
1.38am	Leeds C.S.	2.25	LE	MX	
2.41	Leeds Cen.	3.29	Pass	MX	
5. 7	Manchester Vic.	5.25	ES	MX	
5.39	Irlam C.S.	5.55	LE	MX	
6.15	Newton Heath Shed				
	Leeds C.S.	8. 0am	Pass	SO	(55C/22)
9.44am	Manchester Ex.	9.49	ES	SO	
9.54	Ordsall Lane				
	Ordsall Lane	12.15pm	ES	SO	
12.20pm	Manchester Ex.	12.45	Pass	SO	
2.24	Leeds C.S.		LE	SO	
2.44	Farnley Shed				
	Leeds C.S.	7.17pm	Asst.	SO	
8.42	Manchester Ex.	9.37	ES	SO	55C/19A)
9.42	Ordsall Lane	10.40	ES	SO	
10.45	Manchester Ex.	12.15am	News	Sun	
1.30am	Leeds C.S.			Sun	
	Shunt to 3.00am			Sun	
	Leeds C.S.	3.00am	LE	Sun	
3.10	Farnley Shed				

GREENBANK SIDINGS

◀ **One mile north of Preston Station** and No **45661** *Vernon* can proceed at caution past Greenbank Sidings which are just in view on the Down side of the main line. The Glasgow train has crossed Fylde Road Viaduct and the rear coaches are over the Lancaster Canal. The home signal is off whilst the right pair were for the Oxheys Loop. The imposing yet unmistakeable 303ft tall spire of St Walburge's Church seemingly commands the railway at Maudland Junction.

1958 ● JIM DAVENPORT

BROCK TROUGHS

No 45700 *Amethyst* speeds over Brock Troughs, south of Garstang, on the approach to Preston with the 10.50am Glasgow to Manchester.
22ND JULY 1960 ● PETER FITTON

LANCASTER

A pleasing combination of carmine and cream rolling stock and Brunswick Green loco caught in evening sunlight. No **45712** *Victory* is southbound near Lancaster with the 10.25am ex-Glasgow.

22ND SEPTEMBER 1951 ● I.S. PEARSALL

Still carrying her 1946 LMS livery, despite receiving BR cab side numerals and smokebox numberplate, No **45671** *Prince Rupert* works a similar train in the same vicinity.

23RD JUNE 1949 ● JIM DAVENPORT

CARNFORTH

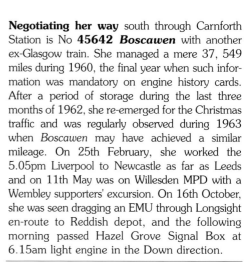

Negotiating her way south through Carnforth Station is No **45642** *Boscawen* with another ex-Glasgow train. She managed a mere 37, 549 miles during 1960, the final year when such information was mandatory on engine history cards. After a period of storage during the last three months of 1962, she re-emerged for the Christmas traffic and was regularly observed during 1963 when *Boscawen* may have achieved a similar mileage. On 25th February, she worked the 5.05pm Liverpool to Newcastle as far as Leeds and on 11th May was on Willesden MPD with a Wembley supporters' excursion. On 16th October, she was seen dragging an EMU through Longsight en-route to Reddish depot, and the following morning passed Hazel Grove Signal Box at 6.15am light engine in the Down direction.

1ST SEPTEMBER 1960 ⦿ **PETER FITTON**

GRANGE OVER SANDS

Newton Heath men had route knowledge over the former Furness line from Carnforth to Barrow and beyond. The driver, aware of the photographer's presence, has beckoned his fireman over to get in on the act. This fine portrait is of No **45706** *Express*, passing through Grange over Sands with a westbound excursion.

1953 ⦿ **PETER WARD**

OXENHOLME

One of the newly delivered members, No 5696 *Arethusa* is about to depart from Oxenholme with a Glasgow train. Notice the Caledonian route indicator suggesting that the loco is working throughout - which wasn't a regular occurrence during the pre-war period. No 5696 still has the vacuum pump under the slidebars (removed 16th November 1938) and is running with tender 3921, previously attached to Royal Scot No 6139. In addition, the name *Arethusa* was duplicated with former LNWR 'Prince of Wales' No 25671.

c1937 ● AUTHOR'S COLLECTION

The Jubilees' overall performance remained somewhat erratic - despite the early superheater modifications which greatly improved their steaming capabilities. No **45702** *Colossus* had been found wanting at Oxenholme with a heavy Manchester to Glasgow train. With steam escaping in every direction, the crew will undoubtedly have problems ahead and may have called for a replacement loco at Carlisle. With safety valves lifting, they are ready for an assault on Grayrigg bank with rear end assistance from a 2-6-4T. The problem was obviously resolved, as during the following month, on 12th September, she was borrowed by York to work the 'Yorkshire Pullman' between Harrogate and Leeds. The following day, No 45671 *Prince Rupert* had the job. The engine arrived with the 7.15am from York and then had a 2 hour wait in the station before departure.

31ST AUGUST 1957 ● W.A. BROWN

LAMBRIGG

Another assault on Grayrigg Bank is being made by No **45578** *United Provinces* which is approaching Lambrigg Crossing with 1S46 - a Liverpool to Glasgow train. Rarely does one see a signal extend high above an engine's exhaust, but the ex-LNWR down home signal does so here. The trailing crossover offered a convenient facility for banking engines to return to Oxenholme, having either failed or dropped off at this point.

13TH JULY 1963 ● PETER FITTON

GRAYRIGG

◀ **Perhaps it was on occasions such as this** that No **45642 *Boscawen*** developed her poor reputation. The loco was diagrammed to work the six coach Manchester portion of the 9.30am departure to Glasgow as far as Preston. From here the Liverpool portion, hauled by Type 4 diesel No D320 would work the combined train forward. Unfortunately *Boscawen* lost so much time before Preston that the connection became impractical. D320 continued north with its lightweight train whilst No 45642 was forced to struggle on as there was no standby engine available. Loco and train had reached the summit of Grayrigg, aided by a banker, Fairburn 2-6-4T No 42299, by which time it was running over two hours late.

5TH OCTOBER 1963 ● PETER FITTON

LOW GILL

Approaching Low Gill with a Down Manchester to Glasgow express is No **45702 *Colossus*.** Those observant passengers travelling north might just catch sight of the rather interesting road vehicle parked in a country lane. This is a Commer 'Gamecock', a larger engined and more robust version of the 'Karrier' which had, in turn, replaced the three wheeled mechanical horse. They were specifically designed for the 'Signal and Telecommunications Department' of the London Midland Region as a crew vehicle and carried the early livery of carmine and cream. They could carry up to nine people, including the driver, and proved both popular and versatile. The 'Gamecock' was capable of carrying telegraph poles, point rodding and timber etc by hinging down the four overhead windows, and in later years became invaluable for maintenance staff covering electrified routes.

1ST SEPTEMBER 1962 ● G.W. MORRISON

DILLICAR TROUGHS

◀ **Throughout the 1950's,** the 'Creative Tourists Agents Conference' organised tours to Scotland, strictly for rail staff only. These all-inclusive affairs were extremely popular and non-standard headboards from different divisions were provided in conjunction with BR. No **45719 *Glorious,*** suitably adorned, picks up water on Dillicar Troughs with a train from the Manchester area. Note the sleepers placed parallel to the track preventing ballast from being washed away.

7TH JUNE 1952 ● AUTHOR'S COLLECTION

DILLICAR

Set amidst fine scenery, the four mile section through the Lune Gorge towards Tebay includes Dillicar cutting and water troughs which were renewed as late as 1961. No **45601** *British Guiana* passes the colour light signal with 1S71 - the 2.00pm Manchester to Glasgow. In earlier days, Tebay No 1 Signal Box's down distant was situated by the troughs, a tall signal which was known as the 'green star' to many enginemen. **13TH JULY 1963 ● PAUL CLAXTON**

TEBAY

Having been put 'inside' for reasons unclear, No **45700** crawls into the platform at Tebay from the Down Loop. From here, she will almost certainly require assistance up to Shap summit. As the photograph is undated, but the tender carries the lettering 'BRITISH RAILWAYS', she could conceivably be either **Britannia** or **Amethyst** - not un-named, as a nameplate can be discerned. The isolated village of Tebay contained a number of stone-built railway properties which survive to this day. One of these was allocated as 'enginemens' lodgings', made use of by Edge Hill and Springs Branch men amongst others. Above the engine can be seen South Terrace, 14 houses which were gas lit, whilst behind the parachute water tank stands the North Terrace.

c1950/1 ● M.L. BOAKES COLLECTION

SHAP FELL

The scenic beauty surrounding Tebay and the northbound ascent of Shap attracted a multitude of photographers over the years and is typically illustrated by this view of No **45706 Express.** A clean exhaust with no trace of escaping steam rather suggests that the engine is in fine mechanical condition. Despite 13 bogies behind the tender, banking assistance wouldn't be called for. Parts of both of Tebay's engine sheds are in view. A new four road building in reinforced concrete replaced the original LNWR structure and was completed during 1950. Situated to the west of the station and on the extreme right, its closure came about on 16th May 1968. To the left of *Express* behind the coke wagons is the surviving outer facing wall of a building constructed by the Stockton & Darlington Railway in 1866 and closed by the North Eastern Railway as early as 31st October 1902. Tebay NE shed served the route to Kirkby Stephen and Darlington via Stainmore.

3RD JUNE 1952 ● AUTHOR'S COLLECTION

A former Caledonian Railway route indicator showing that the train will travel via Beattock is carried by No **5702 Colossus.** This is further up the incline and, once again, no evidence of assistance. **1937 ● AUTHOR'S COLLECTION**

Old favourite, No 45635 *Tobago* finds herself climbing to the summit with another Glasgow train. The last regular 'rostered' Jubilee working over Shap was during the summer of 1965 with the 1.30pm Fridays Only Liverpool to Glasgow which it was scheduled to work throughout. It returned next day with the 2.00pm Glasgow to Liverpool and Manchester although the Bank Hall engines were occasionally relieved at Carlisle, such was their mechanical state by this time. The four Liverpool locos involved were Nos 45627 *Sierra Leone*, 45684 *Jutland*, 45698 *Mars* and 45721 *Impregnable*.

1959 ● AUTHOR'S COLLECTION

A classic location bathed in afternoon sunshine offered the perfect ingredients to record loco and carriages at Greenholme on the approach to Shap summit. Coincidentally photographed by Paul Claxton at Dillicar, the 2.00pm Manchester to Glasgow makes further progress behind No **45601 *British Guiana*** which will probably be relieved at Carlisle. Newton Heath engines working throughout to Glasgow were the exception rather than the rule by this time.   **13TH JULY 1963** ● **A.C. GILBERT**

THRIMBY GRANGE

The approaches to Shap summit from the north were much less photographed. No **45661 *Vernon*** is nearing the end of a 30 mile continual climb from Carlisle and is passing through Strickland Woods in the vicinity of Thrimby Grange.   **1955** ● **N. PREEDY COLLECTION**

A fine study of loco and train attacking the approach to Shap Summit from the north. No **45701** *Conqueror* is at Bessie Ghyll, near Thrimby Grange with the afternoon Glasgow to Manchester service and it's almost time for the fireman to take a well earned rest. *Conqueror* was unique in so far as it spent its entire lifetime at Newton Heath. A similar accolade can only be extended to Leeds Holbeck's No 45658 *Keyes* and No 45659 *Drake*, although the latter is subject to question. No 45701's average annual mileage up to 1960 was 46,500 which is considerably less than the Midland Division locos which averaged 56,000 miles. This reflected Holbeck's regular sorties south to London St. Pancras and Bristol and north to Carlisle and Glasgow St Enoch. The Glasgow run was Newton Heath's only significant long-distance trip.

13TH APRIL 1953 ● E.R. MORTEN

PENRITH

The setting sun nicely picks out the 6' 9" driving wheels and fully lined out Crimson Lake livery of No **5701** *Conqueror* during her first full month of service. She remained attached to this Fowler tender (No 3945, ex-Royal Scot No 6109) for all but the last 4 years in traffic. The train is once again the afternoon Glasgow to Manchester Victoria which will return the Jubilee to its home depot. It would be interesting to speculate just how many times *Conqueror* reached Scottish metals over a lifetime of nearly 27 years.

31ST MAY 1936 ● **AUTHOR'S COLLECTION**

WREAY

No 45706 *Express* was every bit a Lancashire and Yorkshire locomotive, spending her entire lifetime at Leeds (Farnley Junction) and Newton Heath. She was newly delivered on 26th May 1936 with nameplates 'in situ' but the plaques depicting the ship's badge were added early the following year. She moved over to Lancashire during wartime and spent a further 20 years wearing a 26A shedplate. No 45706 was returned to traffic after a Heavy General Overhaul on 29th November 1946 at which time she carried the LMS 1928 style of high cab side numerals as seen here, and the following October it spent a further 2 months at Horwich Works - unusual in itself. With steam leaking badly from the middle cylinder, this photograph may well be just prior to that visit. *Express* is climbing between Carlisle (Upperby) and Wreay, with a Glasgow to Manchester train. On September 4th 1952, she worked home from Carlisle double-headed with stablemate No 45671 *Prince Rupert* - a rare occurrence!

c1947 ● **E.E. SMITH**

CARLISLE

No **45700** *Britannia* losts its nameplates when BR unveiled a new flagship engine in February 1951 - No 70000. New *Britannia*. New plates were cast for the Standard Pacific, meanwhile the Jubilee ran nameless for 7 months. The erstwhile 'Railway Travel and Correspondence Society' (RCTS) apparently suggested the name *Amethyst* and it was subsequently accepted by the powers that be. The loco's grubby condition defies the fact that it carried BR lined black - No 45700 gets away from Carlisle Citadel and past No 5 signal box for the south. Crown Street Goods Depot is also in view.

31ST MAY 1951 ● **H.C. CASSERLEY**

The 8.25am from Heads of Ayr is about to depart from Carlisle Citadel for its journey over the Settle and Carlisle route to Leeds. This rather dismal scene offers little sign of life and the platforms show evidence of early morning rain. Fowler 2-6-4T No **42369**, acting as Station Pilot, stands on the centre road where the Upperby Duchesses once stood proud, waiting to relieve the Polmadie Pacifics. A DMU stands in the bay for the Maryport line and is just discernible behind No **45601** *British Guiana*. 24TH AUGUST 1963 ● PAUL CLAXTON

The Leicester Jubilees loaned for the summer of 1961 were considered rarities in the Manchester area, let alone Carlisle and Glasgow! Brought up on a staple diet of Corkerhill, Kingmoor and Upperby examples, many trainspotters from these parts will have gladly underlined the likes of No **45585** *Hyderabad* in their Ian Allan ABC's as a result. She awaits departure from Platform 4 on a train for the south.

4TH JULY 1961 ● L. B. LAPPER

Many cases of double-heading on both arriving and departing trains from Carlisle have been recorded - sometimes simply a case of the load being too great for Class 6 power whilst on other occasions, because of locomotive problems. It was also the preferred way of returning an engine home off an unbalanced working, rather than sending her forward light engine. This may be the case here, as No **45661** *Vernon* has front end assistance in the form of Preston 2P 4-4-0 No **40677** on a Manchester-bound train.

30TH AUGUST 1958 ●
AUTHOR'S COLLECTION

159

Making a confident ascent of Beattock is No 45710 *Irresistible* with the 11.35am Blackpool Central to Glasgow. The train, which has rear end assistance from No 42214, is approaching Greskine Signal Box, about half way up the bank. This is *Irresistible's* last summer in service and probably one of her last forays into Scotland, but local observers had made record of the engine on three previous occasions. On 20th November 1955 No 45710 worked the 7.15am Glasgow Central to Perth whilst on 9th August 1958 she arrived in Carlisle piloted by No 40576 (68B) off the G&SW route with 15 carriages - considered exceptionally heavy for this line. Finally, she ran hot at Lockerbie on 1st August 1959 with the 12.00 noon Glasgow to Manchester and was replaced by ex-Caledonian 0-4-4T No 55234 (68D).

27TH JULY 1963 ● A.C. GILBERT

BEATTOCK

KILMARNOCK

The 10.50am Glasgow Central to Manchester Victoria via the Glasgow and South Western route was a regular job for a returning Newton Heath Jubilee but on this occasion the train is bound for London Euston. No **45661** *Vernon* has therefore been borrowed as she calls at Kilmarnock and has for company LMS 2P 4-4-0 No **40645** of Hurlford MPD. The distinctive building behind *Vernon* is Kilmarnock MPD which apparently lost its allocation way back in 1875 but was was retained as a servicing point, being adjacent to the station.

27TH JULY 1951 ● E.R. MORTEN

There is still evidence of coal in the Fowler tender belonging to No **45712** *Victory,* pictured here at Beattock with the 2.00pm Manchester to Glasgow express.

27TH JUNE 1953 ● R. BUTTERFIELD

CARSTAIRS

◄ **Pausing at Carstairs** with a Glasgow train is No **45701** *Conqueror* carrying the BR Derby 1928 Scroll (or serif) smokebox numberplate, a style carried by relatively few members. On 30th October 1954, West Coast traffic from Glasgow to the south was diverted via Edinburgh Waverley and the Waverley route to Carlisle owing to floods and landslips. A number of Duchesses and Royal Scots traversed the route along with Newton Heath's Nos 45661 *Vernon* and 45701, still coupled to her smaller Fowler tender, and completing journeys of over 250 miles each!

1950 ● AUTHOR'S COLLECTION

HELLIFIELD

By 1964 there was no work for two of Blackpool's remaining Jubilees - Nos 45653 *Barham* and **45705** *Seahorse.* Both were placed in store at the North MPD before transfer to Newton Heath in June for the Summer Timetable, replacing recently withdrawn locos Nos 45578 *United Provinces*, 45710 *Irresistible* and 45737 *Atlas*. The magnitude of traffic over the West Coast Main Line on Summer Saturdays resulted in the 9.20am Manchester Victoria to Glasgow Central (1S48) being routed via Hellifield and the Settle and Carlisle line before traversing the Glasgow and South Western route via Kilmarnock. On 4th July, *Seahorse* was entrusted to the job with Driver Ernie Lawrence and Fireman Paul Winstanley on the footplate. There were problems from the outset and Winstanley had a constant battle with the steam gauge. The engine eventually 'sat down' at Entwistle, which necessitated setting back after a blow up. The train is pictured labouring into Hellifield where Winstanley 'put the bag in' - but not being familiar with the Midland type of water column, it promptly came back out, swung around and drenched the hapless Winstanley in the process. Meanwhile Driver Lawrence had booked a Conductor forward from Hellifield and as the local shed had closed the previous year, a man from Skipton was deployed. 'We've 17 miles of bank ahead. Cobber it up (a Yorkshire way of saying get plenty of coal on). Pressure dropped to 150psi, but after a successful pick up over Garsdale Troughs and once over Ais Gill summit, some lost time was recovered. They were held at Petteril Bridge Junction and arrived at Carlisle at 12.55pm, where Lawrence and Winstanley were glad to be relieved

in the platforms. They travelled home 'on the cushions'. Kingmoor men unhooked No 45705 and put the engine on shed where she stayed throughout the following day. On Monday 6th July, *Seahorse* was observed at Skew Bridge with an Up Fitted Freight.

4TH JULY 1964 ● AUTHOR'S COLLECTION

LONG PRESTON

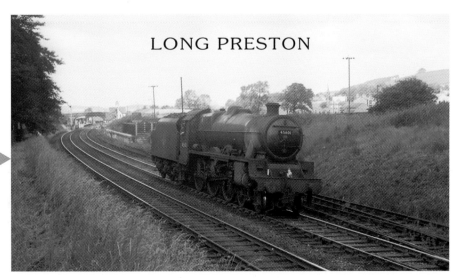

The previous Wednesday, No 45601 ► **British Guiana** worked home light engine over the Settle and Carlisle, presumably off an unbalanced working to Carlisle. She has just passed through the platform at Long Preston heading towards Hellifield, some two miles distant.

1ST JULY 1964 ● PAUL CLAXTON

BROCK TROUGHS

BROUGHTON

DOBBS BROW JUNCTION

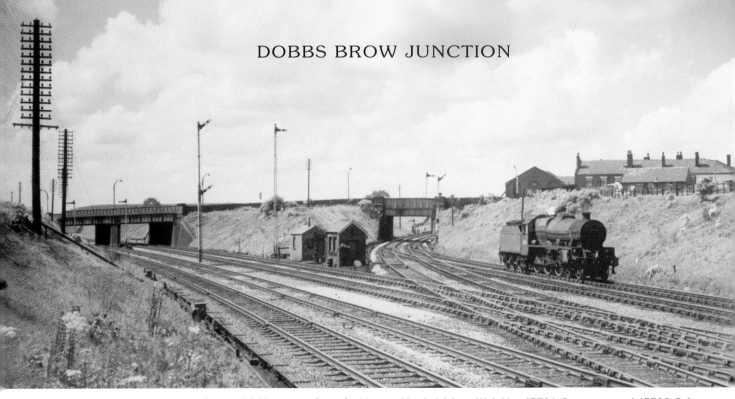

Week-ending Saturday, 22nd June 1963 was significant for Newton Heath Jubilees. With Nos 45701 *Conqueror* and 45702 *Colossus* having been recently withdrawn and No 45700 *Amethyst* moving on loan to Derby, the shed took possession of a quartet from Agecroft MPD deemed surplus to requirements for the Summer Timetable. Nos 45590 *Travancore*, 45654 *Hood*, 45664 *Nelson* and **45716** *Swiftsure* were the engines in question. One of *Swiftsure's* first jobs was to work 1T86 Failsworth to Morecambe before returning home light engine and this movement was captured by no fewer than three different photographers. *Top left:* Passing over Brock Troughs at 2.15pm. *Top right:* Passing through Broughton and *Above:* Taking the Slow Line at Dobbs Brow Junction.

22ND JUNE 1963 ● RAY FARRELL ● PETER FITTON ● DAVE HAMPSON

HINDLEY NORTH

Jubilees could be found on both express and stopping trains over the Southport route. No **45642** *Boscawen* restarts the 3.12pm Manchester Victoria to Southport Chapel Street away from Hindley North. One of her more unusual forays off the beaten track took No 45642 to Mangotsfield, where on 12th May 1956, she appeared on a pigeon special. This traffic brought 4-6-0's from distant sheds over the Midland line to Bristol and Bath.

16TH SEPTEMBER 1961 ● PETER HUTCHINSON

CASTLETON

From November 1955, a new daily diagram was created for a Jubilee or a Class Five locomotive. This was the 12.05am newspaper train from Manchester Exchange to Newcastle-upon-Tyne Central, brought about by the printing of a northern edition of the *Daily Mirror* and its stablemate the *Sunday Pictorial* in Manchester. They had become the UK's best selling daily tabloids. The journey time of 3hrs 33mins was significantly faster than passenger trains, with a first stop at York - where Newton Heath men were relieved by a local crew (they then travelled home on the cushions) and further drops at Darlington and, later, Durham. The engine went on to Gateshead MPD for servicing before returning south as the second engine of the 6.56am Newcastle to York semi-fast, and ran in partnership with a Heaton engine, normally an A2 Pacific. On Tuesdays only, she worked independently on the Inverness to York car sleeper train. After retiring to York MPD, she was diagrammed to work home on the 'Red Bank Vans' - but didn't always do so.

The 'Red Bank Vans', or 'empty vans' as they were officially known, was the daily return of empty newspaper vans from Scotswood Sidings, Newcastle, to Red Bank Sidings, Manchester. This train, often loaded to 20 bogie vehicles, arrived in York in the early afternoon, usually behind a Heaton engine. It was then York MPD's responsibility for providing the ongoing motive power and there would invariably be a pair of engines, Departure was at 2.41pm with a 6.04pm Red Bank scheduled arrival, but the train was prone to late running. Engines were usually the above mentioned and another which had arrived in the city on a fitted freight, also a Newton Heath duty. The 'vans' remained steam hauled for a decade and they produced, arguably, the most unpredictable variety of motive power to run on British Railways on a day-to-day basis. As a consequence, they attracted many enthusiasts and logged observations make for interesting reading. Jubilees featured prominently from a variety of depots including one from Corkerhill (Glasgow)! No surprises above, though, as a pair of Newton Heath engines pass through Castleton with the 'vans'. Class Five No **45202** is piloting No **45578** *United Provinces*.   **18TH AUGUST 1962** ● **I.G. HOLT**

The same location, viewed from Castleton East Junction Signal Box. A short train consisting of three loaded mineral wagons and a dozen or so empty flats is probably destined for Moston Exchange Sidings. It's a pity that the external condition of No **45635** *Tobago* doesn't match the smokebox door on this occasion - but she was rarely clean anyway.   **29TH MAY 1960** ● **R.S. GREENWOOD**

MILLS HILL

The Sunday afternoon Normanton - Manchester Victoria stopping train presents few problems for the crew of No **45635** *Tobago*. The location is Boarshaw Lane bridge approaching Mills Hill, situated between Castleton and Middleton Junction. Many years earlier, on 30th December 1952, this engine was observed leaving Bristol with the 8.45am to Newcastle - unusual in itself - but made even more so by its diversion via Sutton Coldfield and Lichfield to Wichnor Junction owing to a derailment at Castle Bromwich. This also affected the previous express, the 7.35am Bristol to Bradford hauled by Barrow Road's No 45662 *Kempenfelt*. **26TH MARCH 1961** ● **R.S. GREENWOOD**

One of the Leicester contingent to venture north week-ending 1st July 1961 was No **45650** *Blake.* It had been the subject of controversy earlier in the year when, having worked a Whitsuntide excursion on 21st May from Leicester to Brighton via Kew and Herne Hill throughout, the loco was impounded by the powers that be on the Southern Region and a Brighton Schools Class 4-4-0 No 30907 *Dulwich* handled the return working, presumably as far as the north London area. Meanwhile, No 45650 languished at the rear of Brighton MPD until 3rd June when the Running Foreman decided the loco could return home light engine, manned by a Cricklewood crew off a Down excursion. This had apparently been the first Jubilee visit to the south coast since 1953 when Longsight's No 45595 *Southern Rhodesia* worked throughout from Manchester London Road and returned home without incident *(see page 26)*. *Blake* is engaged on weekend duties to the West coast with a Blackpool excursion at Heyside.

9TH JULY 1961 ● **PETER HUTCHINSON**

CLEGG HALL

In the early 1960's, the shed usually provided a Jubilee for the 6.15am (Saturdays Only) Manchester Victoria to Bradford Exchange. The engine returned home later in the morning with a Mytholmroyd to Moston coal train. No **45701** *Conqueror* has clear signals at Clegg Hall on the approaches to Rochdale. **12TH NOVEMBER 1960** ● **I.G. HOLT**

MANCHESTER VICTORIA STATION

The last official day of steam between Manchester and Leeds over the Standedge Route. Having drifted down Miles Platting incline, No **45652** *Hawke* passes through Manchester Victoria before arriving at 11.32am in Manchester Exchange's Platform 3. The journey from Leeds City had taken 2 hours to cover the 43 miles, involving 16 stops. Services were transformed overnight with the introduction of the 'Trans-Pennine' service - Swindon built six-car Inter-City sets which ran hourly between Liverpool Lime Street and Hull, slashing the journey time from Manchester to Leeds to just 1hour 10 minutes.   **30TH DECEMBER 1960 ● PETER FITTON**

An eastbound departure on the 12.45pm to Leeds earlier in the year. No **45706** *Express* thunders through Victoria Middle and past L&Y 'A' Class No **52271** on Wallside Pilot duty.   **2ND APRIL 1960 ● PETER FITTON**

DIGGLE

After a period on loan during the war years, No **45719** *Glorious* became a 26A engine and stayed for a further 10 years. She carried three liveries during that time - LMS Crimson Lake on arrival in October 1942, followed by BR lined black applied in February 1949. Four years later, a Heavy General Overhaul at Crewe involved a coat of Brunswick Green paint. No sooner had she returned than she was off to Bank Hall to work alongside Nos 45698 *Mars* and 45717 *Dauntless*. These three became regular sights through Manchester and are well remembered for working the Liverpool Exchange to Newcastle service over the Calder Valley main line. Looking immaculate in BR lined black, *Glorious* certainly lived up to her name on this occasion, hauling a train of empty stock approaching Diggle before working yet another excursion.

JULY 1949 ● JIM DAVENPORT

DIGGLE JUNCTION

High in the Pennine hills lies Diggle Junction, a bleak spot at the best of times - but an important railway outpost nevertheless, as goods traffic in both Up and Down Sidings will testify. Two WD 2-8-0's are present, the nearest being Mirfield's No **90321**. A clean WD in service was rare - coupled to clean mineral wagons was rarer still! No **45710** *Irrestistible* passes by with a Leeds train.   **1957 ● JIM DAVENPORT**

HUDDERSFIELD

A sunny day in Yorkshire - the result of which is this dramatic lighting effect within the Huddersfield Station interior. With her smokebox door almost in complete shadow, the front numberplate of No **45701** *Conqueror* is just about discernible as she draws her train forward into Platform 2 on another Leeds working. It's doubtful if the sun shone on 26th March 1961 when *Conqueror* worked into Yorkshire again, this time on a ramblers' excursion from Bolton, Blackburn and Burnley to Harrogate and Ripon. She made use of the Wharfedale route via Ilkley to reach her destinations.

c.1957 ● AUTHOR'S COLLECTION

YORK

The Heaton to Red Bank empty stock could always be relied upon to produce unpredictable motive power. On this occasion a pair of filthy Newton Heath Jubilees pass through the environs of York Station with 50A men on each engine as far as Leeds. No **45602 *British Honduras*** is piloting No **45710 *Irresistible.***

10TH AUGUST 1962 ● RAY FARRELL

SHAW

NEWTON HEATH

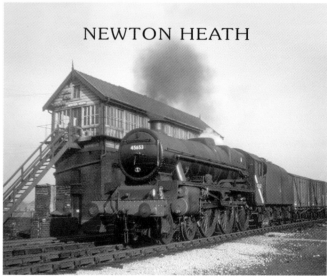

No **45653 *Barham*** takes the Miles Platting line at Newton Heath Junction with a van train from Moston Sidings. On 10th March 1965, she was noted at Huddersfield hauling Brush Type 4 No D1685 eastwards, but was withdrawn the following month.

NOVEMBER 1964 ● DON CASH

◄ **A returning Wakes Week special** from Scarborough to Oldham is nearing the end of its journey. No **45706 *Express*** will have either worked the train throughout or relieved an ex-LNER engine at York. Whatever - she has run round the Gresley stock within the platforms at Rochdale Station before traversing the Oldham Loop tender first. The distant signal, promptly returned to danger, is operated from Royton Junction Sidings Signal Box. This remote location, virtually devoid of trees, is between Shaw and Royton Junction.

25TH JUNE 1960 ● R.S. GREENWOOD

MORECAMBE

The Raleigh Cycle Company, one of Nottingham's major employers, chartered a series of annual excursions after the war, usually to the coast for the benefit of the workforce. In 1952, Morecambe was the chosen destination and this involved no fewer than eleven trains, all carrying duplicate headboards. Departures were from Nottingham Midland and Victoria via various routes and no doubt Jubilees were well to the fore. This train, in all probability, would have travelled by the ex-GC route from Victoria via Sheffield and over Woodhead to Midland Junction, Manchester, from where No **45701** *Conqueror* would complete the journey. Fine weather is in prospect as *Conqueror* nears its destination shortly after leaving the main line at Morecambe South Junction. Sheffield Millhouses' No 45621 *Northern Rhodesia* was also in evidence that day as would have been No 45639 *Raleigh*, always spruced up by Leeds Holbeck for the occasion.

24TH MAY 1952 ● AUTHOR'S COLLECTION

LEA ROAD

Wooden headboards for companies' outings and workingmens' clubs added a touch of colour when affixed to smokebox doors. Sheffield manufacturers 'Batchelors Foods' organised regular outings to the coast and Newton Heath engines were usually on hand for the last leg of the journey.

No 45635 *Tobago* at Lea Road on the Down Slow with a special ▶ from Sheffield (Victoria). **22ND SEPTEMBER 1962** ● PETER FITTON

Two headboards for the price of one! No **45701** *Conqueror* passes the remains of Lea Road Station, whose island platform served the slow lines only. This particular train started out from Worksop. The cameraman in view is of course Peter Fitton.

22ND SEPTEMBER 1962 ● PAUL CLAXTON

▼

LLANDUDNO JUNCTION

A lengthy train of empty stock (3Z46) approaches Llandudno Junction Station on a fine summer's day. Sixteen bogies can be counted and there will be at least two more. This will form two returning holiday specials - probably from Llandudno the following Saturday. No **45654 *Hood*** had brought the carriages to the coast the previous Tuesday - a less busier period over the North Wales main line.

6TH AUGUST 1963 ● PAUL CLAXTON

LLANDUDNO

Up against the buffers at Llandudno ▶ Station isn't an unusual destination for No **45602 *British Honduras*** and her crew. Drivers such as Ken Royale would relish the opportunity to work excursions such as this - from the Lancashire mill towns, in this case Oldham, bound for the North Wales coast and putting to good use the necessary route knowledge gained over many years. Standing alongside in Platform 3 is Class Five No **44842**, a Mold Junction engine.

15TH JUNE 1963 ● G. HARROP

CHESTER (GENERAL)

◀ **As well as the Manchester and Shrewsbury routes,** Crewe also used the Chester line for running-in turns after overhaul. Although the photograph is undated, No **45700 *Amethyst*** went through the shops during August 1962 and was observed at 12.20pm on September 2nd on Chester MPD. She is standing in the platforms at Chester (General) showing slight signs of priming below the smokebox door. *Amethyst* had been recorded as being under repair at Bolton earlier in the year.

SEPTEMBER 1962 ● AUTHOR'S COLLECTION

ROYAL TRAIN DUTY

During the late morning of Saturday 24th March 1956, No **45671 Prince Rupert** left Newton Heath Shed in pristine condition and travelled light engine to Aintree. She would next couple up to No **45580 Burma,** which had been similarly prepared at Blackpool MPD, then the royal carriages and await the arrival of the Royal party. After witnessing 'ESB' win the *Grand National*, The Queen, Prince Philip, The Queen Mother and Princess Margaret travelled via the Midland Main Line to Bedford to spend a few days at a nearby stately home. *Prince Rupert* had been the train engine - notice the polished buffers have been defaced by those belonging to *Burma's* tender! The pair are on Kentish Town MPD the following day, but how they then got home went unrecorded.

27TH MARCH 1956 ● **MIDLAND RAILWAY TRUST**

Immaculate No 45710 Irresistible brings the empty stock of the Royal Train through Manchester Victoria Middle - destination Hollinwood. Having left London Euston the previous day, Monday 7th November 1955, the carriages were stabled overnight at Lowton Manchester Curve, a convenient and secure location, but a copy of the Special Traffic Notice was directed to Springs Branch MPD who presumably supplied the locomotive to steam heat the stock. Other information reveals the return journey to the Capital started out from Styal, so one assumes that much of the Royal itinerary was earmarked for limousine, probably with several points of call. **8TH NOVEMBER 1955** ● **AUTHOR'S COLLECTION**

No 45590 Travancore saw out the 1963 summer season before becoming surplus to requirements and moving on to Warrington. Here she brings empty stock to form an excursion through the centre road at Manchester Exchange Station. **AUGUST 1963** ● **BRIAN MAGILTON**

MADELEY BANK

One of the classic locations on the West Coast Main Line was Madeley Bank, 8 miles south of Crewe and a spot much favoured by Doug Darby and his friend Ronnie Gee, both eminent photographers. One of a constant procession of passing trains is this Liverpool (Lime Street) to London Euston express comprising 14 coaches. Motive power is No **45661 *Vernon,*** presumably borrowed by either Edge Hill or Camden. *Vernon* had been recorded in the area some 8 years previously when on 11th August 1945 she worked a Blackpool to Nuneaton relief. Later in the evening, a Llandudno to Leicester train arrived at Nuneaton behind 'Crab' 2-6-0 No 2885 (Crewe South), which was replaced by No 45661. The engine returned to Rugby MPD the following day. **5TH JULY 1953** ● **J.D. DARBY**

WINWICK QUAY

A northbound excursion on the West Coast Main Line is passing Winwick Quay in the hands of Royal Train engine No **45671 *Prince Rupert.*** Other details are unknown, but on 3rd November 1953, she arrived at Perth with the 9.25am from Crewe. **1956** ● **G. DROUGHT**

WELLINGTON

On Summer Saturdays in 1963, a relief train to the 'Pines Express' left Bournemouth West at 9.28am, travelling via Southampton, Oxford, Birmingham (Snow Hill) and Wolverhampton. No **45664 Nelson** passes Wellington No 4 Signal Box and is on time at 3.05pm en-route to Crewe where the Liverpool (Lime Street) portion will be detached. A fortnight earlier, No 45710 *Irresistible* passed through here with the 12.50pm Bournemouth West to Colne.   **27TH JULY 1963 ● P. WARD**

SANDBACH

The previous week, the same train was in the hands of No **45590 Travancore** but was running considerably late on this occasion. The engine and five-coach Manchester portion are nicely illuminated on the approach to Sandbach. Also on Summer Saturdays, the 'Pines Express' made use of the 'Independent Lines' bypassing Crewe Station (to ease congestion) which are in the right foreground.

20TH JULY 1963 ● M. MENSING

MACCLESFIELD

On Summer Saturdays the 8.00am Colne to London Euston ran as a complete train, but on weekdays a portion was added to the 10.10am from Manchester London Road at Stockport Edgeley. This was usually a job for a Jubilee, but when the loco was diagrammed to continue on to London, Longsight men relieved their Newton Heath counterparts in the platforms at Stockport. No **45635** *Tobago,* hauling a train of 11 carriages, will undoubtedly have the assistance of a Fowler 2-6-4T whilst climbing Moss Bank, south of Macclesfield.   **JULY 1956 ● M.S. WELCH**

PENKRIDGE

The 1962 FA Cup Semi-Final between Fulham and Burnley was played at Villa Park, Birmingham, and involved several Newton Heath locos. No **45642** *Boscawen* is passing through Penkridge with a 'Footex' from Accrington to Birmingham New Street, but much earlier in the day, No 45737 *Atlas* had been entrusted with a similar excursion consisting of 11 carriages, complete with refreshment car, conveying the Burnley team and officials. *Atlas* had only arrived from Crewe (North) six days previously and was in 'good nick'. She travelled over the Copy Pit line to Todmorden and down the Calder Valley to Miles Platting East Junction, then by way of Droylsden and Denton Junctions to Stockport. The passing time at Castleton was 9.03am. The resultant draw involved a replay at Filbert Street, Leicester on Monday, 9th April, kick-off 7.45pm and one assumes excursions were again provided, but their details were unrecorded.   **31ST MARCH 1962 ● R.J. BUCKLEY**

TODMORDEN

A daily job for a Newton Heath engine was the Red Bank to York ECS which occasionally produced a Jubilee. No **45706** *Express* has been put in the Down loop at Hall Royd Junction, Todmorden, to await the passage of a local DMU, as has WD 2-8-0 No 90620 (out of camera) with coal empties off the Copy Pit line. Just visible behind *Express* is the Copy Pit banking engine - a Rose Grove 'Crab' 2-6-0. Another 26A member was in evidence here that day - No 45623 *Palestine,* working a Mytholmroyd to Moston coal train.

13TH OCTOBER 1962 ● R.S. GREENWOOD

◀ **Deep in the heart of the Calder Valley, No 45702 *Colossus*** emerges into bright sunlight at the west end of the 225 yard Millwood Tunnel on the approach to Hall Royd Junction, Todmorden, with an inter-regional excursion. Note the coat of white-wash on the tunnel portal acting as a sighting board in the Down direction. On 19th January 1963, *Colossus* worked a Mirfield to Heaton Mersey coal train and three days later was recorded passing through Sheffield (Midland) on the Up 'Devonian'.

23RD SEPTEMBER 1961 ● JOHN MARSHALL

LEEDS CITY

It was unusual to find a 26A engine ▶ displaying a headboard. The *Thames Clyde Express* was a Leeds Holbeck duty and the flagship engine No **45671 *Prince Rupert*** has been borrowed on both this, and other occasions. On 3rd July 1957 she worked the Up *Waverley* and the following day, a Leeds to St Pancras train. In addition, No 45671 was observed in Bristol early in July, suggesting a prolonged period on loan.

7TH JULY 1953 ● AUTHOR'S COLLECTION

ORRELL

Hastening towards Aintree through the deep cutting at Orrell Station is this Half Day Excursion from Manchester Victoria. The world's premier steeplechase always attracted huge crowds, many of whom travelled courtesy of a bewildering assortment of special trains from far and wide. Having received its final Heavy General Overhaul the previous month, No **45706 *Express*** is as immaculately turned out as the horses would be later in the day for the 'Grand National'.

25TH MARCH 1961 ● A.C. GILBERT

ASHTON-UNDER-LYNE

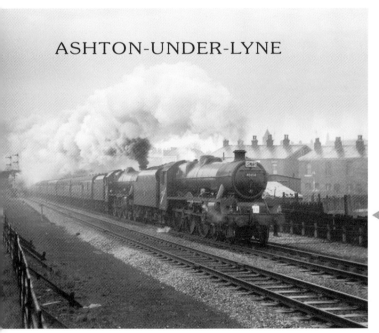

Dank and miserable conditions were hardly conducive for achieving a decent photograph of the two remaining Manchester locos working in tandem. No **45654 *Hood*** is piloting Edgeley's No **45596 *Bahamas*** at Ashton-under-Lyne with the RCTS 'Jubilee Commemorative Railtour' en-route to York. The train started in two portions, one from Crewe, the other from Liverpool Lime Street, combining at Manchester Exchange.

4TH DECEMBER 1965 ● RAY FARRELL

BROUGHTON

Unusual motive power for a Northwich to Corkickle anhydrite train comes in the form of No **45601 *British Guiana.*** The location is between Lightfoot Lane and Broughton, north of Preston. Northwich enginemen worked the train as far as Carnforth.

AUGUST 1963 ● PAUL CLAXTON

BREDBURY

▲

Approaching Ashton Road bridge, Bredbury with a
Moston to Gowhole freight is No **45600 _Bermuda._**
Newton Heath handled a variety of cross-Manchester traffic
via Midland Junction to Gowhole and Rowsley, but the closure
of the former Midland depot at Belle Vue in 1956 brought
about extra diagrams, many emanating from Ancoats Goods
and Ashton Road (Manchester).

9TH OCTOBER 1965 ● N. FIELDS

The 10.07am Ancoats to Gowhole trip working was a ▶
typical Belle Vue duty. This had been a job for a 4F 0-6-0
but by the mid 1960's, Newton Heath had an abundance of
larger engines. No **45601 _British Guiana_** sets back into
Bredbury Goods Yard to offload steel billets for transfer to
the nearby James Mills (Bredbury Steelworks). Other heavy
industry is also in evidence - R.K. Saxton, Pressure Vessel
Manufacturers occupy the premises in view which were
once the domain of the Co-operative Laundry.

1963 ● J. FAIRCLOUGH

THE GOYT VALLEY

◀ **How the mighty have fallen.** Trundling
back from Gowhole between New Mills and
Strines is No **45654 _Hood._** The loco had
barely three months left in service and by this
time was reduced to mundane tasks such as this.
Of course it hadn't always been like this. During
the LMS period, _Hood_ had a fine pedigree as
a Midland engine working out of Derby and
Kentish Town Depots. Later - as a Millhouses
engine, and throughout the 50's, she regularly
worked over this section with the Sheffield
Midland to Manchester Central via Stockport
Tiviot Dale service.

12TH MARCH 1966 ● N. FIELDS

12B CARLISLE UPPERBY

No 45700 *Amethyst* **and Duchess Pacific No 46248** *City of Leeds* **from Crewe (North).**   22ND MAY 1961   ● G.W. MORRISON

24E BLACKPOOL (CENTRAL)

Nos 61315 (41A), 45154 *Lanarkshire Yeomanry* **(26A), D5024 (1A) & 45710** *Irresistible*   7TH OCTOBER 1962 ● PETER FITTON

1A WILLESDEN

No 45716 *Swiftsure*   10TH JUNE 1964 ● M. S. WELCH

24H HELLIFIELD

The former Midland shed at Hellifield ▶
plays host to LMS 4F 0-6-0 No **44479**,
(a visitor from Lower Darwen), their own
Stanier 2-6-4T No **42492** which later
became a Newton Heath engine and No
45602 *British Honduras*, which spent
a greater part of her life standing under
Midland shed roofs whilst working out of
Derby, Nottingham, Bristol and Millhouses.
She was destined to become one of the last
Jubilees stabled within the building here
as the shed closed later that month on 17th
June 1963. The 30 ton BR Breakdown
Crane beyond the Jubilee is RS1087/30.

1ST JUNE 1963 ● H.C. CASSERLEY

8F SPRINGS BRANCH

◀ **Three months earlier and No 45602**
British Honduras managed to find
herself in an almost identical position for
the camera within the confines of Springs
Branch (Wigan) No 1 shed. Keeping her
company on this occasion is a rather clean
Class Five 4-6-0 which may well be one
of the 'Royal Train' engines provided here,
whilst standing alongside is one of their
own Austerity 2-8-0's, No **90261** which
lasted barely a year on allocation before
moving over to Agecroft. Newton Heath
engines remained irregular visitors to
Springs Branch, even after the ex-L&Y
depot at Wigan had closed in April 1964.

23RD MARCH 1963 ●
AUTHOR'S COLLECTION

86C HEREFORD

Newton Heath's Jubilees got far and
wide. For example, engines have been
recorded at Perth, Gateshead and New
England MPD's, but to find No **45661**
Vernon in ex-works condition deep in
the heart of ex-Great Western territory at
Hereford is a real coup. Of further interest
is the GWR pattern 'Not To Be Moved'
sign clipped to the running plate whilst
still displaying a reporting number, which
suggests she has failed in service whilst
working excursion 1V54. The photograph is undated but it may be during
the summer of 1961 as *Vernon* emerged
from Crewe Works after a Heavy General
Overhaul on 5th August.

cAUGUST 1961 ● JOHN TARRANT

AINTREE

No 45706 *Express*   25TH MARCH 1961 ● PETER FITTON

PATRICROFT

No 45710 *Irresistible*   8TH APRIL 1961 ● W.D. COOPER

POLMADIE (GLASGOW)

No 5719 *Glorious*   1948 ● AUTHOR'S COLLECTION

BOLTON

No 45661 *Vernon*   8TH JULY 1962 ● DAVE HAMPSON

CAMDEN

No 45706 *Express*   1957 ● AUTHOR'S COLLECTION

BLACKPOOL (CENTRAL)

No 5700 *Britannia*   1937 ● AUTHOR'S COLLECTION

SHREWSBURY

No 45652 *Hawke*   1962 ● R.K. BLENCOWE COLLECTION

WARRINGTON (DALLAM)

No 45601 *British Guiana*   1962 ● AUTHOR'S COLLECTION

10D LOSTOCK HALL

No 45661 *Vernon*   17TH JULY 1964 ● PETER FITTON

24L CARNFORTH

No 45601 *British Guiana*   1963 ● AUTHOR'S COLLECTION

1A WILLESDEN

No 45635 *Tobago*   1963 ● CHRIS BANKS COLLECTION

12B CARLISLE UPPERBY

No 45652 *Hawke*   1960 ● G.W. MORRISON

5B CREWE SOUTH

No 45600 *Bermuda* (*withdrawn*)   10TH APRIL 1966 ● K. FAIREY

55A LEEDS (HOLBECK)

No 45628 *Somaliland*   AUGUST 1961 ● AUTHOR'S COLLECTION

55C FARNLEY JUNCTION

No 45642 *Boscawen*   1960 ● G.W. MORRISON

12A CARLISLE KINGMOOR

No 45702 *Colossus*   1957 ● AUTHOR'S COLLECTION

LOCOMOTIVE ALLOCATIONS

5552	Silver Jubilee	15.06.35 - 06.07.35	Newton Heath (L)
		28.03.42 - 28.05.49	Longsight
5553	Canada	24.09.49 - 02.06.51	Trafford Park
		02.06.51 - 09.06.56	Longsight
		15.09.56 - 10.11.56	Trafford Park (L)
5554	Ontario	07.10.39 - 18.11.39	Longsight
5555	Quebec	07.07.51 - 12.06.54	Longsight
5556	Nova Scotia	02.06.45 - 12.06.54	Longsight
5558	Manitoba	12.10.46 - 01.11.47	Trafford Park
		02.12.50 - 19.04.64	Patricroft
		09.08.64 - 15.08.64	Newton Heath
5559	British Columbia	10.05.47 - 02.07.60	Patricroft
5561	Saskatchewan	18.07.36 - 03.10.36	Longsight
		15.01.57 - 30.06.58	Trafford Park
		22.07.59 - 07.11.59	Trafford Park (L)
5562	Alberta	18.07.36 - 03.10.36	Longsight
		20.02.37 - 22.05.37	Patricroft
		12.06.37 - 11.09.37	Patricroft (L+P)
5563	Australia	02.07.38 - 23.08.41	Longsight
		29.07.44 - 19.08.44	Longsight
		28.05.49 - 14.09.63	Patricroft
5564	New South Wales	25.07.36 - 14.11.36	Longsight
		12.07.64 - 18.07.64	Newton Heath*
5566	Queensland	01.02.36 - 13.11.37	Patricroft
		13.11.37 - 28.05.38	Longsight
5567	South Australia	30.01.36 - 14.01.39	Patricroft
		22.07.39 - 16.09.39	Patricroft
		05.06.48 - 13.11.48	Longsight
5568	Western Australia	01.02.36 - 22.05.37	Patricroft
		27.07.46 - 14.09.46	Trafford Park (L+P)
		19.04.64 - 25.04.64	Newton Heath*
5569	Tasmania	19.04.64 - 25.04.64	Patricroft*
5570	New Zealand	09.07.38 - 11.10.47	Trafford Park (L+P)
5572	Irish Free State/Eire	11.02.39 - 11.10.47	Trafford Park
5573	Newfoundland	03.09.38 - 11.02.39	Trafford Park (L+P)
5578	United Provinces	05.02.44 - 05.04.47	Longsight
		26.11.49 - 21.01.50	Longsight
		19.09.53 - 20.06.59	Longsight
		17.03.62 - 30.05.64	Newton Heath*
5580	Burma	03.10.64 - 12.12.64	Newton Heath*
5584	North West Frontier	09.03.35 - 20.04.35	Patricroft
5585	Hyderabad	12.10.46 - 16.11.46	Trafford Park
		01.07.61 - 23.09.61	Newton Heath (L)
5586	Mysore	16.03.35 - 16.04.35	Longsight (L+P)
		30.07.38 - 20.08.38	Trafford Park (L+P)
		16.06.45 - 18.08.45	Longsight (L)
5587	Baroda	28.07.51 - 18.06.55	Longsight
		17.09.55 - 14.06.58	Longsight
		20.09.58 - 30.05.59	Longsight
		01.08.59 - 10.06.61	Longsight
5590	Travancore	30.09.39 - 28.10.39	Trafford Park
		25.02.62 - 22.06.63	Agecroft
		22.06.63 - 14.09.63	Newton Heath
5591	Udaipur	30.03.35 - 20.04.35	Newton Heath (L)
		09.05.42 - 21.06.47	Longsight
		08.09.56 - 10.11.56	Trafford Park (L)
5592	Indore	05.06.48 - 30.04.49	Longsight (L)
		21.05.49 - 24.06.50	Longsight
		20.06.64 - 26.09.64	Newton Heath*
5593	Kolhapur**	20.11.43 - 14.07.51	Longsight
		25.09.64 - 02.01.65	Patricroft
		02.01.65 - 28.03.65	Newton Heath
5594	Bhopal	23.03.35 - 20.04.35	Longsight
5595	Southern Rhodesia	16.03.35 - 16.04.35	Longsight
		07.07.51 - 20.06.59	Longsight
5596	Bahamas**	02.07.62 - 23.07.66	Stockport
5597	Barbados	06.04.35 - 20.04.35	Longsight
5599	Bechuanaland	05.09.36 - 22.05.37	Patricroft
		26.06.37 - 16.09.39	Patricroft
5600	Bermuda	29.04.50 - 10.06.50	Longsight
		10.06.50 - 02.01.65	Patricroft
		02.01.65 - 18.12.65	Newton Heath*
5601	British Guiana	25.06.60 - 26.09.64	Newton Heath (L+P)
5602	British Honduras	03.03.62 - 19.04.64	Newton Heath
5603	Solomon Islands	30.04.43 - 05.04.47	Longsight
		29.04.50 - 11.07.53	Longsight
5604	Ceylon	09.05.53 - 04.07.53	Trafford Park (L)
		01.05.54 - 08.05.54	Patricroft (L)
		24.04.65 - 17.07.65	Newton Heath
5606	Falkland Islands	01.05.54 - 12.06.54	Patricroft
5607	Fiji	25.02.62 - 01.12.62	Agecroft
5610	Gold Coast/Ghana	19.07.34 - 21.07.34	Longsight (TT)
		15.06.40 - 29.06.40	Trafford Park (L)
5613	Kenya	18.06.38 - 16.09.39	Patricroft
		27.07.57 - 17.08.57	Longsight (L)
5614	Leeward Islands	11.07.59 - 19.09.59	Newton Heath (L)
		27.02.60 - 19.03.60	Trafford Park
5615	Malay States	08.07.61 - 23.09.61	Newton Heath (L)
5616	Malta G.C.	27.02.60 - 19.03.60	Trafford Park (L)
5617	Mauritius	26.06.37 - 06.12.41	Patricroft
		19.08.50 - 06.12.52	Longsight
		09.05.53 - 13.06.53	Trafford Park (L)
5618	New Hebrides	01.11.47 - 30.06.58	Trafford Park
5619	Nigeria	27.10.34 - 09.02.35	Longsight
5620	North Borneo	27.10.34 - 09.02.35	Longsight
5622	Nyasaland	07.12.46 - 15.09.56	Trafford Park
		15.09.56 - 27.10.56	Longsight (L)
		27.10.56 - 05.07.58	Trafford Park
		20.09.58 - 06.12.58	Trafford Park (L)
		01.07.61 - 15.07.61	Newton Heath (L)
5623	Palestine	25.07.36 - 25.09.37	Longsight (L)
		02.07.38 - 19.11.38	Longsight (L)
		09.05.42 - 20.03.43	Longsight
		30.04.60 - 31.12.60	Longsight
		17.03.62 - 25.07.64	Newton Heath*
5624	St. Helena	25.07.36 - 25.09.37	Longsight (L)
		12.04.52 - 22.06.57	Longsight
5625	Sarawak	25.07.36 - 23.08.41	Longsight (L)
		03.10.42 - 30.11.46	Longsight
		11.01.47 - 21.06.47	Longsight
5626	Seychelles	09.11.34 - 16.03.35	Longsight
5627	Sierra Leone	13.11.34 - 30.03.35	Longsight
		17.12.38 - 08.02.39	Longsight (L)
		29.03.47 - 21.06.47	Trafford Park (L)
5628	Somaliland	13.11.34 - 16.03.35	Longsight
		30.09.39 - 15.09.56	Trafford Park
		15.09.56 - 27.10.56	Longsight
		27.11.56 - 05.07.58	Trafford Park
		10.07.61 - 22.09.61	Newton Heath (L)
5629	Straits Settlements	10.11.34 - 12.01.35	Longsight (TT)
		12.01.35 - 30.03.35	Newton Heath (L)
		11.10.47 - 10.11.56	Trafford Park
		10.11.56 - 14.06.58	Longsight
5630	Swaziland	21.11.42 - 20.03.43	Longsight (L)
5631	Tanganyika	18.06.38 - 16.09.39	Patricroft (L+P)
		09.12.44 - 21.06.47	Longsight
		28.06.47 - 10.06.61	Longsight
5632	Tonga	11.03.39 - 16.09.39	Patricroft
		18.07.42 - 05.04.47	Longsight
		29.04.50 - 21.06.58	Longsight
		21.07.62 - 14.08.65	Stockport
		14.08.65 - 09.10.65	Newton Heath*
5633	Trans Jordan/Aden	03.10.42 - 03.11.51	Longsight
5634	Trinidad	03.10.42 - 25.01.47	Longsight
		29.04.50 - 10.06.50	Longsight
5635	Tobago	01.07.39 - 16.09.39	Longsight
		18.07.42 - 02.01.43	Longsight
		02.01.43 - 08.02.64	Newton Heath (L+P)
5636	Uganda	01.07.61 - 23.09.61	Newton Heath (L)
5637	Windward Islands	11.03.39 - 06.12.41	Patricroft
5638	Zanzibar	05.03.38 - 02.04.38	Longsight (L)
		18.07.42 - 21.11.42	Longsight
		20.03.43 - 10.09.60	Longsight
5639	Raleigh	25.09.48 - 04.12.48	Trafford Park (L)
5642	Boscawen	04.05.40 - 09.01.65	Newton Heath*
5643	Rodney	17.11.56 - 02.02.57	Longsight (L)

5644	Howe	30.08.52 - 31.12.60	Longsight (L+P)		5695	Minotaur	26.03.36 - 04.06.38	Newton Heath (TT)
							01.10.38 - 04.12.39	Newton Heath
5645	Collingwood	07.09.52 - 03.08.63	Patricroft		5696	Arethusa	02.04.36 - 10.08.40	Newton Heath
5647	Sturdee	09.05.42 - 05.04.47	Longsight				02.09.44 - 09.12.44	Newton Heath (L+P)
5648	Wemyss	20.02.37 - 08.05.37	Patricroft				27.07.46 - 17.08.46	Trafford Park (L)
5650	Blake	04.01.36 - 22.05.37	Patricroft				30.11.46 - 21.12.46	Trafford Park (L)
		01.07.61 - 26.08.61	Newton Heath (L)				31.05.47 - 12.07.47	Trafford Park (L)
							15.11.47 - 20.12.47	Trafford Park (L)
5651	Shovell	04.01.36 - 01.02.36	Patricroft		5697	Achilles	18.04.36 - 02.05.36	Newton Heath
		22.05.37 - 05.06.37	Patricroft				29.08.36 - 09.12.39	Newton Heath
5652	Hawke	04.01.36 - 01.02.36	Patricroft		5698	Mars	15.04.36 - 02.10.37	Newton Heath
		30.11.46 - 22.02.47	Trafford Park				10.08.40 - 12.10.46	Newton Heath (L+P)
		11.10.47 - 27.10.56	Trafford Park				04.09.48 - 11.09.48	Newton Heath
		27.10.56 - 10.11.56	Longsight		5699	Galatea**	15.04.36 - 02.10.37	Newton Heath (TT)
		10.11.56 - 05.07.58	Trafford Park		5700	Britannia/Amethyst	20.04.36 - 07.09.57	Newton Heath (TT)
		25.06.60 - 06.07.63	Newton Heath (L+P)				28.09.57 - 09.03.63	Newton Heath
5653	Barham	04.01.36 - 01.02.36	Patricroft		5701	Conqueror	24.04.36 - 23.02.63	Newton Heath* (TT)
		02.10.37 - 13.11.37	Patricroft		5702	Colossus	05.05.36 - 04.06.38	Newton Heath (TT)
		13.11.37 - 16.09.39	Longsight				01.10.38 - 17.04.43	Newton Heath
		18.07.42 - 05.12.42	Longsight				09.12.50 - 23.04.63	Newton Heath*
		05.12.42 - 10.04.43	Newton Heath (L+P)		5703	Thunderer	30.08.47 - 28.05.49	Longsight
		20.06.64 - 03.04.65	Newton Heath*		5704	Leviathan	17.04.43 - 03.07.43	Newton Heath
5654	Hood	25.02.62 - 22.06.63	Agecroft		5705	Seahorse	20.06.64 - 06.11.65	Newton Heath*
		22.06.63 - 14.03.64	Newton Heath		5706	Express	08.05.43 - 28.09.63	Newton Heath*
		14.03.64 - 16.10.65	Stockport		5708	Resolution	10.04.43 - 08.05.43	Newton Heath
		16.10.65 - 25.06.66	Newton Heath*				19.08.44 - 30.09.44	Longsight (L)
5655	Keith	07.10.39 - 24.06.50	Trafford Park				30.09.44 - 09.12.44	Patricroft
		24.06.50 - 02.06.51	Longsight		5709	Implacable	11.03.44 - 22.04.44	Trafford Park
		02.06.51 - 27.10.56	Trafford Park				29.04.50 - 18.06.55	Longsight
		27.10.56 - 09.03.57	Longsight		5710	Irresistible	12.09.36 - 03.10.36	Longsight (L)
		09.03.57 - 23.03.57	Patricroft (L)				15.06.40 - 04.09.48	Newton Heath
		23-03-57 - 22-06-57	Longsight				11.09.48 - 06.06.64	Newton Heath*
5657	Tyrwhitt	26.09.64 - 09.05.65	Patricroft		5711	Courageous	15.06.40 - 04.09.48	Newton Heath
5661	Vernon	11.12.37 - 06.03.43	Newton Heath		5712	Victory	17.10.42 - 23.02.57	Newton Heath
		01.07.44 - 09.08.64	Newton Heath				23.02.57 - 05.07.58	Trafford Park
5663	Jervis	24.10-59 - 14-09-63	Patricroft (L+P)				01.07.61 - 23.09.61	Newton Heath (L)
5664	Nelson	13.09.47 - 17.01.48	Trafford Park		5716	Swiftsure	31.07.62 - 22.06-63	Agecroft (L+P)
		25.02.62 - 22.06.63	Agecroft				22.06.63 - 12.07-64	Newton Heath
		22.06.63 - 14.09.63	Newton Heath		5717	Dauntless	15.06.40 - 03.04-48	Newton Heath
5665	Lord Rutherford of Nelson	09.07.38 - 13.12.41	Trafford Park (L+P)		5718	Dreadnought	29.04.39 - 23.09.39	Longsight
5666	Cornwallis	28.08.37 - 23.08.41	Longsight				29.04.50 - 10.06.50	Longsight
		17.02.45 - 03.03.45	Longsight (L)				07.07.51 - 06.09.52	Longsight
5667	Jellicoe	30.11.57 - 29.03.58	Trafford Park				21.07.62 - 20.10.62	Agecroft (L+P)
		24.05.58 - 31.05.58	Trafford Park		5719	Glorious	23.10.42 - 28.03-53	Newton Heath (L+P)
5668	Madden	01.05.37 - 23.08.41	Longsight		5720	Indomitable	03.10.42 - 27.03.43	Longsight
		26.04.47 - 24.10.59	Patricroft				27.07.46 - 07.09.52	Patricroft
5670	Howard of Effingham	27.07.46 - 15.10-49	Patricroft		5721	Impregnable	22.05.37 - 11.03.39	Patricroft
		26.09.64 - 10.10-64	Stockport* (L+P)		5722	Defence	22.05.37 - 11.03.39	Patricroft
5671	Prince Rupert	18.01.36 - 11.04.36	Newton Heath (L)		5723	Fearless	22.05.37 - 11.03.39	Patricroft
		06.03.43 - 02.09.44	Newton Heath (L+P)				21.03.42 - 07.09.57	Longsight
		09.12.44 - 12.10.46	Newton Heath (L+P)		5724	Warspite	27.07.46 - 03.05.47	Patricroft
		04.09.48 - 19.10.57	Newton Heath				15.10.49 - 10.06.50	Patricroft
		19.10.57 - 10.09.60	Longsight		5726	Vindictive	27.07.46 - 28.05.49	Patricroft
5672	Anson	30.04.38 - 14.05.38	Patricroft				15.05.54 - 19.06.54	Patricroft (L)
		20.03.43 - 25.01.47	Longsight		5728	Defiance	21.07.62 - 20.10.62	Agecroft* (L+P)
5673	Keppel	12.10.46 - 15.04.47	Longsight		5729	Furious	21.07.62 - 20.10.62	Agecroft* (L+P)
5674	Duncan	11.03.39 - 06.12.41	Patricroft		5732	Sanspariel	12.01.63 - 29.02.64	Stockport*
5678	De Robeck	19.01.52 - 28.06.52	Longsight		5734	Meteor	29.04.50 - 07.07.51	Longsight
		25.08.62 - 08.12.62	Stockport*		5736	Phoenix	07.01.56 - 25.02.56	Longsight (L)
5679	Armada	30.04.60 - 25.06.60	Longsight				11.06.60 - 10.09.60	Longsight
		25.06.60 - 29.12.62	Newton Heath (L+P)		5737	Atlas	09.04.49 - 28.05.49	Longsight (L)
5680	Camperdown	11.10.47 - 15.10.60	Longsight				31.03.62 - 30.05.64	Newton Heath
5682	Trafalgar	25.09.48 - 27.11.48	Trafford Park (L)		5738	Samson	05.02.38 - 19.02.38	Longsight (L)
5683	Hogue	28.08.37 - 23.09.39	Longsight		5740	Munster	03.04.43 - 13.06.53	Longsight
5688	Polyphemus	01.07.39 - 16.09.39	Longsight		5741	Leinster	21.03.42 - 25.01.47	Longsight
		29.04.50 - 07.07.51	Longsight		5742	Connaught	04.04.42 - 25.01.47	Longsight (L+P)
5689	Ajax	30.04.38 14.05.38	Patricroft (L)				28.10.50 - 07.07.51	Longsight
		05.09.53 - 19.09.53	Trafford Park (L)					
		19.09.53 - 08.03.58	Longsight					
5692	Cyclops	22.07.39 - 07.12.40	Patricroft					
5693	Agamemnon	29.04.39 - 22.07.39	Longsight					

Notes: (L) - Loan   (P) - Permanent   (TT) - To Traffic   * Withdrawn   ** Preserved

No 5572 renamed Eire on 19th July 1938.   No 5610 renamed Ghana on 12th December 1958.   No 5633 renamed Aden on 4th September 1946.
No 5700 renamed Amethyst during September 1951.   No 5705 Seahorse worked out of Trafford Park from 29.10.64 until withdrawal. It remained officially on Newton Heath's allocation whilst carrying a 9E shedplate.   138 members out of a class total of 191 are accounted for.

CREWE

No 5566 *Queensland* MARCH 1938 ● REAL PHOTOS

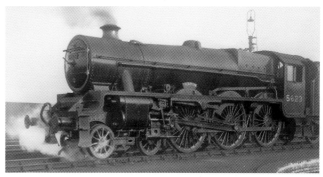

No 5623 *Palestine* SEPTEMBER 1938 ● REAL PHOTOS

No 5633 *Aden* c1947 ● A.G. ELLIS

No 5638 *Zanzibar* APRIL 1947 ● A. BARNARD COLLECTION

No M5661 *Vernon* cAUGUST 1948 ● REAL PHOTOS

No 5668 *Madden* c1948 ● AUTHOR'S COLLECTION

No 5696 *Arethusa* c1938 ● AUTHOR'S COLLECTION

No 5697 *Achilles* 19TH APRIL 1936 ● AUTHOR'S COLLECTION

No 45578 *United Provinces* 1ST NOVEMBER 1953 ● B.K.B.GREEN

No 45592 *Indore* MARCH 1949 ● REAL PHOTOS

No 45629 *Straits Settlements*   1952 ● AUTHOR'S COLLECTION

No 45652 *Hawke*   MAY 1954 ● JIM DAVENPORT

No 45668 *Madden*   1948 ● AUTHOR'S COLLECTION

No 45671 *Prince Rupert*   27TH MARCH 1960 ● M.N. SOCIETY

No 45680 *Camperdown*   SEPTEMBER 1948 ● AUTHOR'S COLLECTION

No 45689 *Ajax*   FEBRUARY 1955 ● D. YOUNG COLLECTION

No 45700 *Britannia*   7TH MAY 1949 ● H.C. CASSERLEY

No 45701 *Conqueror*   8TH NOVEMBER 1959 ● A. SWAIN

No 45710 *Irresistible* 1ST JUNE 1961 ● R. K. BLENCOWE COLLECTION

No 45719 *Glorious*   FEBRUARY 1949 ● REAL PHOTOS

N0 45705 SEAHORSE

Awaiting departure from Buxton (Midland) with the 8.00am commuter service to Manchester Central is No **45705 *Seahorse***. Prior to her 'paper transfer' from Newton Heath to Trafford Park in October 1964, Royal Scots Nos 46115 *Scots Guardsman* and 46129 *The Scottish Horse* had featured amongst others, but the last regular engine had been Rebuilt Patriot No 45522 *Prestatyn*. The Buxton spotting fraternity knew it as the 'half past six namer', and it attracted a good number to the station each evening when a different engine was rostered.

2ND MARCH 1965 ● **KEN TYLER**

The morning train was in the hands of ▶ Buxton men who placed stopping lamps on the engine, but the return service involved a Trafford Park crew as far as Chinley. The relieving Buxton Driver, Tommy Lowe, compares notes with his counterpart on the platform whilst Fireman Mike Bentley, already on the footplate, looks out for the signal. Mike maintained that No **45705 *Seahorse*** had performed indifferently, partly because a superheater element had blown, but once completely removed, she was a different engine and subsequently offered no problems up to the day of her untimely withdrawal. Incidentally, the 5.22pm ran with express lamps, set by the Trafford Park men.

20TH JUNE 1965 ● **A. STEELE**

◀ **Once established as the regular engine,** it soon became obvious that these commuter trains offered the last chance of regular travel behind a Jubilee in the Manchester area. A number of enthusiastic businessmen would detour to Cheadle Heath to experience just that, as would others, and she achieved something of a cult status as a consequence. Buxton enthusiast Ken Tyler took No **45705 *Seahorse*** to heart and produced very convincing wooden replica nameplates which she carried until the end. Along with friend Peter Bentley, brother of fireman Mike, and supported by his family, they 'set-to' on the weekend of 14th and 15th August 1965 at Buxton MPD, cleaning the engine with many buckets of paraffin before fitting the plates. A very proud Ken *(left)* and Peter, kneeling on the running plate, offer *Seahorse* to the backing plate on the fireman's side of the engine.

15TH AUGUST 1965 ● **KEN TYLER**

JUNE 1964

Fri	19	19:30	Farington Jnc	1J63	18.30 Blackpool Central - Manchester Victoria
		17:08	St Annes		15.55 Manchester Victoria - Blackpool Central
Sat	20	10:23	Skew Bridge	1P22	Down Fast
		10:54	Lytham	1P22	
Sun	21	18:54	Skew Bridge	1J63	18.30 Blackpool Central - Manchester Victoria
Mon	22	19:46	Skew Bridge	1J65	19.20 Blackpool Central - Manchester Victoria
Tue	23	21:13	Preston	2J64	18.30 Blackpool North - Manchester Victoria
Wed	24	20:55	Skew Bridge	2J64	18.30 Blackpool North - Manchester Victoria
Thur	25				
Fri	26	14:20	Lytham		Down
Sat	27	15:27	Kings Langley	1X81	Down
			Bletchley	1X81	Down Express
			Hatch End	1X81	Down Express
Sun	28		Wigan Area		
Mon	29	12:50	St Annes		12.40 Blackpool Central - Manchester Victoria
Tue	30				

JULY 1964

Wed	1				
Thur	2		St Annes	1P52	15:55 Manchester Victoria - Blackpool Central
		18:48	St Annes	1J63	18:30 Blackpool Central - Manchester Victoria
Fri	3				
Sat	4		Hellifield	1S48	09:20 Manchester Victoria - Glasgow Central
		12:55	Carlisle Citadel	1S48	09:20 Manchester Victoria - Glasgow Central
Sun	5	08:45	Kingmoor MPD		
Mon	6	19:33	Skew Bridge		Up Fitted Freight
Tue	7				
Wed	8	17:43	St Annes		16:25 Manchester Victoria - Blackpool Central
		19:22	St Annes	2J61	19:05 Blackpool Central - Rochdale
Thur	9	12:28	Preston	1P67	
Fri	10	21:08	Skew Bridge	2J64	20.00 Blackpool North - Manchester Victoria
Sat	11		Newton Heath MPD		
			Blackburn	1S48	09:20 Manchester Victoria - Glasgow Central
			Blea Moor	1S48	09:20 Manchester Victoria - Glasgow Central
		12:52	Carlisle Citadel	1S48	09:20 Manchester Victoria - Glasgow Central
		13:00	Upperby MPD		
		15:15	Upperby MPD		
Sun	12				
Mon	13				
Tue	14	am	Carnforth area		
Wed	15		Preston Station		
Thur	16	12:45	Skew Bridge	0J48	Down Slow Pass
		13:45	Skew Bridge	1J48	Up Fast Pass
Fri	17	08:45	Agecroft		Local Pass
		17:53	Kirkham		16:55 Manchester Victoria - Blackpool North
Sat	18	13:03	Skew Bridge	1F77	Up (8 non-corridor)
		14:12	Walton Old Jnc	1F77	
			Manchester Ex		ECS
			Red Bank CS		LED own
Sun	19	20:19	Lea Road	1Z13	Blackpool Central - Mossley (10 non-corridor)
		20:24	Skew Bridge	1Z13	Blackpool Central - Mossley (10 non-corridor)
Mon	20				
Tue	21				
Wed	22	08:15	Preston Station	1L84	08:15 Preston - Windermere
Thur	23				
Fri	24	16:34	Farington Curve Jnc		15:55 Manchester Victoria - Blackpool Central
		17:12	St Annes		15:55 Manchester Victoria - Blackpool Central
		19:48	Skew Bridge		Up Fast
Sat	25	09:20	Manchester Vic	1S48	09:20 Manchester Victoria - Glasgow Central
		09:40	Bolton	1S48	09:20 Manchester Victoria - Glasgow Central
Sun	26		Springs Branch MPD		
		12:36	Lea Road	1Z12	Down Slow
			Newton Heath MPD		
Mon	27				
Tue	28		St Annes	1Z13	09:30 Manchester Victoria - Blackpool Central
			St Annes		18:25 Blackpool Central - Manchester Victoria
Wed	29	18:10	Newton Heath MPD		
Thur	30		Wigan Area		
Fri	31				

AUGUST 1964

Sat	1	17:32	Carstairs		Up Parcels (4 Bogies)
			Lanark Jnc		15:30 Glasgow - Carlisle Parcels
Sun	2		Kingmoor MPD		
			Carstairs MPD		
Mon	3		Greenhill		14:45 Aberdeen Broad Street Fish
Tue	4				
Wed	5				
Thur	6		Leeds Holbeck MPD		
Fri	7	08:31	Huddersfield		08:31 (FO) - Paignton
Sat	8				
Sun	9	13:55	Newton Heath MPD		
Mon	10				
Tue	11		Newton Heath MPD		
Wed	12				
Thur	13		Manchester Victoria		LE
Fri	14				
Sat	15	14:33	Skew Bridge	2P56	Down Slow (Non-Corridor)

AUGUST 1964 *(contd)*

Sun	16				
Mon	17				
Tue	18	21:20	Bolton MPD		Control Orders to allieviate Bolton shortage
Wed	19		Rochdale		17:40 Liverpool Exchange - Rochdale
Thur	20				
Fri	21				
Sat	22		Bolton		Local Workings
Sun	23		Bolton MPD		
Mon	24		Bolton		Local Workings
Tue	25		Bolton		Local Workings
Wed	26		Rochdale		17:40 Liverpool Exchange - Rochdale
Thur	27		Bolton		Bolton - Leicester Parcels
Fri	28		Newton Heath MPD		
Sat	29		Newton Heath MPD		
Sun	30				
Mon	31				

SEPTEMBER 1964

Tue	1				
Wed	2				
Thur	3	13:31	Preston Stn		12:40 Blackpool Central - Manchester Victoria
			Newton Heath MPD		
Fri	4	17:20	Skew Bridge		Manchester Victoria - Preston
Sat	5	19:00	Carnforth		Morecambe?
Sun	6				
Mon	7				
Tue	8	14:28	Preston		Up Freight
Wed	9				
Thur	10		Wigan Area		
Fri	11				
Sat	12	10:53	Preston		
Sun	13				
Mon	14				
Tue	15				
Wed	16				
Thur	17				
Fri	18				
Sat	19				
Sun	20				
Mon	21				
Tue	22				
Wed	23				
Thur	24				
Fri	25				
Sat	26	16:00	Carstairs MPD		
Sun	27				
Mon	28				
Tue	29				
Wed	30				

OCTOBER 1964

Thur	1				
Fri	2				
Sat	3		Carstairs MPD		Under Repair without leading driving wheels
Sun	4				
Mon	5				
Tue	6				
Wed	7				
Thur	8				
Fri	9				
Sat	10				
Sun	11				
Mon	12				
Tue	13				
Wed	14				
Thur	15				
Fri	16				
Sat	17				
Sun	18				
Mon	19				
Tue	20				
Wed	21				
Thur	22				
Fri	23		Huddersfield		17:38 (FO) Manchester Exchange - York
Sat	24		Neville Hill		Pilot Engine - Scotswood - Red Bank ECS
			Rochdale		Pilot Engine - Scotswood - Red Bank ECS
Sun	25		Patricroft MPD		
			Newton Heath MPD		
Mon	26				
Tue	27				
Wed	28				
Thur	29		Trafford Park MPD		
Fri	30				
Sat	31				

NOVEMBER 1964

Day	Date	Time	Location	Working
Sun	1		Trafford Park MPD	
Mon	2	17:52	Cheadle Heath	17:22 Manchester Central - Buxton
Tue	3	17:22	Manchester Central	17:22 Manchester Central - Buxton
Wed	4			
Thur	5			
Fri	6			
Sat	7			
Sun	8			
Mon	9			
Tue	10			
Wed	11	08:30	Cheadle Heath	08:00 Buxton - Manchester Central
		17:22	Manchester Central	17:22 Manchester Central - Buxton
Thur	12			
Fri	13			
Sat	14			
Sun	15			
Mon	16			
Tue	17			
Wed	18			
Thur	19			
Fri	20			
Sat	21			
Sun	22			
Mon	23			
Tue	24			
Wed	25			
Thur	26	08:30	Cheadle Heath	08:00 Buxton - Manchester Central
		17:22	Manchester Central	17:22 Manchester Central - Buxton
Fri	27			
Sat	28			
Sun	29			
Mon	30	08:30	Cheadle Heath	08:00 Buxton - Manchester Central

DECEMBER 1964

Day	Date	Time	Location	Working
Tue	1	08:30	Cheadle Heath	08:00 Buxton - Manchester Central
Wed	2			
Thur	3			
Fri	4			
Sat	5			
Sun	6			
Mon	7	08:30	Cheadle Heath	08:00 Buxton - Manchester Central
Tue	8			
Wed	9			
Thur	10			
Fri	11			
Sat	12			
Sun	13			
Mon	14			
Tue	15	08:30	Cheadle Heath	08:00 Buxton - Manchester Central
Wed	16	08:30	Cheadle Heath	08:00 Buxton - Manchester Central
		17:22	Manchester Central	17:22 Manchester Central - Buxton
Thur	17			
Fri	18			
Sat	19			
Sun	20			
Mon	21			
Tue	22			
Wed	23	08:30	Cheadle Heath	08:00 Buxton - Manchester Central
Thur	24			
Fri	25			
Sat	26			
Sun	27			
Mon	28			
Tue	29			
Wed	30	08:30	Cheadle Heath	08:00 Buxton - Manchester Central
Thur	31			

JANUARY 1965

Day	Date	Time	Location	Working
Fri	1			
Sat	2			
Sun	3			
Mon	4			
Tue	5			
Wed	6			
Thur	7	08:30	Cheadle Heath	08:00 Buxton - Manchester Central
		17:22	Manchester Central	17:22 Manchester Central - Buxton
Fri	8	08:30	Cheadle Heath	08:00 Buxton - Manchester Central
Sat	9			
Sun	10			
Mon	11			
Tue	12			
Wed	13	08:30	Cheadle Heath	08:00 Buxton - Manchester Central
		17:22	Manchester Central	17:22 Manchester Central - Buxton
Thur	14		Loco stopped for standby	
Fri	15			
Sat	16			

JANUARY 1965 (contd)

Day	Date	Time	Location	Working
Sun	17			
Mon	18			
Tue	19			
Wed	20			
Thur	21			
Fri	22			
Sat	23			
Sun	24			
Mon	25			
Tue	26			
Wed	27			
Thur	28			
Fri	29			
Sat	30			

FEBRUARY 1965

Day	Date	Time	Location	Working
Sun	31		Longsight MPD	
Mon	1			
Tue	2	17:22	Manchester Central	17:22 Manchester Central - Buxton
Wed	3			
Thur	4			
Fri	5	17:22	Manchester Central	17:22 Manchester Central - Buxton
Sat	6			
Sun	7			
Mon	8			
Tue	9			
Wed	10			
Thur	11	08:30	Cheadle Heath	08:00 Buxton - Manchester Central
		17:22	Manchester Central	17:22 Manchester Central - Buxton
Fri	12			
Sat	13			
Sun	14		Buxton MPD	
Mon	15	17:52	Cheadle Heath	17:22 Manchester Central - Buxton
Tue	16	08:30	Cheadle Heath	08:00 Buxton - Manchester Central
Wed	17			Irlam - Manchester Central local
Thur	18			
Fri	19			
Sat	20			
Sun	21			
Mon	22	08:30	Cheadle Heath	08:00 Buxton - Manchester Central
Tue	23			
Wed	24			
Thur	25			
Fri	26	17:22	Manchester Central	17:22 Manchester Central - Buxton
Sat	27			

MARCH 1965

Day	Date	Time	Location	Working
Sun	28			
Mon	1	08:30	Cheadle Heath	08:00 Buxton - Manchester Central
		17:22	Manchester Central	17:22 Manchester Central - Buxton
Tue	2	08:30	Cheadle Heath	08:00 Buxton - Manchester Central
		17:22	Manchester Central	17:22 Manchester Central - Buxton
Wed	3			
Thur	4	08:30	Cheadle Heath	08:00 Buxton - Manchester Central
		17:22	Manchester Central	17:22 Manchester Central - Buxton
Fri	5	08:30	Cheadle Heath	08:00 Buxton - Manchester Central
		17:22	Manchester Central	17:22 Manchester Central - Buxton
Sat	6		Unidentified location	Buxton Working - West Riding News?
Sun	7			
Mon	8			
Tue	9			
Wed	10	17:22	Manchester Central	17:22 Manchester Central - Buxton
Thur	11	08:30	Cheadle Heath	08:00 Buxton - Manchester Central
		17:22	Manchester Central	17:22 Manchester Central - Buxton
Fri	12	08:30	Cheadle Heath	08:00 Buxton - Manchester Central
			Trafford Park MPD	
Sat	13			
Sun	14			
Mon	15			
Tue	16			
Wed	17			
Thur	18			
Fri	19	17:22	Manchester Central	17:22 Manchester Central - Buxton
Sat	20			
Sun	21			
Mon	22	17:22	Manchester Central	17:22 Manchester Central - Buxton
Tue	23			
Wed	24			
Thur	25			
Fri	26	17:22	Manchester Central	17:22 Manchester Central - Buxton
Sat	27			
Sun	28			
Mon	29	08:30	Cheadle Heath	08:00 Buxton - Manchester Central
		17:22	Manchester Central	17:22 Manchester Central - Buxton
Tue	30	08:30	Cheadle Heath	08:00 Buxton - Manchester Central
		17:22	Manchester Central	17:22 Manchester Central - Buxton
Wed	31	17:22	Cheadle Heath	17:22 Manchester Central - Buxton

APRIL 1965

Day		Time	Location	Working
Thur	1			
Fri	2			
Sat	3			
Sun	4			
Mon	5	08:30	Cheadle Heath	08:00 Buxton - Manchester Central
		17:22	Manchester Central	17:22 Manchester Central - Buxton
Tue	6	17:22	Manchester Central	17:22 Manchester Central - Buxton
Wed	7			
Thur	8			
Fri	9			
Sat	10			
Sun	11			
Mon	12			
Tue	13			
Wed	14			
Thur	15			
Fri	16			
Sat	17			
Sun	18			
Mon	19		Buxton MPD	
Tue	20	17:00	Knott Mill	LE for 17:22 Manchester Central - Buxton
Wed	21	17:00	Knott Mill	LE for 17:22 Manchester Central - Buxton
Thur	22	17:00	Knott Mill	LE for 17:22 Manchester Central - Buxton
Fri	23	17:00	Knott Mill	LE for 17:22 Manchester Central - Buxton
Sat	24			
Sun	25		Buxton MPD	
Mon	26	08:30	Cheadle Heath	08:00 Buxton - Manchester Central
		17:00	Knott Mill	LE for 17:22 Manchester Central - Buxton
		17:22	Manchester Central	17:22 Manchester Central - Buxton
Tue	27	08:30	Cheadle Heath	08:00 Buxton - Manchester Central
		17:22	Manchester Central	17:22 Manchester Central - Buxton
Wed	28	08:30	Cheadle Heath	08:00 Buxton - Manchester Central
		17:22	Manchester Central	17:22 Manchester Central - Buxton
Thur	29		Trafford Park MPD	
Fri	30	08:30	Cheadle Heath	08:00 Buxton - Manchester Central
		17:22	Manchester Central	17:22 Manchester Central - Buxton
Sat	1			

MAY 1965

Day		Time	Location	Working
Sun	2			
Mon	3			
Tue	4	17:22	Manchester Central	17:22 Manchester Central - Buxton
Wed	5	08:30	Cheadle Heath	08:00 Buxton - Manchester Central
		17:22	Manchester Central	17:22 Manchester Central - Buxton
Thur	6	08:30	Cheadle Heath	08:00 Buxton - Manchester Central
		17:22	Manchester Central	17:22 Manchester Central - Buxton
Fri	7	08:30	Cheadle Heath	08:00 Buxton - Manchester Central
Sat	8		Northallerton	Class 'C' headcode. ECS train/vans
Sun	9			
Mon	10			
Tue	11			
Wed	12			
Thur	13			
Fri	14			
Sat	15			
Sun	16			
Mon	17			
Tue	18			
Wed	19	17:22	Manchester Central	17:22 Manchester Central - Buxton
Thur	20	08:30	Cheadle Heath	08:00 Buxton - Manchester Central
		17:22	Manchester Central	17:22 Manchester Central - Buxton
Fri	21	08:30	Cheadle Heath	08:00 Buxton - Manchester Central
Sat	22			
Sun	23			
Mon	24			
Tue	25	08:30	Cheadle Heath	08:00 Buxton - Manchester Central
		17:22	Manchester Central	17:22 Manchester Central - Buxton
Wed	26	08:30	Cheadle Heath	08:00 Buxton - Manchester Central
		17:22	Manchester Central	17:22 Manchester Central - Buxton
Thur	27	08:30	Cheadle Heath	08:00 Buxton - Manchester Central
			Trafford Park MPD	
		17:22	Manchester Central	17:22 Manchester Central - Buxton
Fri	28	08:30	Cheadle Heath	08:00 Buxton - Manchester Central
		17:22	Manchester Central	17:22 Manchester Central - Buxton
Sat	29			
Sun	30			
Mon	31			

JUNE 1965

Day		Time	Location	Working
Tue	1	08:30	Cheadle Heath	08:00 Buxton - Manchester Central
		17:22	Manchester Central	17:22 Manchester Central - Buxton
Wed	2	08:30	Cheadle Heath	08:00 Buxton - Manchester Central
		17:22	Manchester Central	17:22 Manchester Central - Buxton
Thur	3	08:30	Cheadle Heath	08:00 Buxton - Manchester Central
		17:22	Manchester Central	17:22 Manchester Central - Buxton
Fri	4	08:30	Cheadle Heath	08:00 Buxton - Manchester Central
Sat	5			

JUNE 1965 (contd)

Day		Time	Location	Working
Sun	6			
Mon	7			
Tue	8	08:30	Cheadle Heath	08:00 Buxton - Manchester Central
		17:22	Manchester Central	17:22 Manchester Central - Buxton
Wed	9	08:30	Cheadle Heath	08:00 Buxton - Manchester Central
Thur	10			
Fri	11	17:00	Knott Mill	17:22 Manchester Central - Buxton
Sat	12			
Sun	13			
Mon	14	17:22	Manchester Central	17:22 Manchester Central - Buxton
Tue	15	08:30	Cheadle Heath	08:00 Buxton - Manchester Central
		17:22	Manchester Central	17:22 Manchester Central - Buxton
Wed	16	08:30	Cheadle Heath	08:00 Buxton - Manchester Central
		17:22	Manchester Central	17:22 Manchester Central - Buxton
Thur	17	08:30	Cheadle Heath	08:00 Buxton - Manchester Central
		17:22	Manchester Central	17:22 Manchester Central - Buxton
Fri	18	08:30	Cheadle Heath	08:00 Buxton - Manchester Central
		17:22	Manchester Central	17:22 Manchester Central - Buxton
Sat	19			
Sun	20			
Mon	21	08:30	Cheadle Heath	08:00 Buxton - Manchester Central
		17:22	Manchester Central	17:22 Manchester Central - Buxton
Tue	22			
Wed	23	08:30	Cheadle Heath	08:00 Buxton - Manchester Central
		17:22	Manchester Central	17:22 Manchester Central - Buxton
Thur	24	08:30	Cheadle Heath	08:00 Buxton - Manchester Central
Fri	25			
Sat	26			
Sun	27			
Mon	28	17:22	Manchester Central	17:22 Manchester Central - Buxton
Tue	29	17:22	Manchester Central	17:22 Manchester Central - Buxton
Wed	30			

JULY 1965

Day		Time	Location	Working
Thur	1			
Fri	2	17:22	Manchester Central	17:22 Manchester Central - Buxton
Sat	3			
Sun	4			
Mon	5	08:30	Cheadle Heath	08:00 Buxton - Manchester Central
Tue	6			
Wed	7			
Thur	8			
Fri	9			
Sat	10	08:45	Manchester Central	08:45 Manchester Central - Sheffield Midland
Sun	11			
Mon	12	17:22	Manchester Central	17:22 Manchester Central - Buxton
			Loco recorded in poor condition. Lost 5 mins to Chinley	
Tue	13	08:30	Cheadle Heath	08:00 Buxton - Manchester Central
Wed	14	17:22	Manchester Central	17:22 Manchester Central - Buxton
Thur	15	08:30	Cheadle Heath	08:00 Buxton - Manchester Central
		17:22	Manchester Central	17:22 Manchester Central - Buxton
Fri	16			
Sat	17			
Sun	18			
Mon	19	08:30	Cheadle Heath	08:00 Buxton - Manchester Central
		17:22	Manchester Central	17:22 Manchester Central - Buxton
Tue	20	08:30	Cheadle Heath	08:00 Buxton - Manchester Central
Wed	21			
Thur	22	08:30	Cheadle Heath	08:00 Buxton - Manchester Central
		17:22	Manchester Central	17:22 Manchester Central - Buxton
Fri	23	20:00	Manchester Central	20:00 Manchester Central - Sheffield Midland
Sat	24			
Sun	25			
Mon	26			
Tue	27	08:30	Cheadle Heath	08:00 Buxton - Manchester Central
		17:22	Manchester Central	17:22 Manchester Central - Buxton
Wed	28			
Thur	29			
Fri	30	08:30	Cheadle Heath	08:00 Buxton - Manchester Central
		17:22	Manchester Central	17:22 Manchester Central - Buxton
Sat	31			

AUGUST 1965

Day		Time	Location	Working
Sun	1			
Mon	2	08:30	Cheadle Heath	08:00 Buxton - Manchester Central
Tue	3			
Wed	4	08:30	Cheadle Heath	08:00 Buxton - Manchester Central
		17:22	Manchester Central	17:22 Manchester Central - Buxton
Thur	5			
Fri	6			
Sat	7			
Sun	8			
Mon	9			
Tue	10	17:22	Manchester Central	17:22 Manchester Central - Buxton
Wed	11	08:30	Cheadle Heath	08:00 Buxton - Manchester Central
		17:22	Manchester Central	17:22 Manchester Central - Buxton
Thur	12	08:30	Cheadle Heath	08:00 Buxton - Manchester Central
		17:22	Manchester Central	17:22 Manchester Central - Buxton
Fri	13	08:30	Cheadle Heath	08:00 Buxton - Manchester Central
		17:22	Manchester Central	17:22 Manchester Central - Buxton

AUGUST 1965 (contd)

Sat	14		
Sun	15	Buxton MPD. Being cleaned and fitted with wooden nameplates by Ken Tyler	
Mon	16		
Tue	17	08:30 Cheadle Heath	08:00 Buxton - Manchester Central
		17:22 Manchester Central	17:22 Manchester Central - Buxton
Wed	18	08:30 Cheadle Heath	08:00 Buxton - Manchester Central
		17:22 Manchester Central	17:22 Manchester Central - Buxton
Thur	19	08:30 Cheadle Heath	08:00 Buxton - Manchester Central
		17:22 Manchester Central	17:22 Manchester Central - Buxton
Fri	20		
Sat	21		
Sun	22		
Mon	23	08:30 Cheadle Heath	08:00 Buxton - Manchester Central
		17:22 Manchester Central	17:22 Manchester Central - Buxton
Tue	24	08:30 Cheadle Heath	08:00 Buxton - Manchester Central
		17:22 Manchester Central	17:22 Manchester Central - Buxton
Wed	25	08:30 Cheadle Heath	08:00 Buxton - Manchester Central
		17:22 Manchester Central	17:22 Manchester Central - Buxton
Thur	26	08:30 Cheadle Heath	08:00 Buxton - Manchester Central
		17:22 Manchester Central	17:22 Manchester Central - Buxton
Fri	27	08:30 Cheadle Heath	08:00 Buxton - Manchester Central
Sat	28		
Sun	29		
Mon	30		
Tue	31	08:30 Cheadle Heath	08:00 Buxton - Manchester Central
		17:22 Manchester Central	17:22 Manchester Central - Buxton

SEPTEMBER 1965

Wed	1	08:30 Cheadle Heath	08:00 Buxton - Manchester Central
		17:22 Manchester Central	17:22 Manchester Central - Buxton
Thur	2	08:30 Cheadle Heath	08:00 Buxton - Manchester Central
Fri	3		
Sat	4		
Sun	5		
Mon	6	17:22 Manchester Central	17:22 Manchester Central - Buxton
Tue	7	08:30 Cheadle Heath	08:00 Buxton - Manchester Central
		17:22 Manchester Central	17:22 Manchester Central - Buxton
Wed	8	08:30 Cheadle Heath	08:00 Buxton - Manchester Central
Thur	9	17:22 Manchester Central	17:22 Manchester Central - Buxton
Fri	10	08:30 Cheadle Heath	08:00 Buxton - Manchester Central
		17:22 Manchester Central	17:22 Manchester Central - Buxton
Sat	11		
Sun	12		
Mon	13		
Tue	14		
Wed	15		
Thur	16		
Fri	17		
Sat	18		
Sun	19	pm Derby MPD	
Mon	20		
Tue	21	17:22 Manchester Central	17:22 Manchester Central - Buxton
Wed	22	17:22 Manchester Central	17:22 Manchester Central - Buxton
Thur	23		
Fri	24		
Sat	25		

SEPTEMBER 1965 (contd)

Sun	26	Buxton MPD	
Mon	27		
Tue	28		
Wed	29		
Thur	30		

OCTOBER 1965

Fri	1		
Sat	2		
Sun	3	Buxton MPD	
Mon	4	17:22 Manchester Central	17:22 Manchester Central - Buxton
Tue	5		
Wed	6		
Thur	7		
Fri	8		
Sat	9		
Sun	10		
Mon	11	08:30 Cheadle Heath	08:00 Buxton - Manchester Central
Tue	12	17:22 Manchester Central	17:22 Manchester Central - Buxton
Wed	13		
Thur	14		
Fri	15	08:30 Cheadle Heath	08:00 Buxton - Manchester Central
Sat	16		
Sun	17		
Mon	18	08:30 Cheadle Heath	08:00 Buxton - Manchester Central
Tue	19		
Wed	20	17:22 Manchester Central	17:22 Manchester Central - Buxton
Thur	21		
Fri	22	17:22 Manchester Central	17:22 Manchester Central - Buxton
Sat	23		
Sun	24		
Mon	25		
Tue	26		08:00 Buxton - Manchester Central
Wed	27	08:30 Cheadle Heath	
Thur	28		
Fri	29		
Sat	30		

NOVEMBER 1965

Sun	31		
Mon	1		
Tue	2	08:30 Cheadle Heath	08:00 Buxton - Manchester Central
		17:22 Manchester Central	17:22 Manchester Central - Buxton
Wed	3	08:30 Cheadle Heath	08:00 Buxton - Manchester Central
Thur	4		
Fri	5	08:30 Cheadle Heath	08:00 Buxton - Manchester Central
		17:22 Manchester Central	17:22 Manchester Central - Buxton
Sat	6		
Sun	7		
Mon	8	08:30 Cheadle Heath	08:00 Buxton - Manchester Central
		17:22 Manchester Central	17:22 Manchester Central - Buxton
Tue	9	17:22 Manchester Central	17:22 Manchester Central - Buxton
Wed	10	08:30 Cheadle Heath	08:00 Buxton - Manchester Central
		12:00 Withdrawn from service	

JANUARY 1966

Tue	18	To Crewe (South) MPD for eventual disposal at Cashmores, Great Bridge. Towed dead by 8F No 48354	

Her finest hour came on 18th September 1965 when she was selected to haul the second leg of the 'High Peak Railtour', an outing from London organised by the Locomotive Club of Great Britain. No **45705** *Seahorse* waits at Cheadle Heath to relieve the preserved ex-LNER Pacific No 4472 *Flying Scotsman,* and take the train forward to Aston, Birmingham where she, in turn, was relieved by Class Five No 45114.

18TH SEPTEMBER 1965 ● AUTHOR'S COLLECTION

SEAHORSE

IRRESISTIBLE

SWIFTSURE

AMETHYST

SIERRA LEONE

VICTORY

NELSON

MADDEN

SOUTHERN RHODESIA

BARHAM

SASKATCHEWAN

ATLAS

CAMPERDOWN

EXPRESS

TOBAGO

TRINIDAD

PHOENIX

LORD RUTHERFORD OF NELSON

EIRE

SANSPAREIL

TRAVANCORE

AJAX

SILVER JUBILEE

IMPLACABLE

CANADA

TONGA

MARS